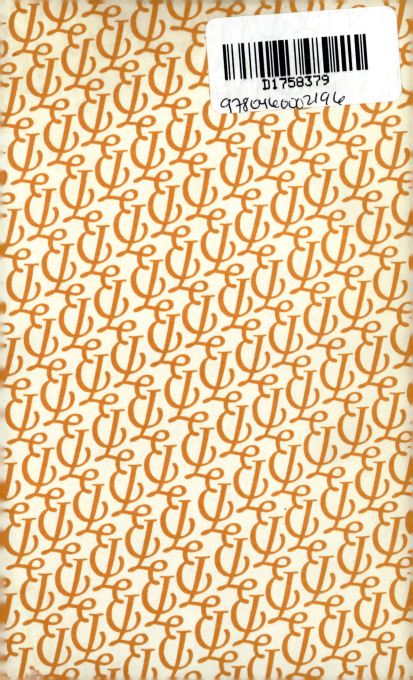

D1758379

9780460002196

824 RUS 20018

EVERYMAN, I will go with thee,

and be thy guide,

In thy most need to go by thy side

JOHN RUSKIN

Born in London on 8th February 1819, the son
a wealthy wine merchant. Educated at King's
College, London, and at Christ Church,
Oxford. Won the Newdigate prize in 1839.
In 1840 his health broke down and he travelled
abroad, chiefly in Italy, returning to Oxford for
his degree in 1842. Married Euphemia Chalmers
Grey in 1848, but the marriage annulled on her
petition in 1855. Inherited a fortune in 1864, and
moved to Brantwood, Coniston Lake, in 1871.
He was already established as the leading critic
on art in England, and was defendant in a libel
action brought by Whistler in 1877. In his
later years he was keenly interested in economics and social reform. Died at Brantwood
20th January 1900.

RUSKIN

Sesame and Lilies
The Two Paths
The King of the Golden River

INTRODUCED BY
SIR OLIVER LODGE

DENT: LONDON
EVERYMAN'S LIBRARY
DUTTON: NEW YORK

NO. *219*

INTRODUCTION

> "Whatever bit of a wise man's work is honestly and benevolently done, that bit is his book or his piece of art."—J. R. 1864.

To introduce writings of John Ruskin to any class of English readers ought to be absurdly unnecessary, notwithstanding the fact that they have been beyond the recognized means of many persons : who nevertheless have, some of them, spent an equal amount in ephemeral or less worthy literature. Others have determined to possess them at any cost ; thereby showing the appreciative and discriminating spirit desired and contemplated by their author in fixing the price high ; for he wished his writings to be bought and used by people who would appreciate them, not bought only, nor yet obtained easily without any sacrifice.

Undoubtedly, however, the price of the books has made them actually if not theoretically unknown to the greater number of the populace ; and so, now that they have become easily accessible, a preface of the most simple character may be a temporary help to new readers.

Such alone shall be the aim of this introduction : it shall make no attempt to re-word anything which the author has already perfectly said ; nor shall it attempt to speak to scholars ; it shall merely give initial information sufficient to introduce another selection from these great writings to the unlearned and the simple.

"Sesame" is a lecture on reading, and the right use of books. It was originally given under the title "Kings' Treasuries" : the idea being that in the silent storehouse of a row of volumes a reader is privileged to hold communion with the Kings and Prophets of all ages ; who are, as it were, awaiting audience—craving it rather than granting it,—and who are ready to share their best thoughts with any

one who comes into their presence bringing with him an
intelligent and sympathetic mind.

Incidentally the lecture contains a discourse on the accurate
and careful employment of words ; wherein the importance
of this branch of culture is forcibly and luminously emphasized,
with illustrations from great writers, and notably from Milton.
Language is so much the instrument of thinking, that probably
no training, not even mathematics, conduces to accuracy of
thought so effectively as does the constantly cultivated
precision of expression here advocated and illustrated.

But the lecture does not conclude in a literary and intellectual atmosphere : it enters with profound emotion and
disquiet into the condition of public and private life in
England at the time—not so very different then from what
it is to-day,—it calls attention to the mistaken aims and
misguided sympathies which are rampant in the land, and
while denouncing with prophetic assurance it exhorts with
inspired fervour.

Incidentally it may be permissible to explain to young
readers that "sesame" is a three-syllabled word, and that
it signifies a kind of corn or grain—"that old enchanted
Arabian grain" which in the legend was supposed to open
doors.

" Lilies," also called " Queens' Gardens," is a lecture on
the ideal of womanhood and on the vital education of girls.
In places its treatment is probably too direct and didactic
to exert the maximum of influence, in the wider outlook of
to-day : some patience, and a willingness to supply or to
detect indirect qualifications, may be required ; but a discriminating and appreciative reader will be richly rewarded.
The lecture is illustrated by the women of Shakespeare, of
Scott, and other poets, and by the atmosphere of chivalry ;
it appeals to the women of to-day to see that their country
is kept beautiful, and that the children in it are given a fair
chance ; it appeals to them also to exercise their power and
cause unnecessary wars to cease ; it holds up a lofty ideal of
service and influence, to be exercised in the most natural
and peaceful ways ; it emphasizes the true function of the

Lady amid the rough and tumble activities of men ; and it
closes in passages of the utmost eloquence.

Mr. Ruskin says that these lectures cost him much thought
and much strong emotion, and that he found it difficult to
rouse his audience into sympathy with the temper into which
he had brought himself by years of thinking over subjects
full of pain. The moral which he finally draws is that the
two most heinous sins are Idleness and Cruelty,—two vices
which, as he shows, penetrate much deeper than may at
first sight be supposed ; and he quotes as two of the most
forcible commands—

> "Work while you have light."

and

> "Be merciful while you have mercy."

Mr. Ruskin explains his meaning in his own preface to
the 1871 edition, where he convicts of both these sins many
who would be horrified at the idea that they could for a
moment be really cruel. It may be remembered that the
form of torture called "sweating" is not extinct ; nor have
purchasers learnt, as yet, how effectively to discourage it.
Young readers would do well to refer to this preface if they
can get the opportunity. Another form of torture—a form
operating chiefly on the mind, and called imprisonment—is
still enforced among us ; possibly because few are able keenly
to realize what it means. It seems to be a form of punishment which does not forcibly arouse the imagination beforehand, and, therefore, is but slightly deterrent ; but it will
soon become a question whether, as a punishment, and
except as an opportunity for reformation, confinement is a
penalty we have any right to inflict on free and responsible
beings—whether in fact a more frankly brutal and bodily
form of torment might not righteously be substituted for it,
and be more legitimate. The particular phase of cruelty
involved in prolonged removal of liberty and suspension of
will is not indeed referred to by Mr. Ruskin in the text, but
the general utterances of a prophet must be held capable of
wide specific application.

"The Two Paths" is the name given to a short collection of lectures on Art, and its application to Decoration and Manufacture. They recall the artist and designer of every kind to the importance of following organic form, and of learning to utilize and represent truly, in architecture as well as in all other constructive arts, the truths of simple natural beauty. These lectures insist that Art is not for the select few alone : that it should be accessible to all : that it should be made in fact by the people for the people, and applied to the most homely and every-day uses, as representing the conscious joy of the maker and increasing the unconscious pleasure of the user.

Lastly there is incorporated in this small volume that remarkable fairy tale—the only one, so far as we know, that Ruskin ever attempted—called "The King of the Golden River." To some people it has seemed one of the best fairy tales that ever was written. It is not nearly so widely known as it ought to be, perhaps because it is barely simple enough for small children ; but it is a beautiful allegory, and it has the advantage of not having become so hackneyed as to be utilized for purposes of parody. It ought to appear with Doyle's illustrations : and it might well be issued in still cheaper form separately.

The parable is in two halves, a sort of Paradise Lost and a Paradise Regained—lost by selfishness, regained by love. The definition of "holy water" may be quoted as typical of its central theme—

"The water which has been refused to the cry of the weary and dying, is unholy, though it had been blessed by every saint in heaven ; and the water which is found in the vessel of mercy is holy, though it had been defiled with corpses."

And the restoration of wealth to Treasure Valley, by restoring the fertility of its soil instead of by metalliferous undertakings, is entirely in harmony with the author's consistent teaching that all true material increase must come from the soil. For land is a means of receiving and utilizing the energy of the sun ; and to that energy every terrestrial activity is necessarily due. Upon the surface of the planet the solar energy falls, and thereby the earth is enabled to bring forth all her increase. Ownership of the earth's surface is therefore lordship over man ; and it used to be accompanied by the openly-admitted slavery or serfdom of those who, being born without such traditional possession, were unable to receive directly and independently any of the sun's rays except those which fell upon their bodies or upon the king's highway.

It may be that private and individual ownership of a large tract of country is the system best adapted to develop its usefulness and beauty for the good of all. It may be so,— this is not the place to discuss questions of economics ; but whatever be the recognized condition of tenure, whereby the earth's surface is parcelled out among the generation living on it at any given moment, it is clearly a human arrangement, and is properly subject to reconsideration from time to time. It is not a matter in which the future is necessarily dominated and controlled by the past.

OLIVER LODGE

SELECT BIBLIOGRAPHY

SEPARATE WORKS. *Modern Painters : their Superiority in the Art of Landscape Painting to all the Ancient Masters . . .*, 5 vols.: vol. i, 1843; vol. ii, 1846; vols. iii and iv, 1856; vol. v, 1860. *The Seven Lamps of Architecture*, 1849; *The King of the Golden River; or The Black Brothers : A Legend of Styria*, 1851; *The Stones of Venice*, 3 vols., 1851, 1853; *Pre-Raphaelitism*, 1851; *Lectures on Architecture and Painting* (delivered at Edinburgh, 1853), 1854; *The Elements of Drawing*, 1857; *The Political Economy of Art*, 1857; reprinted, with three supplementary papers, as *A Joy for Ever*, 1880 (in collected works, vol. xi); *The Two Paths* (lectures on art and its application to decoration and manufacture), 1859; *The Elements of Perspective*, 1859; '*Unto this Last*' (essays on political economy), 1862; *Sesame and Lilies* (two lectures delivered 1864), 1865; *The Crown of Wild Olive* (three lectures on Work, Traffic and War), 1866; *Time and Tide by Weare and Tyne* (twenty-five letters to a working man), 1867; *The Queen of the Air, a Study of the Greek Myths of Cloud and Storm*, 1869; *Lectures on Art* (delivered at Oxford), 1870; *Fors Clavigera. Letters to the Workmen and Labourers of Great Britain*, 8 vols., 1871–4; *Munera Pulveris* (six essays on political economy), 1872 (collected works, vol. ii); *Aratra Pontelici* (six lectures on the elements of sculpture), 1872 (collected works, vol. iii); *The Eagle's Nest* (ten lectures delivered at Oxford on the relation of natural science to art), 1872 (collected works, vol. iv); *Love's Meinie. Lectures on Greek and English Birds* (three lectures delivered at Oxford), 1873, 1881; *The Poetry of Architecture*, 1873; *Ariadne Florentina* (six lectures on wood and metal engraving, delivered at Oxford, 1872), in seven parts, 1873–5; *Val D'Arno* (ten lectures on Tuscan art), 1874; *Proserpina. Studies of Wayside Flowers . . .*, in six parts, 1875–9; *Deucalion. Collected Studies of the Lapse of Waves, and Life of Stones*, in six parts, 1875–9; *St Mark's Rest. The History of Venice*, 1879; *The Art of England* (lectures delivered at Oxford), in seven parts, 1883–4; *The Pleasures of England* (lectures delivered at Oxford), 1884; *On the Old Road* (essays, pamphlets, etc., 1834–85), 1885; *Praeterita*, 3 vols., 1886–9; *Dilecta* (diary-notes, etc., illustrating *Praeterita*, in three parts, 1886–1900.

CORRESPONDENCE. *Stray Letters to a London Bibliophile*, 1892; *Letters upon Subjects of General Interest to various Correspondents*, 1892; *Letters to William Ward*, 1893; *Letters addressed to a College Friend*, 1894; Separate Collections of Letters, edited by T. J. Wise, were published 1894, 1895, 1896 and 1897; *Letters to Charles Eliot Norton*, edited by C. E. Norton, 1897; *Lectures on Landscape*, 1897; *Letters to Mary and Helen Gladstone*, 1903.

COLLECTED EDITIONS. *Works*, in eleven volumes, 1871–83; *The Life and Letters and Complete Works*, Library Edition, edited by E. T. Cook and A. Wedderburn, 1903, etc., in about 38 volumes.

BIOGRAPHY AND CRITICISM. W. E. Collingwood, *Life of John Ruskin*, 1900; Frederick Harrison (English Men of Letters), 1902; J. R. Morley, *John Ruskin and Social Ethics*, 1917; A. Strachey, 'The Tragedy of John Ruskin', 1928; R. H. Wilenski, 1933; D. G. Lang, 1937; R. W. Livingstone (British Academy Lecture, 1945); H. B. Hagstotz, *The Educational Theories of John Ruskin*, 1942; Sir K. Clark, *Ruskin at Oxford*, 1947; Sir W. M. James, *The Order of Release*, 1947; J. H. Whitehouse, *Ruskin the Painter*, 1938; *Ruskin's Influence To-day*, 1945; *Vindication of Ruskin*, 1950, and sundry lectures to the Ruskin Society; D. Leon, *Ruskin, the Great Victorian*, 1949; P. Quennell, *John Ruskin*, etc., 1949; F. G. Townsend, *Ruskin and the Landscape Feeling*, 1951.

CONTENTS

CONTENTS

SESAME AND LILIES

TWO LECTURES
DELIVERED AT MANCHESTER IN 1864

By JOHN RUSKIN

I. OF KINGS' TREASURIES
II. OF QUEENS' GARDENS

"ἀπὸ τῆς χαρᾶς αὐτοῦ ὑπάγει, καὶ ἀγοράζει τὸν ἀγρὸν ἐκεῖνον."

SESAME AND LILIES

LECTURE I.—SESAME

OF KINGS' TREASURIES

ἐξ αὐτῆς ἐξελεύσεται ἄρτος, . . . καὶ χῶμα χρυσίον.[1]

I BELIEVE, ladies and gentlemen, that my first duty this evening is to ask your pardon for the ambiguity of title under which the subject of lecture has been announced; and for having endeavoured, as you may ultimately think, to obtain your audience under false pretences. For indeed I am not going to talk of kings, known as regnant, nor of treasuries, understood to contain wealth; but of quite another order of royalty, and material of riches, than those usually acknowledged. And I had even intended to ask your attention for a little while on trust, and (as sometimes one contrives in taking a friend to see a favourite piece of scenery) to hide what I wanted most to show, with such imperfect cunning as I might, until we had unexpectedly reached the best point of view by winding paths. But since my good plain-spoken friend, Canon Anson, has already partly anticipated my reserved "trot for the avenue" in his first advertised title of subject, "How and What to Read;" —and as also I have heard it said, by men practised in public address, that hearers are never so much fatigued as by the endeavour to follow a speaker who gives them no clue to his purpose, I will take the slight mask off at once, and tell you plainly that I want to speak to you about books; and about the way we read them, and could, or should read them. A grave subject, you will say; and a wide one! Yes; so wide that I shall make

[1] Job xxviii. 5, 6.

no effort to touch the compass of it. I will try only to bring before you a few simple thoughts about reading, which press themselves upon me every day more deeply, as I watch the course of the public mind with respect to our daily enlarging means of education, and the answeringly wider spreading, on the levels, of the irrigation of literature. It happens that I have practically some connexion with schools for different classes of youth ; and I receive many letters from parents respecting the education of their children. In the mass of these letters, I am always struck by the precedence which the idea of a "position in life" takes above all other thoughts in the parents'—more especially in the mothers'—minds. "The education befitting such and such a *station in life*"—this is the phrase, this the object, always. They never seek, as far as I can make out, an education good in itself : the conception of abstract rightness in training rarely seems reached by the writers. But an education "which shall keep a good coat on my son's back ;—an education which shall enable him to ring with confidence the visitors' bell at double-belled doors ;—education which shall result ultimately in establishment of a double-belled door to his own house ; in a word, which shall lead to advancement in life." It never seems to occur to the parents that there may be an education which, in itself, *is* advancement in Life ;—that any other than that may perhaps be advancement in Death ;—and that this essential education might be more easily got, or given, than they fancy, if they set about it in the right way ; while it is for no price, and by no favour, to be got, if they set about it in the wrong.

Indeed, among the ideas most prevalent and effective in the mind of this busiest of countries, I suppose the first—at least that which is confessed with the greatest frankness, and put forward as the fittest stimulus to youthful exertion—is this of "Advancement in life." My main purpose this evening is to determine, with you, what this idea practically includes, and what it should include.

Practically, then, at present, "advancement in life " means becoming conspicuous in life ;—obtaining a position which shall be acknowledged by others to be respectable or honourable. We do not understand by this advancement, in general, the mere making of money, but the being known to have made it; not the accomplishment of any great aim, but the being seen to have accomplished it. In a word, we mean the gratification of our thirst for applause. That thirst, if the last infirmity of noble minds, is also the first infirmity of weak ones; and, on the whole, the strongest impulsive influence of average humanity: the greatest efforts of the race have always been traceable to the love of praise, as its greatest catastrophes to the love of pleasure.

I am not about to attack or defend this impulse. I want you only to feel how it lies at the root of effort; especially of all modern effort. It is the gratification of vanity which is, with us, the stimulus of toil, and balm of repose; so closely does it touch the very springs of life that the wounding of our vanity is always spoken of (and truly) as in its measure *mortal;* we call it " mortification," using the same expression which we should apply to a gangrenous and incurable bodily hurt. And although few of us may be physicians enough to recognise the various effect of this passion upon health and energy, I believe most honest men know, and would at once acknowledge, its leading power with them as a motive. The seaman does not commonly desire to be made captain only because he knows he can manage the ship better than any other sailor on board. He wants to be made captain that he may be *called* captain. The clergyman does not usually want to be made a bishop only because he believes that no other hand can, as firmly as his, direct the diocese through its difficulties. He wants to be made bishop primarily that he may be called " My Lord." And a prince does not usually desire to enlarge, or a subject to gain, a kingdom because he believes that no one else can as well serve the state upon the throne; but, briefly, because he wishes to be addressed as " Your Majesty," by as many lips as may be brought to such utterance.

This, then, being the main idea of advancement in life, the force of it applies, for all of us, according to our station, particularly to that secondary result of such advancement which we call "getting into good society." We want to get into good society, not that we may have it, but that we may be seen in it; and our notion of its goodness depends primarily on its conspicuousness.

Will you pardon me if I pause for a moment to put what I fear you may think an impertinent question? I never can go on with an address unless I feel, or know, that my audience are either with me or against me : (I do not much care which, in beginning) ; but I must know where they are ; and I would fain find out, at this instant, whether you think I am putting the motives of popular action too low. I am resolved, to-night, to state them low enough to be admitted as probable ; for whenever, in my writings on Political Economy, I assume that a little honesty, or generosity,—or what used to be called "virtue"—may be calculated upon as a human motive of action, people always answer me, saying, "You must not calculate on that : that is not in human nature : you must not assume anything to be common to men but acquisitiveness and jealousy ; no other feeling ever has influence on them, except accidentally, and in matters out of the way of business." I begin accordingly to-night low down in the scale of motives ; but I must know if you think me right in doing so. Therefore, let me ask those who admit the love of praise to be usually the strongest motive in men's minds in seeking advancement, and the honest desire of doing any kind of duty to be an entirely secondary one, to hold up their hands. (*About a dozen of hands held up—the audience partly not being sure the lecturer is serious, and partly shy of expressing opinion.*) I am quite serious—I really do want to know what you think ; however, I can judge by putting the reverse question. Will those who think that duty is generally the first, and love of praise the second, motive, hold up their hands? (*One hand reported to have been held up, behind the lecturer.*) Very good : I see you are with me, and that you think I have not begun too near the ground. Now, without teasing you by putting farther question, I venture to assume that you will admit duty as at least a secondary or tertiary motive. You think that the desire of doing something useful, or obtaining some real good, is indeed an existent collateral idea, though a secondary one, in most men's desire of advancement. You will grant that moderately honest men desire place and office, at least in some measure for the sake of their beneficent power ; and would wish to associate rather with sensible and well-informed persons than with fools and ignorant persons, whether they are seen in the company of the sensible ones or not. And finally, without being troubled by repetition of any common truisms about the precious-ness of friends, and the influence of companions, you will admit, doubtless, that according to the sincerity of our desire that our friends may be true, and our companions wise,—and in proportion to the earnestness and discretion with which we choose both, will be the general chances of our happiness and usefulness.

But, granting that we had both the will and the sense to choose our friends well, how few of us have the power ! or, at least, how limited, for most, is the sphere of choice ! Nearly all our associations are determined by chance, or necessity ; and restricted within a narrow circle. We cannot know whom we would ; and those whom we know, we cannot have at our side when we most need them. All the higher circles of human intelligence are, to those beneath, only momentarily and partially open. We may, by good fortune, obtain a glimpse of a great poet, and hear the sound of his voice ; or put a question to a man of science, and be answered good-humouredly. We may intrude ten minutes' talk on a cabinet minister, answered probably with words worse than silence, being deceptive ; or snatch, once or twice in our lives, the privilege of throwing a bouquet in the path of a Princess, or arresting the kind glance of a Queen. And yet these momentary chances we covet ; and spend our years, and passions, and powers in pursuit of little more than these; while, meantime, there is a society continually open to us, of people who will talk to us as long as we like, whatever our rank or occupation;—talk to us in the best words they can choose, and with thanks if we listen to them. And this society, because it is so numerous and so gentle,—and can be kept waiting round us all day long, not to grant audience, but to gain it;—kings and statesmen lingering patiently in those plainly furnished and narrow anterooms, our bookcase shelves,—we make no account of that company,—perhaps never listen to a word they would say, all day long!

You may tell me, perhaps, or think within yourselves, that the apathy with which we regard this company of the noble, who are praying us to listen to them, and the passion with which we pursue the company, probably of the ignoble, who despise us, or who have nothing to teach us, are grounded in this,—that we can see the faces of the living men, and it is themselves, and not their sayings, with which we desire to become familiar. But it is not so. Suppose you never were to see their faces;—suppose you could be put behind a screen in the statesman's cabinet, or the prince's chamber, would you not be glad to listen to their words, though you were forbidden to advance beyond the screen? And when the screen is only a little less, folded in two, instead of four, and you can be hidden behind the cover of the two boards that bind a book, and listen, all day long, not to the casual talk, but to the studied, determined, chosen addresses of the wisest of men;—this station of audience, and honourable privy council, you despise!

But perhaps you will say that it is because the living people talk of things that are passing, and are of immediate interest to you, that you desire to hear them. Nay; that cannot be so, for the living people will themselves tell you about passing matters, much better in their writings than in their careless talk. But I admit that this motive does influence you, so far as you prefer those rapid and ephemeral writings to slow and enduring writings—books, properly so called. For all books are divisible into two classes, the books of the hour, and the books of all time. Mark this distinction—it is not one of quality only. It is not merely the bad book that does not last, and the good one that does. It is a distinction of species. There are good books for the hour, and good ones for all time; bad books for the hour, and bad ones for all time. I must define the two kinds before I go farther.

The good book of the hour, then,—I do not speak of the bad ones—is simply the useful or pleasant talk of some person whom you cannot otherwise converse with, printed for you. Very useful often, telling you what you need to know; very pleasant often, as a sensible friend's present talk would be. These bright accounts of travels; good-humoured and witty discussions of question; lively or pathetic story-telling in the form of novel; firm fact-telling, by the real agents concerned in the events of passing history;—all these books of the hour, multiplying among us as education becomes more general, are a peculiar characteristic and possession of the present age: we ought to be entirely thankful for them, and entirely ashamed of ourselves if we make no good use of them. But we make the worst possible use, if we allow them to usurp the place of true books: for, strictly speaking, they are not books at all, but merely letters or news-papers in good print. Our friend's letter may be delight-ful, or necessary, to-day: whether worth keeping or not, is to be considered. The newspaper may be entirely proper at breakfast time, but assuredly it is not reading for all day. So, though bound up in a volume, the long letter which gives you so pleasant an account of the inns, and roads, and weather last year at such a place, or which tells you that amusing story, or gives you the real circum-stances of such and such events, however valuable for occasional reference, may not be, in the real sense of the word, a "book" at all, nor, in the real sense, to be "read." A book is essentially not a talked thing, but a written thing; and written, not with the view of mere communication, but of permanence. The book of talk is printed only because its author cannot speak to thousands of people at once; if he could, he would—the volume is mere *multiplication* of his voice. You cannot talk to your friend in India; if you could, you would; you write instead: that is mere *conveyance* of voice. But a book is written, not to multiply the voice merely, not to carry it merely, but to preserve it. The author has something to say which he perceives to be true and useful, or helpfully beautiful. So far as he knows, no one has yet said it; so far as he knows, no one else can say it. He is bound to say it, clearly and melodiously if he may; clearly, at all events. In the sum of his life he finds this to be the thing, or group of things, manifest to him;—this the piece of true knowledge, or sight, which his share of sunshine and earth has permitted him to seize. He would fain set it down for ever; engrave it on rock, if he could; saying, "This is the best of me; for the rest, I ate, and drank, and slept, loved, and hated, like another; my life was as the vapour, and is not; but this I saw and knew: this, if anything of mine, is worth your memory." That is his " writing ;" it is, in his small human way, and with whatever degree of true inspiration is in him, his inscription, or scripture. That is a " Book."

Perhaps you think no books were ever so written ?

But, again, I ask you, do you at all believe in honesty, or at all in kindness ? or do you think there is never any honesty or benevolence in wise people ? None of us, I hope, are so unhappy as to think that. Well, whatever bit of a wise man's work is honestly and benevolently done, that bit is his book, or his piece of art. It is mixed always with evil fragments—ill-done, redundant, affected work. But if you read rightly, you will easily discover the true bits, and those *are* the book.

Now books of this kind have been written in all ages by their greatest men :—by great leaders, great statesmen, and great thinkers. These are all at your choice; and life is short. You have heard as much before ;—yet have you measured and mapped out this short life and its possibilities ? Do you know, if you read this, that you cannot read that—that what you lose to-day you cannot gain to-morrow? Will you go and gossip with your housemaid, or your stable-boy, when you may talk with queens and kings; or flatter yourselves that it is with any worthy consciousness of your own claims to respect that you jostle with the common crowd for *entrée* here, and audience there, when all the while this eternal court is open to you, with its society wide as the world, multitudinous as its days, the chosen, and the mighty, of every place and time? Into that you may enter always; in that you may take fellowship and rank according to your wish; from that, once entered into it, you can never be outcast but by your own fault; by your aristocracy of companionship there, your own inherent aristocracy will be assuredly tested, and the motives with which you strive to take high place in the society of the living, measured, as to all the truth and sincerity that are in them, by the place you desire to take in this company of the Dead.

" The place you desire," and the place you *fit yourself for*, I must also say; because, observe, this court of the past differs from all living aristocracy in this :—it is open to labour and to merit, but to nothing else. No wealth will bribe, no name overawe, no artifice deceive, the guardian of those Elysian gates. In the deep sense, no vile or vulgar person ever enters there. At the portières of that silent Faubourg St. Germain, there is but brief question, " Do you deserve to enter? Pass. Do you ask to be the companion of nobles? Make yourself noble, and you shall be. Do you long for the conversation of the wise? Learn to understand it, and you shall hear it. But on other terms?—no. If you will not rise to us, we cannot stoop to you. The living lord may assume courtesy, the living philosopher explain his thought to you with considerate pain; but here we neither feign nor interpret; you must rise to the level of our thoughts if you would be gladdened by them, and share our feelings, if you would recognise our presence."

This, then, is what you have to do, and I admit that it is much. You must, in a word, love these people, if you are to be among them. No ambition is of any use. They scorn your ambition. You must love them, and show your love in these two following ways.

I.—First, by a true desire to be taught by them, and to enter into their thoughts. To enter into theirs, observe; not to find your own expressed by them. If the person who wrote the book is not wiser than you, you need not read it; if he be, he will think differently from you in many respects.

Very ready we are to say of a book, "How good this is—that's exactly what I think!" But the right feeling is, "How strange that is! I never thought of that before, and yet I see it is true; or if I do not now, I hope I shall, some day." But whether thus submissively or not, at least be sure that you go to the author to get at *his* meaning, not to find yours. Judge it afterwards, if you think yourself qualified to do so; but ascertain it first. And be sure also, if the author is worth anything, that you will not get at his meaning all at once;—nay, that at his whole meaning you will not for a long time arrive in any wise. Not that he does not say what he means, and in strong words too; but he cannot say it all; and what is more strange, will not, but in a hidden way and in parables, in order that he may be sure you want it. I cannot quite see the reason of this, nor analyse that cruel reticence in the breasts of wise men which makes them always hide their deeper thought. They do not give it you by way of help, but of reward, and will make themselves sure that you deserve it before they allow you to reach it. But it is the same with the physical type of wisdom, gold. There seems, to you and me, no reason why the electric forces of the earth should not carry whatever there is of gold within it at once to the mountain tops, so that kings and people might know that all the gold they could get was there; and without any trouble of digging, or anxiety, or chance, or waste of time, cut it away, and coin as much as they needed. But Nature does not manage it so. She puts it in little fissures in the earth, nobody knows where:

you may dig long and find none ; you must dig painfully to find any.

And it is just the same with men's best wisdom. When you come to a good book, you must ask yourself, "Am I inclined to work as an Australian miner would ? Are my pickaxes and shovels in good order, and am I in good trim myself, my sleeves well up to the elbow, and my breath good, and my temper ? " And, keeping the figure a little longer, even at cost of tiresomeness, for it is a thoroughly useful one, the metal you are in search of being the author's mind or meaning, his words are as the rock which you have to crush and smelt in order to get at it. And your pickaxes are your own care, wit, and learning ; your smelting furnace is your own thoughtful soul. Do not hope to get at any good author's meaning without those tools and that fire ; often you will need sharpest, finest chiselling, and patientest fusing, before you can gather one grain of the metal.

And, therefore, first of all, I tell you, earnestly and authoritatively, (I *know* I am right in this,) you must get into the habit of looking intensely at words, and assuring yourself of their meaning, syllable by syllable—nay, letter by letter. For though it is only by reason of the opposition of letters in the function of signs, to sounds in function of signs, that the study of books is called "literature," and that a man versed in it is called, by the consent of nations, a man of letters instead of a man of books, or of words, you may yet connect with that accidental nomenclature this real principle :—that you might read all the books in the British Museum (if you could live long enough), and remain an utterly "illiterate," uneducated person ; but that if you read ten pages of a good book, letter by letter,—that is to say, with real accuracy,—you are for evermore in some measure an educated person. The entire difference between education and non-education (as regards the merely intellectual part of it), consists in this accuracy. A well-educated gentleman may not know many lan-guages,—may not be able to speak any but his own,—

may have read very few books. But whatever language he knows, he knows precisely ; whatever word he pronounces he pronounces rightly ; above all, he is learned in the *peerage* of words ; knows the words of true descent and ancient blood, at a glance, from words of modern canaille ; remembers all their ancestry—their inter-marriages, distantest relationships, and the extent to which they were admitted, and offices they held, among the national noblesse of words at any time, and in any country. But an uneducated person may know by memory any number of languages, and talk them all, and yet truly know not a word of any,—not a word even of his own. An ordinarily clever and sensible seaman will be able to make his way ashore at most ports ; yet he has only to speak a sentence of any language to be known for an illiterate person : so also the accent, or turn of expression of a single sentence will at once mark a scholar. And this is so strongly felt, so conclusively admitted, by educated persons, that a false accent or a mistaken syllable is enough, in the parliament of any civilized nation, to assign to a man a certain degree of inferior standing for ever. And this is right ; but it is a pity that the accuracy insisted on is not greater, and required to a serious purpose. It is right that a false Latin quantity should excite a smile in the House of Commons ; but it is wrong that a false English meaning should *not* excite a frown there. Let the accent of words be watched, by all means, but let their meaning be watched more closely still, and fewer will do the work. A few words well chosen and well distinguished, will do work that a thousand cannot, when every one is acting, equivocally, in the function of another. Yes ; and words, if they are not watched, will do deadly work sometimes. There are masked words droning and skulking about us in Europe just now,—(there never were so many, owing to the spread of a shallow, blotching, blundering, infectious "information," or rather deformation, everywhere, and to the teaching of catechisms and phrases at schools instead of human meanings)—there are masked words abroad, I say, which nobody understands, but which everybody uses, and most people will also fight for, live for, or even die for, fancying they mean this, or that, or the other, of things dear to them : for such words wear chamæleon cloaks— "groundlion" cloaks, of the colour of the ground of any man's fancy : on that ground they lie in wait, and rend him with a spring from it. There were never creatures of prey so mischievous, never diplomatists so cunning, never poisoners so deadly, as these masked words ; they are the unjust stewards of all men's ideas : whatever fancy or favourite instinct a man most cherishes, he gives to his favourite masked word to take care of for him ; the word at last comes to have an infinite power over him,—you cannot get at him but by its ministry. And in languages so mongrel in breed as the English, there is a fatal power of equivocation put into men's hands, almost whether they will or no, in being able to use Greek or Latin forms for a word when they want it to be respectable, and Saxon or otherwise common forms when they want to discredit it. What a singular and salutary effect, for instance, would be produced on the minds of people who are in the habit of taking the Form of the words they live by, for the Power of which those words tell them, if we always either retained, or refused, the Greek form "biblos," or "biblion," as the right expression for "book"—instead of employing it only in the one instance in which we wish to give dignity to the idea, and translating it everywhere else. How wholesome it would be for the many simple persons who worship the Letter of God's Word instead of its Spirit, (just as other idolaters worship His picture instead of His presence,) if, in such places (for instance) as Acts xix. 19 we retained the Greek expression, instead of translating it, and they had to read—"Many of them also which used curious arts, brought their bibles together, and burnt them before all men ; and they counted the price of them, and found it fifty thousand pieces of silver !" Or if, on the other hand, we translated instead of retaining it, and always spoke of "the Holy Book," instead of "Holy Bible," it might come into more heads than it does at present that the Word of God, by which the heavens were, of old, and by which they are now kept in store,[1] cannot be made a present of to anybody in morocco binding; nor sown on any wayside by help either of steam plough or steam press; but is nevertheless being offered to us daily, and by us with contumely refused; and sown in us daily, and by us as instantly as may be, choked.

So, again, consider what effect has been produced on the English vulgar mind by the use of the sonorous Latin form "damno," in translating the Greek κατακρίνω, when people charitably wish to make it forcible; and the substitution of the temperate "condemn" for it, when they choose to keep it gentle. And what notable sermons have been preached by illiterate clergymen on— "He that believeth not shall be damned;" though they would shrink with horror from translating, Heb. xi. 7, "The saving of his house, by which he damned the world," or John viii. 12, "Woman, hath no man damned thee? She saith, No man, Lord. Jesus answered her, Neither do I damn thee; go and sin no more." And divisions in the mind of Europe, which have cost seas of blood, and in the defence of which the noblest souls of men have been cast away in frantic desolation, countless as forest-leaves—though, in the heart of them, founded on deeper causes—have nevertheless been rendered practically possible, namely, by the European adoption of the Greek word for a public meeting, to give peculiar respectability to such meetings, when held for religious purposes; and other collateral equivocations, such as the vulgar English one of using the word "priest" as a contraction for "presbyter."

Now, in order to deal with words rightly, this is the habit you must form. Nearly every word in your language has been first a word of some other language

[1] 3. Peter iii. 5–7.

—of Saxon, German, French, Latin, or Greek; (not to speak of eastern and primitive dialects). And many words have been all these;—that is to say, have been Greek first, Latin next, French or German next, and English last: undergoing a certain change of sense and use on the lips of each nation; but retaining a deep vital meaning which all good scholars feel in employing them, even at this day. If you do not know the Greek alphabet, learn it; young or old—girl or boy—whoever you may be, if you think of reading seriously (which, of course, implies that you have some leisure at command), learn your Greek alphabet; then get good dictionaries of all these languages, and whenever you are in doubt about a word, hunt it down patiently. Read Max Müller's lectures thoroughly, to begin with; and, after that, never let a word escape you that looks suspicious. It is severe work; but you will find it, even at first, interesting, and at last, endlessly amusing. And the general gain to your character, in power and precision, will be quite incalculable.

Mind, this does not imply knowing, or trying to know, Greek, or Latin, or French. It takes a whole life to learn any language perfectly. But you can easily ascertain the meanings through which the English word has passed; and those which in a good writer's work it must still bear.

And now, merely for example's sake, I will, with your permission, read a few lines of a true book with you, carefully; and see what will come out of them. I will take a book perfectly known to you all; No English words are more familiar to us, yet nothing perhaps has been less read with sincerity. I will take these few following lines of Lycidas.

> " Last came, and last did go,
> The pilot of the Galilean lake;
> Two massy keys he bore of metals twain,
> (The golden opes, the iron shuts amain),
> He shook his mitred locks, and stern bespake,
> How well could I have spar'd for thee, young swain,

> Enow of such as for their bellies' sake
> Creep, and intrude, and climb into the fold!
> Of other care they little reckoning make,
> Than how to scramble at the shearers' feast,
> And shove away the worthy bidden guest;
> Blind mouths! that scarce themselves know how to hold
> A sheep-hook, or have learn'd aught else, the least
> That to the faithful herdman's art belongs!
> What recks it them? What need they? They are sped
> And when they list, their lean and flashy songs
> Grate on their scrannel pipes of wretched straw;
> The hungry sheep look up, and are not fed,
> But swoln with wind, and the rank mist they draw,
> Rot inwardly, and foul contagion spread;
> Besides what the grim wolf with privy paw
> Daily devours apace, and nothing said."

Let us think over this passage, and examine its words. First, is it not singular to find Milton assigning to St. Peter, not only his full episcopal function, but the very types of it which Protestants usually refuse most passionately? His "mitred" locks! Milton was no Bishop-lover; how comes St. Peter to be "mitred?" "Two massy keys he bore." Is this, then, the power of the keys claimed by the Bishops of Rome, and is it acknowledged here by Milton only in a poetical licence, for the sake of its picturesqueness, that he may get the gleam of the golden keys to help his effect? Do not think it. Great men do not play stage tricks with the doctrines of life and death: only little men do that. Milton means what he says; and means it with his might too—is going to put the whole strength of his spirit presently into the saying of it. For though not a lover of false bishops, he *was* a lover of true ones; and the Lake-pilot is here, in his thoughts, the type and head of true episcopal power. For Milton reads that text, "I will give unto thee the keys of the kingdom of Heaven" quite honestly. Puritan though he be, he would not blot it out of the book because there have been bad bishops; nay, in order to understand him, we must understand that verse first; it will not do to eye it askance, or whisper it under our breath, as if it were a weapon of an adverse sect. It is a solemn, universal assertion, deeply to be kept in mind by all sects. But perhaps we shall be better able to reason on it if we go on a little farther, and come back to it. For clearly, this marked insistance on the power of the true episcopate is to make us feel more weightily what is to be charged against the false claimants of episcopate ; or generally, against false claimants of power and rank in the body of the clergy ; they who, " for their bellies' sake, creep, and intrude, and climb into the fold."

Do not think Milton uses those three words to fill up his verse, as a loose writer would. He needs all the three ; specially those three, and no more than those—" creep," and "intrude," and " climb ;" no other words would or could serve the turn, and no more could be added. For they exhaustively comprehend the three classes, correspondent to the three characters, of men who dishonestly seek ecclesiastical power. First, those who "*creep*" into the fold ; who do not care for office, nor name, but for secret influence, and do all things occultly and cunningly, consenting to any servility of office or conduct, so only that they may intimately discern, and unawares direct, the minds of men. Then those who "intrude" (thrust, that is) themselves into the fold, who by natural insolence of heart, and stout eloquence of tongue, and fearlessly perseverant self-assertion, obtain hearing and authority with the common crowd. Lastly, those who " climb," who, by labour and learning, both stout and sound, but selfishly exerted in the cause of their own ambition, gain high dignities and authorities, and become "lords over the heritage," though not " ensamples to the flock."

Now go on :—

> " Of other care they little reckoning make,
> Than how to scramble at the shearers' feast.
> *Blind mouths—*"

I pause again, for this is a strange expression ; a broken metaphor, one might think, careless and un-scholarly.

Not so : its very audacity and pithiness are intended to make us look close at the phrase and remember it. Those two monosyllables express the precisely accurate contraries of right character, in the two great offices of the Church—those of bishop and pastor.

A Bishop means a person who sees.

A Pastor means one who feeds.

The most unbishoply character a man can have is therefore to be Blind.

The most unpastoral is, instead of feeding, to want to be fed,—to be a Mouth.

Take the two reverses together, and you have "blind mouths." We may advisably follow out this idea a little. Nearly all the evils in the Church have arisen from bishops desiring *power* more than *light*. They want authority, not outlook. Whereas their real office is not to rule ; though it may be vigorously to exhort and rebuke ; it is the king's office to rule ; the bishop's office is to *oversee* the flock ; to number it, sheep by sheep ; to be ready always to give full account of it. Now it is clear he cannot give account of the souls, if he has not so much as numbered the bodies of his flock. The first thing, therefore, that a bishop has to do is at least to put himself in a position in which, at any moment, he can obtain the history from childhood of every living soul in his diocese, and of its present state. Down in that back street, Bill, and Nancy, knocking each other's teeth out !—Does the bishop know all about it ? Has he his eye upon them ? Has he *had* his eye upon them ? Can he circumstantially explain to us how Bill got into the habit of beating Nancy about the head ? If he cannot, he is no bishop, though he had a mitre as high as Salisbury steeple ; he is no bishop,—he has sought to be at the helm instead of the masthead ; he has no sight of things. "Nay," you say, it is not his duty to look after Bill in the back street. What ! the fat sheep that have full fleeces—you think it is only those he should look after, while (go back to your Milton) "the hungry sheep look up, and are not fed, besides what the grim wolf, with privy paw" (bishops knowing nothing about it) "daily devours apace, and nothing said?"

"But that's not our idea of a bishop." Perhaps not; but it was St. Paul's; and it was Milton's. They may be right, or we may be; but we must not think we are reading either one or the other by putting our meaning into their words.

I go on.

> "But swoln with wind, and the rank mist they draw."

This is to meet the vulgar answer that "if the poor are not looked after in their bodies, they are in their souls; they have spiritual food."

And Milton says, "They have no such thing as spiritual food; they are only swollen with wind." At first you may think that is a coarse type, and an obscure one. But again, it is a quite literally accurate one. Take up your Latin and Greek dictionaries, and find out the meaning of "Spirit." It is only a contraction of the Latin word "breath," and an indistinct translation of the Greek word for "wind." The same word is used in writing, "The wind bloweth where it listeth;" and in writing, "So is every one that is born of the Spirit;" born of the *breath*, that is; for it means the breath of God, in soul and body. We have the true sense of it in our words "inspiration" and "expire." Now, there are two kinds of breath with which the flock may be filled; God's breath, and man's. The breath of God is health, and life, and peace to them, as the air of heaven is to the flocks on the hills; but man's breath—the word which *he* calls spiritual,—is disease and contagion to them, as the fog of the fen. They rot inwardly with it; they are puffed up by it, as a dead body by the vapours of its own decomposition. This is literally true of all false religious teaching; the first, and last, and fatalest sign of it is that "puffing up." Your converted children, who teach their parents; your converted convicts, who teach honest men; your converted dunces, who, having lived in cretinous stupefaction half their lives, suddenly awaking to the fact of there being a God, fancy themselves therefore His peculiar people and messengers ; your sectarians of every species, small and great, Catholic or Protestant, of high church or low, in so far as they think themselves exclusively in the right and others wrong ; and pre-eminently, in every sect, those who hold that men can be saved by thinking rightly instead of doing rightly, by word instead of act, and wish instead of work :—these are the true fog children—clouds, these, without water ; bodies, these, of putrescent vapour and skin, without blood or flesh : blown bag-pipes for the fiends to pipe with—corrupt, and corrupting,—" Swollen with wind, and the rank mist they draw."

Lastly, let us return to the lines respecting the power of the keys, for now we can understand them. Note the difference between Milton and Dante in their interpretation of this power : for once, the latter is weaker in thought ; he supposes *both* the keys to be of the gate of heaven ; one is of gold, the other of silver : they are given by St. Peter to the sentinel angel ; and it is not easy to determine the meaning either of the substances of the three steps of the gate, or of the two keys. But Milton makes one, of gold, the key of heaven ; the other, of iron, the key of the prison, in which the wicked teachers are to be bound who " have taken away the key of knowledge, yet entered not in themselves."

We have seen that the duties of bishop and pastor are to see, and feed ; and, of all who do so, it is said, " He that watereth, shall be watered also himself." But the reverse is truth also. He that watereth not, shall be *withered* himself ; and he that seeth not, shall himself be shut out of sight,—shut into the perpetual prison-house. And that prison opens here, as well as hereafter : he who is to be bound in heaven must first be bound on earth. That command to the strong angels, of which the rock-apostle is the image, " Take him, and bind him hand and foot, and cast him out," issues, in its measure, against the teacher, for every help withheld, and for every truth refused and for every falsehood enforced ; so that

he is more strictly fettered the more he fetters, and farther
outcast, as he more and more misleads, till at last the
bars of the iron cage close upon him, and as "the
golden opes, the iron shuts amain."

We have got something out of the lines, I think, and
much more is yet to be found in them ; but we have
done enough by way of example of the kind of word-by-
word examination of your author which is rightly called
"reading ;" watching every accent and expression, and
putting ourselves always in the author's place, annihilating
our own personality, and seeking to enter into his, so as
to be able assuredly to say, "Thus Milton thought," not
"Thus I thought, in mis-reading Milton." And by this
process you will gradually come to attach less weight to
your own "Thus I thought" at other times. You will
begin to perceive that what *you* thought was a matter of
no serious importance ;—that your thoughts on any
subject are not perhaps the clearest and wisest that could
be arrived at thereupon :—in fact, that unless you are a
very singular person, you cannot be said to have any
"thoughts" at all ; that you have no materials for them,
in any serious matters ;—no right to "think," but only
to try to learn more of the facts. Nay, most probably
all your life (unless, as I said, you are a singular person)
you will have no legitimate right to an "opinion" on
any business, except that instantly under your hand.
What must of necessity be done, you can always find
out, beyond question, how to do. Have you a house to
keep in order, a commodity to sell, a field to plough,
a ditch to cleanse? There need be no two opinions
about these proceedings; it is at your peril if you have
not much more than an "opinion" on the way to
manage such matters. And also, outside of your own
business, there are one or two subjects on which you are
bound to have but one opinion. T at roguery and
lying are objectionable, and are instantly to be flogged
out of the way whenever discovered ;—that covetousness
and love of quarrelling are dangerous dispositions even
in children, and deadly dispositions in men and nations ;

—that in the end, the God of heaven and earth loves active, modest, and kind people, and hates idle, proud, greedy, and cruel ones;—on these general facts you are bound to have but one, and that a very strong, opinion. For the rest, respecting religions, governments, sciences, arts, you will find that, on the whole, you can know NOTHING,—judge nothing; that the best you can do, even though you may be a well-educated person, is to be silent, and strive to be wiser every day, and to understand a little more of the thoughts of others, which so soon as you try to do honestly, you will discover that the thoughts even of the wisest are very little more than pertinent questions. To put the difficulty into a clear shape, and exhibit to you the grounds for *in*decision, that is all they can generally do for you!—and well for them and for us, if indeed they are able "to mix the music with our thoughts, and sadden us with heavenly doubts." This writer, from whom I have been reading to you, is not among the first or wisest : he sees shrewdly as far as he sees, and therefore it is easy to find out his full meaning; but with the greater men, you cannot fathom their meaning; they do not even wholly measure it themselves,—it is so wide. Suppose I had asked you, for instance, to seek for Shakespeare's opinion, instead of Milton's, on this matter of Church authority?—or for Dante's? Have any of you, at this instant, the least idea what either thought about it? Have you ever balanced the scene with the bishops in Richard III. against the character of Cranmer? the description of St. Francis and St. Dominic against that of him who made Virgil wonder to gaze upon him,—" disteso, tanto vilmente, nell' eterno esilio ; " or of him whom Dante stood beside, "come 'l frate che confessa lo perfido assassin?"[1] Shakespeare and Alighieri knew men better than most of us, I presume! They were both in the midst of the main struggle between the temporal and spiritual powers. They had an opinion, we may guess?

[1] Inf. xix. 71 ; xxiii. 117.

But where is it? Bring it into court! Put Shakespeare's or Dante's creed into articles, and send *that* up into the Ecclesiastical Courts!

You will not be able, I tell you again, for many and many a day, to come at the real purposes and teaching of these great men; but a very little honest study of them will enable you to perceive that what you took for your own "judgment" was mere chance prejudice, and drifted, helpless, entangled weed of castaway thought: nay, you will see that most men's minds are indeed little better than rough heath wilderness, neglected and stubborn, partly barren, partly overgrown with pestilent brakes and venomous wind-sown herbage of evil surmise; that the first thing you have to do for them, and yourself, is eagerly and scornfully to set fire to *this;* burn all the jungle into wholesome ash-heaps, and then plough and sow. All the true literary work before you, for life, must begin with obedience to that order, "Break up your fallow ground, and *sow not among thorns.*"

II. Having then faithfully listened to the great teachers, that you may enter into their Thoughts, you have yet this higher advance to make;—you have to enter into their Hearts. As you go to them first for clear sight, so you must stay with them that you may share at last their just and mighty Passion. Passion, or "sensation." I am not afraid of the word; still less of the thing. You have heard many outcries against sensation lately; but, I can tell you, it is not less sensation we want, but more. The ennobling difference between one man and another,—between one animal and another,—is precisely in this, that one feels more than another. If we were sponges, perhaps sensation might not be easily got for us; if we were earth-worms, liable at every instant to be cut in two by the spade, perhaps too much sensation might not be good for us. But being human creatures, *it is* good for us; nay, we are only human in so far as we are sensitive, and our honour is precisely in proportion to our passion.

You know I said of that great and pure society of the

dead, that it would allow "no vain or vulgar person to enter there." What do you think I meant by a "vulgar" person? What do you yourselves mean by "vulgarity?" You will find it a fruitful subject of thought; but, briefly, the essence of all vulgarity lies in want of sensation. Simple and innocent vulgarity is merely an untrained and undeveloped bluntness of body and mind; but in true inbred vulgarity, there is a deathful callousness, which, in extremity, becomes capable of every sort of bestial habit and crime, without fear, without pleasure, without horror, and without pity. It is in the blunt hand and the dead heart, in the diseased habit, in the hardened conscience, that men become vulgar; they are for ever vulgar, precisely in proportion as they are incapable of sympathy,—of quick understanding,—of all that, in deep insistance on the common, but most accurate term, may be called the "tact" or touch-faculty of body and soul: that tact which the Mimosa has in trees, which the pure woman has above all creatures;—fineness and fulness of sensation, beyond reason;—the guide and sanctifier of reason itself. Reason can but determine what is true:— it is the God-given passion of humanity which alone can recognise what God has made good.

We come then to that great concourse of the Dead, not merely to know from them what is True, but chiefly to feel with them what is Righteous. Now, to feel with them, we must be like them; and none of us can become that without pains. As the true knowledge is disciplined and tested knowledge,—not the first thought that comes, —so the true passion is disciplined and tested passion, —not the first passion that comes. The first that come are the vain, the false, the treacherous; if you yield to them they will lead you wildly and far, in vain pursuit, in hollow enthusiasm, till you have no true purpose and no true passion left. Not that any feeling possible to humanity is in itself wrong, but only wrong when un-disciplined. Its nobility is in its force and justice; it is wrong when it is weak, and felt for paltry cause. There is a mean wonder, as of a child who sees a juggler tossing golden balls, and this is base, if you will. But do you think that the wonder is ignoble, or the sensation less, with which every human soul is called to watch the golden balls of heaven tossed through the night by the Hand that made them? There is a mean curiosity, as of a child opening a forbidden door, or a servant prying into her master's business;—and a noble curiosity, questioning, in the front of danger, the source of the great river beyond the sand,—the place of the great continents beyond the sea;—a nobler curiosity still, which questions of the source of the River of Life, and of the space of the Continent of Heaven,—things which "the angels desire to look into." So the anxiety is ignoble, with which you linger over the course and catastrophe of an idle tale; but do you think the anxiety is less, or greater, with which you watch, or *ought* to watch, the dealings of fate and destiny with the life of an agonised nation? Alas! it is the narrowness, selfishness, minuteness, of your sensation that you have to deplore in England at this day;—sensation which spends itself in bouquets and speeches; in revellings and junketings; in sham fights and gay puppet shows, while you can look on and see noble nations murdered, man by man, woman by woman, child by child, without an effort, or a tear.

I said "minuteness" and "selfishness" of sensation, but in a word, I ought to have said "injustice" or "unrighteousness" of sensation. For as in nothing is a gentleman better to be discerned from a vulgar person, so in nothing is a gentle nation (such nations have been) better to be discerned from a mob, than in this,—that their feelings are constant and just, results of due contemplation, and of equal thought. You can talk a mob into anything; its feelings may be—usually are—on the whole generous and right; but it has no foundation for them, no hold of them; you may tease or tickle it into any, at your pleasure; it thinks by infection, for the most part, catching a passion like a cold, and there is nothing so little that it will not roar itself wild about,

when the fit is on;—nothing so great but it will forget
in an hour, when the fit is past.   But a gentleman's, or
a gentle nation's, passions are just, measured, and continuous.   A great nation, for instance, does not spend
its entire national wits for a couple of months in weighing evidence of a single ruffian's having done a single
murder; and for a couple of years, see its own children
murder each other by their thousands or tens of thousands
a day, considering only what the effect is likely to be on
the price of cotton, and caring nowise to determine which
side of battle is in the wrong.   Neither does a great
nation send its poor little boys to jail for stealing six
walnuts; and allow its bankrupts to steal their hundreds
of thousands with a bow, and its bankers, rich with poor
men's savings, to close their doors "under circumstances
over which they have no control," with a "by your
leave;" and large landed estates to be bought by men
who have made their money by going with armed
steamers up and down the China Seas, selling opium at
the cannon's mouth, and altering, for the benefit of the
foreign nation, the common highwayman's demand of
"your money *or* your life," into that of "your money
and your life."   Neither does a great nation allow the
lives of its innocent poor to be parched out of them by
fog fever, and rotted out of them by dunghill plague, for
the sake of sixpence a life extra per week to its land-
lords;[1] and then debate, with drivelling tears, and

---

[1] See the evidence in the Medical officer's report to the Privy
Council, just published.   There are suggestions in its preface which
will make some stir among us, I fancy, respecting which let me
note these points following:—
There are two theories on the subject of land now abroad, and in
contention; both false.
The first is that by Heavenly law, there have always existed, and
must continue to exist, a certain number of hereditarily sacred
persons, to whom the earth, air, and water of the world belong, as
personal property; of which earth, air, and water these persons
may, at their pleasure permit, or forbid, the rest of the human race
to eat, to breathe or to drink.   This theory is not for many years
longer tenable.   The adverse theory is that a division of the land
of the world among the mob of the world would immediately

diabolical sympathies, whether it ought not piously to save, and nursingly cherish, the lives of its murderers.

elevate the said mob into sacred personages; that houses would then build themselves, and corn grow of itself; and that everybody would be able to live, without doing any work for his living. This theory would also be found highly untenable in practice.

It will, however, require some rough experiments, and rougher catastrophes, even in this magnesium-lighted epoch, before the generality of persons will be convinced that no law concerning anything, least of all concerning land, for either holding or dividing it, or renting it high, or renting it low, would be of the smallest ultimate use to the people, so long as the general contest for life, and for the means of life, remains one of mere brutal competition. That contest, in an unprincipled nation, will take one deadly form or another, whatever laws you make for it. For instance, it would be an entirely wholesome law for England, if it could be carried, that maximum limits should be assigned to incomes, according to classes; and that every nobleman's income should be paid to him as a fixed salary or pension by the nation; and not squeezed by him in a variable sum, at discretion, out of the tenants of his land. But if you could get such a law passed to-morrow; and if, which would be farther necessary, you could fix the value of the assigned incomes by making a given weight of pure wheat-flour legal tender for a given sum, a twelvemonth would not pass before another currency would have been tacitly established, and the power of accumulative wealth would have re-asserted itself in some other article, or some imaginary sign. Forbid men to buy each other's lives for sovereigns, and they will for shells, or slates. There is only one cure for public distress—and that is public education, directed to make men thoughtful, merciful, and just. There are, indeed, many laws conceivable which would gradually better and strengthen the national temper; but, for the most part, they are such as the national temper must be much bettered before it would bear. A nation in its youth may be helped by laws, as a weak child by backboards, but when it is old, it cannot that way straighten its crooked spine.

And besides; the problem of land, at its worst, is a bye one; distribute the earth as you will, the principal question remains inexorable,—Who is to dig it? Which of us, in brief words, is to do the hard and dirty work for the rest—and for what pay? Who is to do the pleasant and clean work, and for what pay? Who is to do no work, and for what pay? And there are curious moral and religious questions connected with these. How far is it lawful to suck a portion of the soul out of a great many persons, in order to put the abstracted psychical quantities together, and make one very beautiful or ideal soul? If we had to deal with mere blood, instead of spirit, and the thing might literally be done (as it has been done with infants before now) so that it were possible, by

Also, a great nation having made up its mind that hanging is quite the wholesomest process for its homicides in general, can yet with mercy distinguish between the degrees of guilt in homicides; and does not yelp like a pack of frost-pinched wolf-cubs on the blood-track of an unhappy crazed boy, or grey-haired clodpate Othello, "perplexed i' the extreme," at the very moment that it is sending a Minister of the Crown to make polite speeches to a man who is bayoneting young girls in their fathers' sight, and killing noble youths in cool blood, faster than a country butcher kills lambs in spring. And, lastly, a great nation does not mock Heaven and its Powers, by pretending belief in a revelation which asserts the love of money to be the root of *all* evil, and declaring, at the same time, that it is actuated, and intends to be actuated, in all chief national deeds and measures, by no other love.

My friends, I do not know why any of us should talk about reading. We want some sharper discipline than that of reading; but, at all events, be assured, we cannot read. No reading is possible for a people with its mind

taking a certain quantity of blood from the arms of a given number of the mob, and putting it all into one person, to make a more azure-blooded gentleman of him, the thing would of course be managed; but secretly, I should conceive. But now, because it is brain and soul that we abstract, not visible blood, it can be done quite openly; and we live, we gentlemen, on delicatest prey, after the manner of weasels; that is to say we keep a certain number of clowns digging and ditching, and genera'ly stupefied, in order that we, being fed gratis, may have all the thinking and feeling to ourselves. Yet there is a great deal to be said for this. A highly-bred and trained English, French, Austrian, or Italian gentleman (much more a lady) is a great production; a better production than most statues; being beautifully coloured as well as shaped, and plus all the brains; a glorious thing to look at, a wonderful thing to talk to; and you cannot have it, any more than a pyramid or a church, but by sacrifice of much contributed life. And it is, perhaps, better to build a beautiful human creature than a beautiful dome or steeple; and more delightful to look up reverently to a creature far above us, than to a wall; only the beautiful human creature will have some duties to do in return —duties of living belfry and rampart—of which presently.

in this state. No sentence of any great writer is intelligible to them. It is simply and sternly impossible
for the English public, at this moment, to understand any
thoughtful writing,—so incapable of thought has it become in its insanity of avarice. Happily, our disease is,
as yet, little worse than this incapacity of thought; it is
not corruption of the inner nature; we ring true still,
when anything strikes home to us; and though the idea
that everything should "pay" has infected our every
purpose so deeply, that even when we would play the
good Samaritan, we never take out our twopence and
give them to the host, without saying, "When I come
again, thou shalt give me fourpence," there is a capacity
of noble passion left in our hearts' core. We show it in
our work—in our war,—even in those unjust domestic
affections which make us furious at a small private wrong,
while we are polite to a boundless public one: we are
still industrious to the last hour of the day, though we
add the gambler's fury to the labourer's patience; we
are still brave to the death, though incapable of discerning true cause for battle, and are still true in
affection to our own flesh, to the death, as the sea-
monsters are, and the rock-eagles. And there is hope
for a nation while this can be still said of it. As long as
it holds its life in its hand, ready to give it for its honour
(though a foolish honour), for its love (though a selfish
love), and for its business (though a base business) there
is hope for it. But hope only; for this instinctive, reckless virtue cannot last. No nation can last, which has
made a mob of itself, however generous at heart. It
must discipline its passions, and direct them, or they
will discipline it, one day, with scorpion whips. Above
all, a nation cannot last as a money-making mob: it
cannot with impunity,—it cannot with existence,—go
on despising literature, despising science, despising art,
despising nature, despising compassion, and concentrat-
ing its soul on Pence. Do you think these are harsh or
wild words? Have patience with me but a little longer.
I will prove their truth to you, clause by clause.

I.   I say first we have despised literature.   What do
we, as a nation, care about books?   How much do you
think we spend altogether on our libraries, public or
private, as compared with what we spend on our horses?
If a man spends lavishly on his library, you call him mad
—a biblio-maniac.   But you never call any one a horse-
maniac, though men ruin themselves every day by their
horses, and you do not hear of people ruining themselves
by their books.   Or, to go lower still, how much do you
think the contents of the book-shelves of the United
Kingdom, public and private, would fetch, as compared
with the contents of its wine-cellars?   What position
would its expenditure on literature take, as compared
with its expenditure on luxurious eating?   We talk of
food for the mind, as of food for the body: now a good
book contains such food inexhaustibly; it is a provision
for life, and for the best part of us; yet how long most
people would look at the best book before they would
give the price of a large turbot for it!   Though there
have been men who have pinched their stomachs and
bared their backs to buy a book, whose libraries were
cheaper to them, I think, in the end, than most men's
dinners are.   We are few of us put to such trial, and
more the pity; for, indeed, a precious thing is all the
more precious to us if it has been won by work or
economy; and if public libraries were half as costly as
public dinners, or books cost the tenth part of what
bracelets do, even foolish men and women might sometimes suspect there was good in reading, as well as in
munching and sparkling; whereas the very cheapness
of literature is making even wise people forget that if a
book is worth reading, it is worth buying.   No book is
worth anything which is not worth *much*; nor is it
serviceable, until it has been read, and reread, and loved,
and loved again; and marked, so that you can refer to
the passages you want in it, as a soldier can seize the
weapon he needs in an armoury, or a housewife bring
the spice she needs from her store.   Bread of flour is
good; but there is bread, sweet as honey, if he would

eat it, in a good book; and the family must be poor indeed which, once in their lives, cannot, for such multipliable barley-loaves, pay their baker's bill. We call ourselves a rich nation, and we are filthy and foolish enough to thumb each other's books out of circulating libraries !

II. I say we have despised science. "What!" (you exclaim) "are we not foremost in all discovery, and is not the whole world giddy by reason, or unreason, of our inventions?" Yes; but do you suppose that is national work? That work is all done in spite of the nation; by private people's zeal and money. We are glad enough, indeed, to make our profit of science; we snap up anything in the way of a scientific bone that has meat on it, eagerly enough; but if the scientific man comes for a bone or a crust to *us*, that is another story. What have we publicly done for science? We are obliged to know what o'clock it is, for the safety of our ships, and therefore we pay for an observatory; and we allow ourselves, in the person of our Parliament, to be annually tormented into doing something, in a slovenly way, for the British Museum; sullenly apprehending that to be a place for keeping stuffed birds in, to amuse our children. If anybody will pay for their own telescope, and resolve another nebula, we cackle over the discernment as if it were our own; if one in ten thousand of our hunting squires suddenly perceives that the earth was indeed made to be something else than a portion for foxes, and burrows in it himself, and tells us where the gold is, and where the coals, we understand that there is some use in that; and very properly knight him: but is the accident of his having found out how to employ himself usefully any credit to *us*? (The negation of such discovery among his brother squires may perhaps be some *dis*credit to us, if we would consider of it.) But if you doubt these generalities, here is one fact for us all to meditate upon, illustrative of our love of science. Two years ago there was a collection of the fossils of Solenhofen to be sold in Bavaria; the best in existence, containing many specimens unique for perfectness, and one, unique as an example of a species (a whole kingdom of unknown living creatures being announced by that fossil). This collection, of which the mere market worth, among private buyers, would probably have been some thousand or twelve hundred pounds, was offered to the English nation for seven hundred: but we would not give seven hundred, and the whole series would have been in the Munich museum at this moment, if Professor Owen[1] had not, with loss of his own time, and patient tormenting of the British public in person of its representatives, got leave to give four hundred pounds at once, and himself become answerable for the other three! which the said public will doubtless pay him eventually, but sulkily, and caring nothing about the matter all the while; only always ready to cackle if any credit comes of it. Consider, I beg of you, arithmetically, what this fact means. Your annual expenditure for public purposes (a third of it for military apparatus), is at least 50 millions. Now 700*l.* is to 50,000,000*l.* roughly, as seven pence to two thousand pounds. Suppose then, a gentleman of unknown income, but whose wealth was to be conjectured from the fact that he spent two thousand a year on his park-walls and footmen only, professes himself fond of science; and that one of his servants comes eagerly to tell him that an unique collection of fossils, giving clue to a new era of creation, is to be had for the sum of seven pence sterling; and that the gentleman, who is fond of science, and spends two thousand a year on his park, answers, after keeping his servant waiting several months, "Well! I'll give you fourpence for them, if you will be answerable for the extra threepence yourself, till next year!"

III. I say you have despised Art! "What!" you again answer, "have we not Art exhibitions, miles long? and do not we pay thousands of pounds for single

---

[1] I state this fact without Professor Owen's permission: which of course he could not with propriety have granted, had I asked it; but I consider it so important that the public should be aware of the fact, that I do what seems to me right, though rude.

pictures? and have we not Art schools and institutions, more than ever nation had before?" Yes, truly, but all that is for the sake of the shop. You would fain sell canvas as well as coals, and crockery as well as iron; you would take every other nation's bread out of its mouth if you could; not being able to do that, your ideal of life is to stand in the thoroughfares of the world, like Ludgate apprentices, screaming to every passer by, "What d'ye lack?" You know nothing of your own faculties or circumstances; you fancy that, among your damp, flat, fat fields of clay, you can have as quick art-fancy as the Frenchman among his bronzed vines, or the Italian under his volcanic cliffs;—that Art may be learned as book-keeping is, and when learned, will give you more books to keep. You care for pictures, absolutely, no more than you do for the bills pasted on your dead walls. There is always room on the walls for the bills to be read,—never for the pictures to be seen. You do not know what pictures you have (by repute), in the country, nor whether they are false or true, nor whether they are taken care of or not; in foreign countries, you calmly see the noblest existing pictures in the world rotting in abandoned wreck—(and, in Venice, with the Austrian guns deliberately pointed at the palaces containing them), and if you heard that all the Titians in Europe were made sand-bags to-morrow on the Austrian forts, it would not trouble you so much as the chance of a brace or two of game less in your own bags in a day's shooting. That is your national love of Art.

IV. You have despised nature; that is to say, all the deep and sacred sensations of natural scenery. The French revolutionists made stables of the cathedrals of France; you have made racecourses of the cathedrals of the earth. Your *one* conception of pleasure is to drive in railroad carriages round their aisles, and eat off their altars. You have put a railroad bridge over the fall of Schaffhausen. You have tunnelled the cliffs of Lucerne by Tell's chapel; you have destroyed the Clarens shore of the Lake of Geneva; there is not a quiet valley in England that you have not filled with bellowing fire; there is no particle left of English land which you have not trampled coal ashes into—nor any foreign city in which the spread of your presence is not marked among its fair old streets and happy gardens by a consuming white leprosy of new hotels and perfumers' shops: the Alps themselves, which your own poets used to love so reverently, you look upon as soaped poles in a bear-garden, which you set yourselves to climb, and slide down again, with "shrieks of delight." When you are past shrieking, having no human articulate voice to say you are glad with, you fill the quietude of their valleys with gunpowder blasts, and rush home, red with cutaneous eruption of conceit, and voluble with convulsive hiccough of self-satisfaction. I think nearly the two sorrowfullest spectacles I have ever seen in humanity, taking the deep inner significance of them, are the English mobs in the valley of Chamouni, amusing themselves with firing rusty howitzers; and the Swiss vintagers of Zurich expressing their Christian thanks for the gift of the vine, by assembling in knots in the "towers of the vineyards," and slowly loading and firing horse-pistols from morning till evening. It is pitiful, to have dim conceptions of duty; more pitiful, it seems to me, to have conceptions like these, of mirth.

Lastly. You despise compassion. There is no need of words of mine for proof of this. I will merely print one of the newspaper paragraphs which I am in the habit of cutting out and throwing into my store-drawer; here is one from a *Daily Telgraph* of an early date this year; date which, though by me carelessly left unmarked, is easily discoverable; for on the back of the slip, there is the announcement that "yesterday the seventh of the special services of this year was performed by the Bishop of Ripon in St. Paul's;" and there is a pretty piece of modern political economy besides, worth preserving note of, I think, so I print it in the note below.[1] But my

---

[1] It is announced that an arrangement has been concluded between the Ministry of Finance and the Bank of Credit for the payment of

business is with the main paragraph, relating one of such facts as happen now daily, which, by chance, has taken a form in which it came before the coroner. I will print the paragraph in red.[1] Be sure, the facts themselves are written in that colour, in a book which we shall all of us, literate or illiterate, have to read our page of, some day.

" **An inquiry was held on Friday by Mr. Richards, deputy coroner, at the White Horse Tavern, Christ Church, Spitalfields, respecting the death of Michael Collins, aged 58 years.** Mary Collins, a miserable-looking woman, said that she lived with the deceased and his son in a room at 2, Cobb's court, Christ Church. Deceased was a 'translator' of boots. Witness went out and bought old boots; deceased and his son made them into good ones, and then witness sold them for what she could get at the shops, which was very little indeed. Deceased and his son used to work night and day to try and get a little bread and tea, and pay for the room (2s. a week), so as to keep the home together. On Friday-night week deceased got up from his bench and began to shiver. He threw down the boots, saying, ' Somebody else must finish them when I am gone, for I can do no more.' There was no fire, and he said, ' I would be better if I was warm.' Witness therefore took two pairs of translated boots to sell at the shop, but she could only get** 14d. **for the two pairs, for the people at the shop said, ' We must have our profit.' Witness got 14lb. of coal, and a little tea and bread. Her son sat up the whole night to make the ' translations,' to get money, but deceased died on Saturday morning. The family never had enough to eat.—**

the eleven millions which the State has to pay to the National Bank by the 14th inst. This sum will be raised as follows:—The eleven commercial members of the committee of the Bank of Credit will each borrow a million of florins for three months of this bank, which will accept their bills, which again will be discounted by the National Bank. By this arrangement *the National Bank will itself furnish the funds with which it will be paid.*

[1] In this edition the red is indicated by heavy type.

Coroner: ' It seems to me deplorable that you did not go into the workhouse.'—Witness: ' We wanted the comforts of our little home.'   A juror asked what the comforts were, for he only saw a little straw in the corner of the room, the windows of which were broken. The witness began to cry, and said that they had a quilt and other little things.   The deceased said he never would go into the workhouse.   In summer, when the season was good, they sometimes made as much as 10s. profit in the week.   They then always saved towards the next week, which was generally a bad one. In winter they made not half so much.   For three years they had been getting from bad to worse.—Cornelius Collins said that he had assisted his father since 1847. They used to work so far into the night that both nearly lost their eyesight.   Witness now had a film over his eyes.   Five years ago deceased applied to the parish for aid.   The relieving officer gave him a 4lb. loaf, and told him if he came again he should ' get the stones.' [1] That disgusted deceased, and he would have nothing to do with them since.   They got worse and worse until

[1] I do not know what this means.   It is curiously coincident in verbal form, with a certain passage which some of us may remember. It may perhaps be well to preserve beside this paragraph, another cutting out of my store-drawer, from the *Morning Post*, of about a parallel date, Friday, March 10th, 1865:—"The *salons* of Mme. C——, who did the honours with clever imitative grace and elegance, were crowded with princes, dukes, marquises, and counts—in fact, with the same *male* company as one meets at the parties of the Princess Metternich and Madame Drouyn de Lhuys.   Some English peers and members of Parliament were present, and appeared to enjoy the animated and dazzlingly improper scene.   On the second floor the supper tables were loaded with every delicacy of the season.   That your readers may form some idea of the dainty fare of the Parisian demi-monde, I copy the menu of the supper, which was served to all the guests (about 200) seated at four o'clock. Choice Yquem, Johannisberg, Laffitte, Tokay, and Champagne of the finest vintages were served most lavishly throughout the morning. After supper dancing was resumed with increased animation, and the ball terminated with a *chaîne diabolique* and a *cancan d'enfer* at seven in the morning.   (Morning service—'Ere the fresh lawns appeared, under the opening eyelids of the Morn.—')   Here is the menu:—'Consommé de volaille à la Bagration; 16 hors-d'œuvres variés. Bouchées à la Talleyrand. Saumons froids, sauce Ravigote.

last Friday week, when they had not even a halfpenny
to buy a candle.   Deceased then lay down on the straw,
and said he could not live till morning.—A juror: ' You
are dying of starvation yourself, and you ought to go
into the house until the summer.'—Witness: ' If we
went in we should die.   When we come out in the
summer we should be like people dropped from the sky.
No one would know us, and we would not have even a
room.   I could work now if I had food, for my sight
would get better.'—Dr. G. P. Walker said deceased
died from syncope, from exhaustion from want of food.
The deceased had had no bed-clothes.   For four
months he had had nothing but bread to eat.   There
was not a particle of fat in the body.   There was no
disease, but, if there had been medical attendance, he
might have survived the syncope or fainting.—The
coroner having remarked upon the painful nature of
the case, the jury returned the following verdict, ' That
deceased died from exhaustion from want of food and
the common necessaries of life; also through want of
medical aid.' "

'Why would witness not go into the workhouse?" you
ask. Well, the poor seem to have a prejudice against
the workhouse which the rich have not; for of course
every one who takes a pension from Government goes
into the workhouse on a grand scale: only the work-
houses for the rich do not involve the idea of work, and
should be called play-houses.   But the poor like to die
independently, it appears; perhaps if we made the
play-houses for them pretty and pleasant enough, or
gave them their pensions at home, and allowed them
a little introductory peculation with the public money,
their minds might be reconciled to it.   Meantime, here
are the facts: we make our relief either so insulting to
them, or so painful, that they rather die than take it at

Filets de bœuf en Bellevue, timbales milanaises chaudfroid de gibier.
Dindes truffées.   Pâtés de foies gras, buissons d'écrevisses, salades
vénétiennes, gelées blanches aux fruits, gateaux mancini, parisiens
et parisiennes.   Fromages glacés.   Ananas.   Dessert.'"

our hands ; or, for third alternative, we leave them so
untaught and foolish that they starve like brute creatures,
wild and dumb, not knowing what to do, or what to
ask. I say, you despise compassion ; if you did not,
such a newspaper paragraph would be as impossible in a
Christian country as a deliberate assassination permitted
in its public streets.[1] " Christian " did I say? Alas, if
we were but wholesomely un-Christian, it would be
impossible : it is our imaginary Christianity that helps
us to commit these crimes, for we revel and luxuriate
in our faith, for the lewd sensation of it; dressing
it up, like everything else, in fiction. The dramatic

[1] I am heartily glad to see such a paper as the *Pall Mall Gazette*
established ; for the power of the press in the hands of highly-
educated men, in independent position, and of honest purpose, may
indeed become all that it has been hitherto vainly vaunted to be.
Its editor will therefore, I doubt not, pardon me, in that, by very
reason of my respect for the journal, I do not let pass unnoticed an
article in its third number, page 5, which was wrong in every word
of it, with the intense wrongness which only an honest man can
achieve who has taken a false turn of thought in the outset, and is
following it, regardless of consequences. It contained at the end
this notable passage :—
   " The bread of affliction, and the water of affliction—aye, and
the bedsteads and blankets of affliction, are the very utmost that
the law ought to give to *outcasts merely as outcasts.*" I merely put
beside this expression of the gentlemanly mind of England in 1865,
a part of the message which Isaiah was ordered to " lift up his
voice like a trumpet " in declaring to the gentlemen of his day :
" Ye fast for strife, and to smite with the fist of wickedness. Is
not this the fast that I have chosen, to deal thy bread to the
hungry, and that thou bring the poor *that are cast out* (margin,
' afflicted ') to *thy* house." The falsehood on which the writer had
mentally founded himself, as previously stated by him, was this :
" To confound the functions of the dispensers of the poor-rates
with those of the dispensers of a charitable institution is a great
and pernicious error." This sentence is so accurately and exquisitely wrong, that its substance must be thus reversed in our minds
before we can deal with any existing problem of national distress.
" To understand that the dispensers of the poor-rates are the
almoners o the nation, and should distribute its alms with a
gentleness and freedom of hand as much greater and franker than
that possible to individual charity, as the collective national wisdom
and power may be supposed greater than those of any single person,
is the foundation of all law respecting pauperism."

Christianity of the organ and aisle, of dawn-service and twilight-revival—the Christianity which we do not fear to mix the mockery of, pictorially, with our play about the devil, in our Satanellas,—Roberts,—Fausts, chanting hymns through traceried windows for back-ground effect, and artistically modulating the "Dio" through variation on variation of mimicked prayer: (while we distribute tracts, next day, for the benefit of uncultivated swearers, upon what we suppose to be the signification of the Third Commandment);—this gas-lighted, and gas-inspired, Christianity, we are triumphant in, and draw back the hem of our robes from the touch of the heretics who dispute it. But to do a piece of common Christian righteousness in a plain English word or deed ; to make Christian law any rule of life, and found one National act or hope thereon,—we know too well what our faith comes to for that ! You might sooner get lightning out of incense smoke than true action or passion out of your modern English religion. You had better get rid of the smoke, and the organ pipes, both : leave them, and the Gothic windows, and the painted glass, to the property man ; give up your carburetted hydrogen ghost in one healthy expiration, and look after Lazarus at the door-step. For there is a true Church wherever one hand meets another helpfully, and that is the only holy or Mother Church which ever was, or ever shall be.

All these pleasures then, and all these virtues, I repeat, you nationally despise. You have, indeed, men among you who do not; by whose work, by whose strength, by whose life, by whose death, you live, and never thank them. Your wealth, your amusement, your pride would all be alike impossible, but for those whom you scorn or forget. The policeman, who is walking up and down the black lane all night to watch the guilt you have created there ; and may have his brains beaten out and be maimed for life at any moment, and never be thanked : the sailor wrestling with the sea's rage, the quiet student poring over his book or his vial, the common worker, without praise, and nearly without bread, fulfilling his task as your horses drag your carts, hopeless, and spurned of all : these are the men by whom England lives ; but they are not the nation ; they are only the body and nervous force of it, acting still from old habit in a convulsive perseverance, while the mind is gone.   Our National mind and purpose are to be amused ; our National religion, the performance of church ceremonies, and preaching of soporific truths (or untruths) to keep the mob quietly at work, while we amuse ourselves ; and the necessity for this amuse- ment is fastening on us as a feverous disease of parched throat and wandering eyes—senseless, dissolute, merciless. When men are rightly occupied, their amusement grows out of their work, as the colour-petals out of a fruitful flower ;—when they are faithfully helpful and compas- sionate, all their emotions become steady, deep, per- petual, and vivifying to the soul as the natural pulse to the body.   But now, having no true business, we pour our whole masculine energy into the false business of money-making ; and having no true emotion, we must have false emotions dressed up for us to play with, not innocently, as children with dolls, but guiltily and darkly, as the idolatrous Jews with their pictures on cavern walls, which men had to dig to detect.   The justice we do not execute, we mimic in the novel and on the stage ; for the beauty we destroy in nature, we substitute the metamorphosis of the pantomime, and (the human nature of us imperatively requiring awe and sorrow of *some* kind) for the noble grief we should have borne with our fellows, and the pure tears we should have wept with them, we gloat over the pathos of the police court, and gather the night-dew of the grave.

It is difficult to estimate the true significance of these things ; the facts are frightful enough ;—the measure of national fault involved in them is perhaps not as great as it would at first seem.   We permit, or cause, thousands of deaths daily, but we mean no harm ; we set fire to houses, and ravage peasants' fields ; yet we should be sorry to find we had injured anybody.   We are still kind at heart; still capable of virtue, but only as children are. Chalmers, at the end of his long life, having had much power with the public, being plagued in some serious matter by a reference to "public opinion," uttered the impatient exclamation, "The public is just a great baby!" And the reason that I have allowed all these graver subjects of thought to mix themselves up with an inquiry into methods of reading, is that, the more I see of our national faults or miseries, the more they resolve themselves into conditions of childish illiterateness, and want of education in the most ordinary habits of thought. It is, I repeat, not vice, not selfishness, not dulness of brain, which we have to lament; but an unreachable schoolboy's recklessness, only differing from the true schoolboy's in its incapacity of being helped, because it acknowledges no master. There is a curious type of us given in one of the lovely, neglected works of the last of our great painters. It is a drawing of Kirkby Lonsdale churchyard, and of its brook, and valley, and hills, and folded morning sky beyond. And unmindful alike of these, and of the dead who have left these for other valleys and for other skies, a group of schoolboys have piled their little books upon a grave, to strike them off with stones. So do we play with the words of the dead that would teach us, and strike them far from us with our bitter, reckless will, little thinking that those leaves which the wind scatters had been piled, not only upon a gravestone, but upon the seal of an enchanted vault—nay, the gate of a great city of sleeping kings, who would awake for us, and walk with us, if we knew but how to call them by their names. How often, even if we lift the marble entrance gate, do we but wander among those old kings in their repose, and finger the robes they lie in, and stir the crowns on their foreheads; and still they are silent to us, and seem but a dusty imagery; because we know not the incantation of the heart that would wake them;—which, if they once heard, they would start up to meet us in their power of long ago, narrowly to look upon us, and consider us; and, as the fallen kings of Hades meet the newly fallen, saying, "Art thou also become weak as we—art thou also become one of us?" so would these kings, with their undimmed, unshaken diadems, meet us, saying, "Art thou also become pure and mighty of heart as we? art thou also become one of us?"

Mighty of heart, mighty of mind—"magnanimous"—to be this, is indeed to be great in life; to become this increasingly, is, indeed, "to advance in life,"—in life itself—not in the trappings of it. My friends, do you remember that old Scythian custom, when the head of a house died? How he was dressed in his finest dress, and set in his chariot, and carried about to his friends' houses; and each of them placed him at his table's head, and all feasted in his presence? Suppose it were offered to you, in plain words, as it *is* offered to you in dire facts, that you should gain this Scythian honour, gradually, while you yet thought yourself alive. Suppose the offer were this: "You shall die slowly; your blood shall daily grow cold, your flesh petrify, your heart beat at last only as a rusted group of iron valves. Your life shall fade from you, and sink through the earth into the ice of Caina; but, day by day, your body shall be dressed more gaily, and set in higher chariots, and have more orders on its breast—crowns on its head, if you will. Men shall bow before it, stare and shout round it, crowd after it up and down the streets; build palaces for it, feast with it at their tables' heads all the night long; your soul shall stay enough within it to know what they do, and feel the weight of the golden dress on its shoulders, and the furrow of the crown-edge on the skull;—no more. Would you take the offer, verbally made by the death-angel? Would the meanest among us take it, think you? Yet practically and verily we grasp at it, every one of us, in a measure; many of us grasp at it in its fulness of horror. Every man accepts it, who desires to advance in life without knowing what life is; who means only that he is to get more horses, and more footmen, and more fortune, and more public honour, and—*not* more personal soul. He only is advancing in life, whose heart is getting softer, whose blood warmer, whose brain quicker, whose spirit is entering into Living[1] peace. And the men who have this life in them are the true lords or kings of the earth— they, and they only. All other kingships, so far as they are true, are only the practical issue and expression of theirs; if less than this, they are either dramatic royalties, —costly shows, with real jewels instead of tinsel—the toys of nations; or else, they are no royalties at all, but tyrannies, or the mere active and practical issue of national folly; for which reason I have said of them elsewhere, "Visible governments are the toys of some nations, the diseases of others, the harness of some, the burdens of more."

But I have no words for the wonder with which I hear Kinghood still spoken of, even among thoughtful men, as if governed nations were a personal property, and might be bought and sold, or otherwise acquired, as sheep, of whose flesh their king was to feed, and whose fleece he was to gather; as if Achilles' indignant epithet of base kings, "people-eating" were the constant and proper title of all monarchs; and enlargement of a king's dominion meant the same thing as the increase of a private man's estate! Kings who think so, however powerful, can no more be the true kings of the nation than gad-flies are the kings of a horse; they suck it, and may drive it wild, but do not guide it. They, and their courts, and their armies are, if one could see clearly, only a large species of marsh mosquito, with bayonet proboscis and melodious, band-mastered, trumpeting in the summer air; the twilight being, perhaps, sometimes fairer, but hardly more whole-some, for its glittering mists of midge companies. The true kings, meanwhile, rule quietly, if at all, and hate ruling; too many of them make "il gran refiúto;" and if they do not, the mob, as soon as they are likely to become useful to it, is pretty sure to make *its* "gran refiúto" of *them*.

Yet the visible king may also be a true one, some day,

---

[1] " το δὲ φρόνημα τοῦ πνεύματος ζωὴ καὶ εἰρήνη."

if ever day comes when he will estimate his dominion by the *force* of it,—not the geographical boundaries. It matters very little whether Trent cuts you a cantel out here, or Rhine rounds you a castle less there. But it does matter to you, king of men, whether you can verily say to this man, "Go," and he goeth; and to another, "Come," and he cometh. Whether you can turn your people as you can Trent—and where it is that you bid them come, and where go. It matters to you, king of men, whether your people hate you, and die by you, or love you, and live by you. You may measure your dominion by multitudes, better than by miles; and count degrees of love-latitude, not from, but to, a wonderfully warm and infinite equator. Measure!—nay, you cannot measure. Who shall measure the difference between the power of those who "do and teach," and who are greatest in the kingdoms of earth, as of heaven—and the power of those who undo, and consume—whose power, at the fullest, is only the power of the moth and the rust? Strange! to think how the Moth-kings lay up treasures for the moth, and the Rust-kings, who are to their peoples' strength as rust to armour, lay up treasures for the rust; and the Robber-kings, treasures for the robber; but how few kings have ever laid up treasures that needed no guarding—treasures of which, the more thieves there were, the better! Broidered robe, only to be rent—helm and sword, only to be dimmed; jewel and gold, only to be s attered—there have been three kinds of kings who have gathered these. Suppose there ever should arise a Fourth order of kings, who had read, in some obscure writing of long ago, that there was a Fourth kind of treasure, which the jewel and gold could not equal, neither should it be valued with pure gold. A web more fair in the weaving, by Athena's shuttle; an armour, forged in diviner fire by Vulcanian force—a gold only to be mined in the sun's red heart, where he sets over the Delphian cliffs;—deep-pictured tissue, impenetrable armour, potable gold!—the three great Angels of Conduct, Toil, and Thought, still calling to us, and waiting at the posts of our doors, to lead us, if we would, with their winged power, and guide us, with their inescapable eyes, by the path which no fowl knoweth, and which the vulture's eye has not seen ! Suppose kings should ever arise, who heard and believed this word, and at last gathered and brought forth treasures of—Wisdom—for their people ?

Think what an amazing business *that* would be ! How inconceivable, in the state of our present national wisdom. That we should bring up our peasants to a book exercise instead of a bayonet exercise !—organize, drill, maintain with pay, and good generalship, armies of thinkers, instead of armies of stabbers !—find national amusement in reading-rooms as well as rifle-grounds ; give prizes for a fair shot at a fact, as well as for a leaden splash on a target. What an absurd idea it seems, put fairly in words, that the wealth of the capitalists of civilized nations should ever come to support literature instead of war ! Have yet patience with me, while I read you a single sentence out of the only book, properly to be called a book, that I have yet written myself, the one that will stand, (if anything stand), surest and longest of all work of mine.

" It is one very awful form of the operation of wealth in Europe that it is entirely capitalists' wealth which supports unjust wars. Just wars do not need so much money to support them ; for most of the men who wage such, wage them gratis ; but for an unjust war, men's bodies and souls have both to be bought ; and the best tools of war for them besides, which makes such war costly to the maximum ; not to speak of the cost of base fear, and angry suspicion, between nations which have not grace nor honesty enough in all their multitudes to buy an hour's peace of mind with ; as, at present France and England, purchasing of each other ten millions' sterling worth of consternation, annually (a remarkably light crop, half thorns and half aspen leaves, sown, reaped, and granaried by the 'science' of the modern political economist, teaching covetousness instead of truth). And, all unjust war being supportable, if not by pillage of the enemy, only by loans from capitalists, these loans are repaid by subsequent taxation of the people, who appear to have no will in the matter, the capitalists' will being the primary root of the war; but its real root is the covetousness of the whole nation, rendering it incapable of faith, frankness, or justice, and bringing about, therefore, in due time, his own separate loss and punishment to each person."

France and England literally, observe, buy *panic* of each other; they pay, each of them, for ten thousand thousand pounds worth of terror, a year. Now suppose, instead of buying these ten millions' worth of panic annually, they made up their minds to be at peace with each other, and buy ten millions' worth of knowledge annually; and that each nation spent its ten thousand thousand pounds a year in founding royal libraries, royal art galleries, royal museums, royal gardens, and places o rest. Might it not be better somewhat for both French and English?

It will be long, yet, before that comes to pass. Nevertheless, I hope it will not be long before royal or national libraries will be founded in every considerable city, with a royal series of books in them; the same series in every one of them, chosen books, the best in every kind, prepared for that national series in the most perfect way possible; their text printed all on leaves of equal size, broad of margin, and divided into pleasant volumes, light in the hand, beautiful, and strong, and thorough as examples of binders' work; and that these great libraries will be accessible to all clean and orderly persons at all times of the day and evening; strict law being enforced for this cleanliness and quietness.

I could shape for you other plans, for art-galleries, and for natural history galleries, and for many precious, many, it seems to me, needful, things; but this book plan is the easiest and needfullest, and would prove a considerable tonic to what we call our British constitution, which has fallen dropsical of late, and has an evil thirst, and evil hunger, and wants healthier feeding. You have got its corn laws repealed for it ; try if you cannot get corn laws established for it, dealing in a better bread ;—bread made of that old enchanted Arabian grain, the Sesame, which opens doors ;—doors, not of robbers', but of Kings' Treasuries.

Friends, the treasuries of true kings are the streets of their cities ; and the gold they gather, which for others is as the mire of the streets, changes itself, for them and their people, into a crystalline pavement for evermore.

LECTURE II.—LILIES

OF QUEENS' GARDENS

" ὡς κρίνον ἐν μέσῳ ἀκανθῶν, οὕτως ἡ πλησίον μοῦ." [1]

It will, perhaps, be well, as this Lecture is the sequel of one previously given, that I should shortly state to you my general intention in both. The questions specially proposed to you in the first, namely, How and What to Read, rose out of a far deeper one, which it was my endeavour to make you propose earnestly to yourselves, namely, *Why* to Read. I want you to feel, with me, that whatever advantages we possess in the present day in the diffusion of education and of literature, can only be rightly used by any of us when we have apprehended clearly what education is to lead to, and literature to teach. I wish you to see that both well-directed moral training and well-chosen reading lead to the possession of a power over the ill-guided and illiterate, which is, according to the measure of it, in the truest sense, *kingly ;* conferring indeed the purest kingship that can exist among men : too many other kingships, (however distinguished by visible insignia or material power) being either spectral, or tyrannous ;—Spectral—that is to say, aspects and shadows only of royalty, hollow as death, and which only the " Likeness of a kingly crown have on ; " or else tyrannous—that is to say, substituting their own will for the law of justice and love by which all true kings rule.

There is, then, I repeat—and as I want to leave this idea with you, I begin with it, and shall end with it—only one pure kind of kingship ; an inevitable and eternal kind, crowned or not : the kingship, namely, which consists in a stronger moral state, and a truer thoughtful state, than that of others ; enabling you, therefore, to guide, or to raise them. Observe that word "State ; " we

[1] Canticles, ii. 2.

have got into a loose way of using it. It means literally the standing and stability of a thing; and you have the full force of it in the derived word "statue"—"the immoveable thing." A king's majesty or "state," then, and the right of his kingdom to be called a state, depends on the movelessness of both :—without tremor, without quiver of balance; established and enthroned upon a foundation of eternal law which nothing can alter nor overthrow.

Believing that all literature and all education are only useful so far as they tend to confirm this calm, beneficent, and *therefore* kingly, power—first, over ourselves, and, through ourselves, over all around us, I am now going to ask you to consider with me farther, what special portion or kind of this royal authority, arising out of noble education, may rightly be possessed by women; and how far they also are called to a true queenly power. Not in their households merely, but over all within their sphere. And in what sense, if they rightly understood and exercised this royal or gracious influence, the order and beauty induced by such benignant power would justify us in speaking of the territories over which each of them reigned, as "Queens' Gardens."

And here, in the very outset, we are met by a far deeper question, which—strange though this may seem —remains among many of us yet quite undecided, in spite of its infinite importance.

We cannot determine what the queenly power of women should be, until we are agreed what their ordinary power should be. We cannot consider how education may fit them for any widely extending duty, until we are agreed what is their true constant duty. And there never was a time when wilder words were spoken, or more vain imagination permitted, respecting this question—quite vital to all social happiness. The relations of the womanly to the manly nature, their different capacities of intellect or of virtue, seem never to have been yet measured with entire consent. We hear of the mission and of the rights of Woman, as if these

C 219

could ever be separate from the mission and the rights of Man ;—as if she and her lord were creatures of independent kind and of irreconcileable claim. This, at least, is wrong. And not less wrong—perhaps even more foolishly wrong (for I will anticipate thus far what I hope to prove)—is the idea that woman is only the shadow and attendant image of her lord, owing him a thoughtless and servile obedience, and supported altogether in her weakness by the pre-eminence of his fortitude.

This, I say, is the most foolish of all errors respecting her who was made to be the helpmate of man. As if he could be helped effectively by a shadow, or worthily by a slave !

Let us try, then, whether we cannot get at some clear and harmonious idea (it must be harmonious if it is true) of what womanly mind and virtue are in power and office, with respect to man's ; and how their relations, rightly accepted, aid, and increase, the vigour, and honour, and authority of both.

And now I must repeat one thing I said in the last lecture : namely, that the first use of education was to enable us to consult with the wisest and the greatest men on all points of earnest difficulty. That to use books rightly, was to go to them for help : to appeal to them, when our own knowledge and power of thought failed ; to be led by them into wider sight, purer conception than our own, and receive from them the united sentence of the judges and councils of all time, against our solitary and unstable opinion.

Let us do this now. Let us see whether the greatest, the wisest, the purest-hearted of all ages are agreed in any wise on this point : let us hear the testimony they have left respecting what they held to be the true dignity of woman, and her mode of help to man.

And first let us take Shakespeare.

Note broadly in the outset, Shakespeare has no heroes ;—he has only heroines. There is not one entirely heroic figure in all his plays, except the slight

sketch of Henry the Fifth, exaggerated for the purposes
of the stage ; and the still slighter Valentine in The Two
Gentlemen of Verona. In his laboured and perfect
plays you have no hero. Othello would have been one,
if his simplicity had not been so great as to leave him
the prey of every base practice round him ; but he is
the only example even approximating to the heroic type.
Coriolanus—Cæsar—Antony, stand in flawed strength,
and fall by their vanities ;—Hamlet is indolent, and
drowsily speculative ; Romeo an impatient boy ; the
Merchant of Venice languidly submissive to adverse
fortune ; Kent, in King Lear, is entirely noble at heart,
but too rough and unpolished to be of true use at the
critical time, and he sinks into the office of a servant
only. Orlando, no less noble, is yet the despairing toy
of chance, followed, comforted, saved, by Rosalind.
Whereas there is hardly a play that has not a perfect
woman in it, steadfast in grave hope, and errorless
purpose . Cordelia, Desdemona, Isabella, Hermione,
Imogen, Queen Katherine, Perdita, Sylvia, Viola, Rosalind, Helena, and last, and perhaps loveliest, Virgilia,
are all faultless ; conceived in the highest heroic type
of humanity.

Then observe, secondly,

The catastrophe of every play is caused always by the
folly or fault of a man ; the redemption, if there be any,
is by the wisdom and virtue of a woman, and, failing that,
there is none. The catastrophe of King Lear is owing to
his own want of judgment, his impatient vanity, his mis-
understanding of his children ; the virtue of his one true
daughter would have saved him from all the injuries of
the others, unless he had cast her away from him ; as it is,
she all but saves him.

Of Othello I need not trace the tale ;—nor the one
weakness of his so mighty love ; nor the inferiority of his
perceptive intellect to that even of the second woman
character in the play, the Emilia who dies in wild testimony against his error :—" Oh, murderous coxcomb !
What should such a fool Do with so good a wife ? "

In Romeo and Juliet, the wise and entirely brave stratagem of the wife is brought to ruinous issue by the reckless impatience of her husband. In Winter's Tale, and in Cymbeline, the happiness and existence of two princely households, lost through long years, and imperilled to the death by the folly and obstinacy of the husbands, are redeemed at last by the queenly patience and wisdom of the wives. In Measure for Measure, the injustice of the judges, and the corrupt cowardice of the brother, are opposed to the victorious truth and adamantine purity of a woman. In Coriolanus, the mother's counsel, acted upon in time, would have saved her son from all evil; his momentary forgetfulness of it is his ruin; her prayer, at last granted, saves him—not, indeed, from death, but from the curse of living as the destroyer of his country.

And what shall I say of Julia, constant against the fickleness of a lover who is a mere wicked child?—of Helena, against the petulance and insult of a careless youth?—of the patience of Hero, the passion of Beatrice, and the calmly devoted wisdom of the "unlessoned girl," who appears among the helplessness, the blindness, and the vindictive passions of men, as a gentle angel, to save merely by her presence, and defeat the worst intensities of crime by her smile?

Observe, further, among all the principal figures in Shakespeare's plays, there is only one weak woman— Ophelia; and it is because she fails Hamlet at the critical moment, and is not, and cannot in her nature be, a guide to him when he needs her most, that all the bitter catastrophe follows. Finally, though there are three wicked women among the principal figures, Lady Macbeth, Regan, and Goneril, they are felt at once to be frightful exceptions to the ordinary laws of life; fatal in their influence also in proportion to the power for good which they have abandoned.

Such, in broad light, is Shakespeare's testimony to the position and character of women in human life. He represents them as infallibly faithful and wise counsellors,

—incorruptibly just and pure examples—strong always to sanctify, even when they cannot save.

Not as in any wise comparable in knowledge of the nature of man,—still less in his understanding of the causes and courses of fate,—but only as the writer who has given us the broadest view of the conditions and modes of ordinary thought in modern society, I ask you next to receive the witness of Walter Scott.

I put aside his merely romantic prose writings as of no value : and though the early romantic poetry is very beautiful, its testimony is of no weight, other than that of a boy's ideal. But his true works, studied from Scottish life, bear a true witness, and in the whole range of these there are but three men who reach the heroic type—Dandie Dinmont, Rob Roy, and Claverhouse : of these, one is a border farmer; another a freebooter; the third a soldier in a bad cause. And these touch the ideal of heroism only in their courage and faith, together with a strong, but uncultivated, or mistakenly applied, intellectual power ; while his younger men are the gentlemanly playthings of fantastic fortune, and only by aid (or accident) of that fortune, survive, not vanquish, the trials they involuntarily sustain. Of any disciplined, or consistent character, earnest in a purpose wisely conceived, or dealing with forms of hostile evil, definitely challenged, and resolutely subdued, there is no trace in his conceptions of men. Whereas in his imaginations of women, —in the characters of Ellen Douglas, of Flora MacIvor, Rose Bradwardine, Catherine Seyton, Diana Vernon, Lilias Redgauntlet, Alice Bridgenorth, Alice Lee, and Jeanie Deans,—with endless varieties of grace, tenderness, and intellectual power, we find in all a quite infallible and inevitable sense of dignity and justice ; a fearless, instant, and untiring self-sacrifice to even the appearance of duty, much more to its real claims ; and, finally, a patient wisdom of deeply restrained affection, which does infinitely more than protect its objects from a momentary error ; it gradually forms, animates, and exalts the characters of the unworthy lovers, until, at the close of the tale, we are just able, and no more, to take patience in hearing of their unmerited success.

So that in all cases, with Scott as with Shakespeare, it is the woman who watches over, teaches, and guides the youth ; it is never, by any chance, the youth who watches over or educates his mistress.

Next, take, though more briefly, graver and deeper testimony—that of the great Italians and Greeks. You know well the plan of Dante's great poem—that it is a love-poem to his dead lady, a song of praise for her watch over his soul. Stooping only to pity, never to love, she yet saves him from destruction—saves him from hell. He is going eternally astray in despair ; she comes down from heaven to his help, and throughout the ascents of Paradise is his teacher, interpreting for him the most difficult truths, divine and human ; and leading him, with rebuke upon rebuke, from star to star.

I do not insist upon Dante's conception ; if I began I could not cease : besides, you might think this a wild imagination of one poet's heart. So I will rather read to you a few verses of the deliberate writing of a knight of Pisa to his living lady, wholly characteristic of the feeling of all the noblest men of the thirteenth century, preserved among many other such records of knightly honour and love, which Dante Rossetti has gathered for us from among the early Italian poets.

> For lo ! thy law is passed
> That this my love should manifestly be
>   To serve and honour thee :
> And so I do ; and my delight is full,
> Accepted for the servant of thy rule.

> Without almost, I am all rapturous,
>   Since thus my will was set
>   To serve, thou flower of joy, thine excellence :
> Nor ever seems it anything could rouse
>   A pain or a regret,
>   But on thee dwells mine every thought and sense ;
> Considering that from thee all virtues spread
>   As from a fountain head, —

That in thy gift is wisdom's best avail,
　　And honour without fail;
With whom each sovereign good dwells separate,
Fulfilling the perfection of thy state.

　　　　Lady, since I conceived
Thy pleasurable aspect in my heart,
　　My life has been apart
In shining brightness and the place of truth;
　　Which till that time, good sooth,
Groped among shadows in a darken'd place,
　　Where many hours and days
It hardly ever had remember'd good.
　　But now my servitude
Is thine, and I am full of joy and rest.
　　A man from a wild beast
Thou madest me, since for thy love I lived.

You may think, perhaps, a Greek knight would have had a lower estimate of women than this Christian lover. His own spiritual subjection to them was indeed not so absolute; but as regards their own personal character, it was only because you could not have followed me so easily, that I did not take the Greek women instead of Shakespeare's; and instance, for chief ideal types of human beauty and faith, the simple mother's and wife's heart of Andromache; the divine, yet rejected wisdom of Cassandra; the playful kindness and simple princess-life of happy Nausicaa; the housewifely calm of that of Penelope, with its watch upon the sea; the ever patient, fearless, hopelessly devoted piety of the sister, and daughter, in Antigone; the bowing down of Iphigenia, lamb-like and silent; and, finally, the expectation of the resurrection, made clear to the soul of the Greeks in the return from her grave of that Alcestis, who, to save her husband, had passed calmly through the bitterness of death.

Now I could multiply witness upon witness of this kind upon you if I had time. I would take Chaucer, and show you why he wrote a Legend of Good Women; but no Legend of Good Men. I would take Spenser, and show you how all his fairy knights are sometimes deceived and sometimes vanquished; but the soul of Una is never darkened, and the spear of Britomart is never broken. Nay, I could go back into the mythical teaching of the most ancient times, and show you how the great people,—by one of whose princesses it was appointed that the Lawgiver of all the earth should be educated, rather than by his own kindred;—how that great Egyptian people, wisest then of nations, gave to their Spirit of Wisdom the form of a woman; and into her hand, for a symbol, the weaver's shuttle: and how the name and the form of that spirit, adopted, believed, and obeyed by the Greeks, became that Athena of the olive-helm, and cloudy shield, to whose faith you owe, down to this date, whatever you hold most precious in art, in literature, or in types of national virtue.

But I will not wander into this distant and mythical element; I will only ask you to give its legitimate value to the testimony of these great poets and men of the world,—consistent as you see it is on this head. I will ask you whether it can be supposed that these men, in the main work of their lives, are amusing themselves with a fictitious and idle view of the relations between man and woman;—nay, worse than fictitious or idle; for a thing may be imaginary, yet desirable, if it were possible; but this, their ideal of women, is, according to our common idea of the marriage relation, wholly un-desirable. The woman, we say, is not to guide, nor even to think, for herself. The man is always to be the wiser; he is to be the thinker, the ruler, the superior in knowledge and discretion, as in power. Is it not somewhat important to make up our minds on this matter? Are all these great men mistaken, or are we? Are Shakespeare and Æschylus, Dante and Homer, merely dressing dolls for us; or, worse than dolls, un-natural visions, the realization of which, were it possible, would bring anarchy into all households and ruin into all affections? Nay, if you could suppose this, take lastly the evidence of facts, given by the human heart itself. In all Christian ages which have been remarkable

for their purity or progress, there has been absolute
yielding of obedient devotion, by the lover, to his
mistress. I say *obedient*—not merely enthusiastic and
worshipping in imagination, but entirely subject, receiving
from the beloved woman, however young, not only the
encouragement, the praise, and the reward of all toil,
but, so far as any choice is open, or any question difficult
of decision, the *direction* of all toil. That chivalry, to the
abuse and dishonour of which are attributable primarily
whatever is cruel in war, unjust in peace, or corrupt and
ignoble in domestic relations ; and to the original purity
and power of which we owe the defence alike of faith,
of law, and of love ;—that chivalry, I say, in its very first
conception of honourable life, assumes the subjection of
the young knight to the command—should it even be
the command in caprice—of his lady. It assumes this,
because its masters knew that the first and necessary
impulse of every truly taught and knightly heart is this
of blind service to its lady: that where that true faith
and captivity are not, all wayward and wicked passion
must be ; and that in this rapturous obedience to the
single love of his youth, is the sanctification of all man's
strength, and the continuance of all his purposes. And
this, not because such obedience would be safe, or
honourable, were it ever rendered to the unworthy ;
but because it ought to be impossible for every noble
youth—it *is* impossible for every one rightly trained—
to love any one whose gentle counsel he cannot trust,
or whose prayerful command he can hesitate to
obey.

I do not insist by any farther argument on this, for I
think it should commend itself at once to your knowledge
of what has been and to your feeling of what should be.
You cannot think that the buckling on of the knight's
armour by his lady's hand was a mere caprice of romantic
fashion. It is the type of an eternal truth—that the
soul's armour is never well set to the heart unless a
woman's hand has braced it ; and it is only when she
braces it loosely that the honour of manhood fails.

Know you not those lovely lines—I would they were
learned by all youthful ladies of England :—

> " Ah wasteful woman !—she who may
> On her sweet self set her own price,
> Knowing he cannot choose but pay—
> How has she cheapen'd Paradise !
> How given for nought her priceless gift,
> How spoiled the bread and spill'd the wine,
> Which, spent with due, respective thrift,
> Had made brutes men, and men divine." [1]

Thus much, then, respecting the relations of lovers I
believe you will accept.   But what we too often doubt
is the fitness of the continuance of such a relation
throughout the whole of human life.   We think it right
in the lover and mistress, not in the husband and wife.
That is to say, we think that a reverent and tender duty
is due to one whose affection we still doubt, and whose
character we as yet do but partially and distantly discern ;
and that this reverence and duty are to be withdrawn,
when the affection has become wholly and limitlessly our
own, and the character has been so sifted and tried that
we fear not to entrust it with the happiness of our lives.
Do you not see how ignoble this is, as well as how un-
reasonable ?   Do you not feel that marriage—when it is
marriage at all,—is only the seal which marks the vowed
transition of temporary into untiring service, and of fitful
into eternal love ?

But how, you will ask, is the idea of this guiding
function of the woman reconcileable with a true wifely
subjection ?   Simply in that it is a *guiding*, not a deter-
mining, function.   Let me try to show you briefly how
these powers seem to be rightly distinguishable.

We are foolish, and without excuse foolish, in speaking
of the " superiority " of one sex to the other, as if they
could be compared in similar things.   Each has what
the other has not : each completes the other, and is
completed by the other : they are in nothing alike, and
the happiness and perfection of both depends on each

[1] Coventry Patmore.

asking and receiving from the other what the other only can give.

Now their separate characters are briefly these. The man's power is active, progressive, defensive. He is eminently the doer, the creator, the discoverer, the defender. His intellect is for speculation and invention ; his energy for adventure, for war, and for conquest, wherever war is just, wherever conquest necessary. But the woman's power is for rule, not for battle,—and her intellect is not for invention or creation, but for sweet ordering, arrangement, and decision. She sees the qualities of things, their claims, and their places. Her great function is Praise : she enters into no contest, but infallibly adjudges the crown of contest. By her office, and place, she is protected from all danger and temptation. The man, in his rough work in open world, must encounter all peril and trial :—to him, therefore, the failure, the offence, the inevitable error : often he must be wounded, or subdued, often misled, and *always* hardened. But he guards the woman from all this ; within his house, as ruled by her, unless she herself has sought it, need enter no danger, no temptation, no cause of error or offence. This is the true nature of home—it is the place of Peace ; the shelter, not only from all injury, but from all terror, doubt, and division. In so far as it is not this, it is not home ; so far as the anxieties of the outer life penetrate into it, and the inconsistently-minded, unknown, unloved, or hostile society of the outer world is allowed by either husband or wife to cross the threshold, it ceases to be home ; it is then only a part of that outer world which you have roofed over, and lighted fire in. But so far as it is a sacred place, a vestal temple, a temple of the hearth watched over by Household Gods, before whose faces none may come but those whom they can receive with love,—so far as it is this, and roof and fire are types only of a nobler shade and light,—shade as of the rock in a weary land, and light as of the Pharos in the stormy sea ;—so far it vindicates the name, and fulfils the praise, of Home.

And wherever a true wife comes, this home is always round her. The stars only may be over her head ; the glowworm in the night-cold grass may be the only fire at her foot : but home is yet wherever she is ; and for a noble woman it stretches far round her, better than ceiled with cedar, or painted with vermilion, shedding its quiet light far, for those who else were homeless.

This, then, I believe to be,—will you not admit it to be,—the woman's true place and power? But do not you see that, to fulfil this, she must—as far as one can use such terms of a human creature—be incapable of error? So far as she rules, all must be right, or nothing is. She must be enduringly, incorruptibly good ; instinctively, infallibly wise—wise, not for self-development, but for self-renunciation : wise, not that she may set herself above her husband, but that she may never fail from his side : wise, not with the narrowness of insolent and loveless pride, but with the passionate gentleness of an infinitely variable, because infinitely applicable, modesty of service—the true changefulness of woman. In that great sense—"La donna e mobile," not "Qual piùm' al vento ;" no, nor yet "Variable as the shade, by the light quivering aspen made ;" but variable as the *light*, manifold in fair and serene division, that it may take the colour of all that it falls upon, and exalt it.

II. I have been trying, thus far, to show you what should be the place, and what the power of woman. Now, secondly, we ask, What kind of education is to fit her for these?

And if you indeed think this a true conception of her office and dignity, it will not be difficult to trace the course of education which would fit her for the one, and raise her to the other.

The first of our duties to her—no thoughtful persons now doubt this,—is to secure for her such physical training and exercise as may confirm her health, and perfect her beauty ; the highest refinement of that beauty being unattainable without splendour of activity and of delicate strength. To perfect her beauty, I say, and

increase its power; it cannot be too powerful, nor shed
its sacred light too far: only remember that all physical
freedom is vain to produce beauty without a correspond-
ing freedom of heart.   There are two passages of that
poet who is distinguished, it seems to me, from all others
—not by power, but by exquisite *right*ness—which point
you to the source, and describe to you, in a few syllables,
the completion of womanly beauty.   I will read the
introductory stanzas, but the last is the one I wish you
specially to notice :—

> " Three years she grew in sun and shower,
>   Then Nature said, a lovelier flower
>   On earth was never sown.
>   This child I to myself will take ;
>   She shall be mine, and I will make
>   A lady of my own.
>
> " Myself will to my darling be
>   Both law and impulse ; and with me
>   The girl, in rock and plain,
>   In earth and heaven, in glade and bower,
>   Shall feel an overseeing power
>   To kindle, or restrain.
>
> " The floating clouds their state shall lend
>   To her, for her the willow bend ;
>   Nor shall she fail to see
>   Even in the motions of the storm,
>   Grace that shall mould the maiden's form
>   By silent sympathy.
>
> " And *vital feelings of delight*
>   Shall rear her form to stately height,—
>   Her virgin bosom swell.
>   Such *thoughts* to Lucy I will give,
>   While she and I together live,
>   Here in this happy dell."

" *Vital* feelings of delight," observe.   There are deadly
feelings of delight; but the natural ones are vital,
necessary to very life.

And they must be feelings of delight, if they are to be
vital.   Do not think you can make a girl lovely, if you
do not make her happy.   There is not one restraint you

put on a good girl's nature—there is not one check you give to her instincts of affection or of effort—which will not be indelibly written on her features, with a hardness which is all the more painful because it takes away the brightness from the eyes of innocence, and the charm from the brow of virtue.

This for the means : now note the end.   Take from the same poet, in two lines, a perfect description of womanly beauty—

> " A countenance in which did meet
> Sweet records, promises as sweet."

The perfect loveliness of a woman's countenance can only consist in that majestic peace, which is founded in the memory of happy and useful years,—full of sweet records ; and from the joining of this with that yet more majestic childishness, which is still full of change and promise ;—opening always—modest at once, and bright, with hope of better things to be won, and to be bestowed. There is no old age where there is still that promise—it is eternal youth.

Thus, then, you have first to mould her physical frame, and then, as the strength she gains will permit you, to fill and temper her mind with all knowledge and thoughts which tend to confirm its natural instincts of justice, and refine its natural tact of love.

All such knowledge should be given her as may enable her to understand, and even to aid, the work of men : and yet it should be given, not as knowledge,—not as if it were, or could be, for her an object to know ; but only to feel, and to judge.   It is of no moment, as a matter of pride or perfectness in herself, whether she knows many languages or one ; but it is of the utmost, that she should be able to show kindness to a stranger, and to understand the sweetness of a stranger's tongue.   It is of no moment to her own worth or dignity that she should be acquainted with this science or that ; but it is of the highest that she should be trained in habits of accurate thought ; that she should understand the meaning, the inevitableness, and the loveliness of natural laws, and follow at least some one path of scientific attainment, as far as to the threshold of that bitter Valley of Humiliation, into which only the wisest and bravest of men can descend, owning themselves for ever children, gathering pebbles on a boundless shore. It is of little consequence how many positions of cities she knows, or how many dates of events, or how many names of celebrated persons —it is not the object of education to turn a woman into a dictionary; but it is deeply necessary that she should be taught to enter with her whole personality into the history she reads; to picture the passages of it vitally in her own bright imagination; to apprehend, with her fine instincts, the pathetic circumstances and dramatic relations, which the historian too often only eclipses by his reasoning, and disconnects by his arrangement; it is for her to trace the hidden equities of divine reward, and catch sight, through the darkness, of the fateful threads of woven fire that connect error with its retribution. But, chiefly of all, she is to be taught to extend the limits of her sympathy with respect to that history which is being for ever determined, as the moments pass in which she draws her peaceful breath; and to the contemporary calamity which, were it but rightly mourned by her, would recur no more hereafter. She is to exercise herself in imagining what would be the effects upon her mind and conduct, if she were daily brought into the presence of the suffering which is not the less real because shut from her sight. She is to be taught somewhat to understand the nothingness of the proportion which that little world in which she lives and loves, bears to the world in which God lives and loves;—and solemnly she is to be taught to strive that her thoughts of piety may not be feeble in proportion to the number they embrace, nor her prayer more languid than it is for the momentary relief from pain of her husband or her child, when it is uttered for the multitudes of those who have none to love them,— and is "for all who are desolate and oppressed."

Thus far, I think, I have had your concurrence;

perhaps you will not be with me in what I believe is most needful for me to say. There *is* one dangerous science for women—one which let them indeed beware how they profanely touch—that of theology. Strange, and miserably strange, that while they are modest enough to doubt their powers, and pause at the threshold of sciences where every step is demonstrable and sure, they will plunge headlong, and without one thought of incompetency, into that science in which the greatest men have trembled, and the wisest erred. Strange, that they will complacently and pridefully bind up whatever vice or folly there is in them, whatever arrogance, petulance, or blind incomprehensiveness, into one bitter bundle of consecrated myrrh. Strange, in creatures born to be Love visible, that where they can know least, they will condemn first, and think to recommend themselves to their Master by scrambling up the steps of His judgment-throne, to divide it with Him. Most strange, that they should think they were led by the Spirit of the Comforter into habits of mind which have become in them the unmixed elements of home discomfort ; and that they dare to turn the Household Gods of Christianity into ugly idols of their own—spiritual dolls, for them to dress according to their caprice ; and from which their husbands must turn away in grieved contempt, lest they should be shrieked at for breaking them.

I believe, then, with this exception, that a girl's education should be nearly, in its course and material of study, the same as a boy's ; but quite differently directed. A woman, in any rank of life, ought to know whatever her husband is likely to know, but to know it in a different way. His command of it should be foundational and progressive, hers, general and accomplished for daily and helpful use. Not but that it would often be wiser in men to learn things in a womanly sort of way, for present use, and to seek for the discipline and training of their mental powers in such branches of study as will be afterwards fittest for social service ; but, speaking broadly, a man ought to know any language or science he learns, thoroughly, while a woman ought to know the same language, or science, only so far as may enable her to sympathise in her husband's pleasures, and in those of his best friends.

Yet, observe, with exquisite accuracy as far as she reaches. There is a wide difference between elementary knowledge and superficial knowledge—between a firm beginning, and a feeble smattering. A woman may always help her husband by what she knows, however little; by what she half-knows, or mis-knows, she will only teaze him.

And indeed, if there were to be any difference between a girl's education and a boy's, I should say that of the two the girl should be earlier led, as her intellect ripens faster, into deep and serious subjects; and that her range of literature should be, not more, but less frivolous, calculated to add the qualities of patience and serious-ness to her natural poignancy of thought and quickness of wit; and also to keep her in a lofty and pure element of thought. I enter not now into any question of choice of books; only be sure that her books are not heaped up in her lap as they fall out of the package of the circu-lating library, wet with the last and lightest spray of the fountain of folly

Or even of the fountain of wit; for with respect to that sore temptation of novel reading, it is not the badness of a novel that we should dread, but its over-wrought interest. The weakest romance is not so stupifying as the lower forms of religious exciting literature, and the worst romance is not so corrupting as false history, false philosophy, or false political essays. But the best romance becomes dangerous, if, by its excitement, it renders the ordinary course of life uninteresting, and increases the morbid thirst for useless acquaintance with scenes in which we shall never be called upon to act.

I speak therefore of good novels only; and our modern literature is particularly rich in types of such. Well read, indeed, these books have serious use, being nothing less than treatises on moral anatomy and chemistry ; studies of human nature in the elements of it. But I attach little weight to this function : they are hardly ever read with earnestness enough to permit them to fulfil it. The utmost they usually do is to enlarge somewhat the charity of a kind reader, or the bitterness of a malicious one ; for each will gather, from the novel, food for her own disposition. Those who are naturally proud and envious will learn from Thackeray to despise humanity ; those who are naturally gentle, to pity it ; those who are naturally shallow, to laugh at it. So, also, there might be a serviceable power in novels to bring before us, in vividness, a human truth which we had before dimly conceived ; but the temptation to picturesqueness of statement is so great, that often the best writers of fiction cannot resist it ; and our views are rendered so violent and one-sided, that their vitality is rather a harm than good.

Without, however, venturing here on any attempt at decision how much novel reading should be allowed, let me at least clearly assert this, that whether novels, or poetry, or history be read, they should be chosen, not for what is *out* of them, but for what is *in* them. The chance and scattered evil that may here and there haunt, or hide itself in, a powerful book, never does any harm to a noble girl ; but the emptiness of an author oppresses her, and his amiable folly degrades her. And if she can have access to a good library of old and classical books, there need be no choosing at all. Keep the modern magazine and novel out of your girl's way : turn her loose into the old library every wet day, and let her alone. She will find what is good for her ; you cannot : for there is just this difference between the making of a girl's character and a boy's—you may chisel a boy into shape, as you would a rock, or hammer him into it, if he be of a better kind, as you would a piece of bronze. But you cannot hammer a girl into anything. She grows as a flower does,—she will wither without sun ; she will decay in her sheath, as the narcissus does, if you do not give her air enough ; she may fall, and defile her head in dust, if you leave her without help at some moments of her life ; but you cannot fetter her ; she must take her own fair form and way, if she take any, and in mind as in body, must have always

> " Her household motions light and free
> And steps of virgin liberty."

Let her loose in the library, I say, as you do a fawn in a field. It knows the bad weeds twenty times better than you ; and the good ones too, and will eat some bitter and prickly ones, good for it, which you had not the slightest thought were good.

Then, in art, keep the finest models before her, and let her practice in all accomplishments be accurate and thorough, so as to enable her to understand more than she accomplishes. I say the finest models—that is to say, the truest, simplest, usefullest. Note those epithets ; they will range through all the arts. Try them in music, where you might think them the least applicable. I say the truest, that in which the notes most closely and faithfully express the meaning of the words, or the character of intended emotion ; again, the simplest, that in which the meaning and melody are attained with the fewest and most significant notes possible ; and, finally, the usefullest, that music which makes the best words most beautiful, which enchants them in our memories each with its own glory of sound, and which applies them closest to the heart at the moment we need them.

And not only in the material and in the course, but yet more earnestly in the spirit of it, let a girl's education be as serious as a boy's. You bring up your girls as if they were meant for sideboard ornaments, and then complain of their frivolity. Give them the same advantages that you give their brothers—appeal to the same grand instincts of virtue in them ; teach *them* also that courage and truth are the pillars of their being : do you think that they would not answer that appeal, brave and true as they are even now, when you know that there is hardly a girl's school in this Christian kingdom where the children's courage or sincerity would be thought of half so much importance as their way of coming in at a door ; and when the whole system of society, as respects the mode of establishing them in life, is one rotten plague of cowardice and imposture—cowardice, in not daring to let them live, or love, except as their neighbours choose ; and imposture, in bringing, for the purposes of our own pride, the full glow of the world's worst vanity upon a girl's eyes, at the very period when the whole happiness of her future exist-ence depends upon her remaining undazzled?

And give them, lastly, not only noble teachings, but noble teachers. You consider somewhat, before you send your boy to school, what kind of a man the master is ;—whatsoever kind of man he is, you at least give him full authority over your son, and show some respect to him yourself : if he comes to dine with you, you do not put him at a side table ; you know also that, at his college, your child's immediate tutor will be under the direction of some still higher tutor, for whom you have absolute reverence. You do not treat the Dean of Christ Church or the Master of Trinity as your inferiors.

But what teachers do you give your girls, and what reverence do you show to the teachers you have chosen? Is a girl likely to think her own conduct, or her own intellect, of much importance, when you trust the entire formation of her character, moral and intellectual, to a person whom you let your servants treat with less respect than they do your housekeeper (as if the soul of your child were a less charge than jams and groceries), and whom you yourself think you confer an honour upon by letting her sometimes sit in the drawing-room in the evening?

Thus, then, of literature as her help, and thus of art. There is one more help which she cannot do without— one which, alone, has sometimes done more than all other influences besides,—the help of wild and fair nature. Hear this of the education of Joan of Arc ;

"The education of this poor girl was mean according to the present standard ; was ineffably grand, according to a purer philosophic standard ; and only not good for our age, because for us it would be unattainable. * * *

"Next after her spiritual advantages, she owed most to the advantages of her situation. The fountain of Domrémy was on the brink of a boundless forest ; and it was haunted to that degree by fairies, that the parish priest (curé) was obliged to read mass there once a year, in order to keep them in any decent bounds. * * *

"But the forests of Domrémy—those were the glories of the land ; for in them abode mysterious powers and ancient secrets that towered into tragic strength. ' Abbeys there were, and abbey windows,'—' like Moorish temples of the Hindoos,' that exercised even princely power both in Touraine and in the German Diets. These had their sweet bells that pierced the forests for many a league at matins or vespers, and each its own dreamy legend. Few enough, and scattered enough, were these abbeys, so as in no degree to disturb the deep solitude of the region ; yet many enough to spread a network or awning of Christian sanctity over what else might have seemed a heathen wilderness." [1]

Now, you cannot, indeed, have here in England, woods eighteen miles deep to the centre ; but you can, perhaps, keep a fairy or two for your children yet, if you wish to keep them. But *do* you wish it ? Suppose you had each, at the back of your houses, a garden, large enough for your children to play in, with just as much lawn as would give them room to run,—no more—and that you could not change your abode ; but that, if you chose, you could double your income, or quadruple it, by digging a coal shaft in the middle of the lawn, and turning the flower-beds into heaps of coke. Would you do it ? I think not. I can tell you, you would be wrong if you did, though it gave you income sixty-fold instead of four-fold.

[1] "Joan of Arc : in reference to M. Michelet's History of France." De Quincey's Works. Vol. iii. p. 217.

Yet this is what you are doing with all England. The whole country is but a little garden, not more than enough for your children to run on the lawns of, if you would let them *all* run there. And this little garden you will turn into furnace-ground, and fill with heaps of cinders, if you can; and those children of yours, not you, will suffer for it. For the fairies will not be all banished; there are fairies of the furnace as of the wood, and their first gifts seem to be "sharp arrows of the mighty;" but their last gifts are "coals of juniper."

And yet I cannot—though there is no part of my subject that I feel more—press this upon you; for we made so little use of the power of nature while we had it that we shall hardly feel what we have lost. Just on the other side of the Mersey you have your Snowdon, and your Menai Straits, and that mighty granite rock beyond the moors of Anglesea, splendid in its heathery crest, and foot planted in the deep sea, once thought of as sacred—a divine promontory, looking westward; the Holy Head or Headland, still not without awe when its red light glares first through storm. These are the hills, and these the bays and blue inlets, which, among the Greeks, would have been always loved, always fateful in influence on the national mind. That Snowdon is your Parnassus; but where are its Muses? That Holyhead mountain is your Island of Ægina, but where is its Temple to Minerva?

Shall I read you what the Christian Minerva had achieved under the shadow of our Parnassus, up to the year 1848?—Here is a little account of a Welsh School, from page 261 of the Report on Wales, published by the Committee of Council on Education. This is a school close to a town containing 5,000 persons:—

"I then called up a larger class, most of whom had recently come to the school. Three girls repeatedly declared they had never heard of Christ, and two that they had never heard of God. Two out of six thought

Christ was on earth now" (they might have had a worse thought, perhaps), "three knew nothing about the crucifixion. Four out of seven did not know the names of the months, nor the number of days in a year. They had no notion of addition beyond two and two, or three and three; their minds were perfect blanks."

Oh ye women of England! from the Princess of that Wales to the simplest of you, do not think your own children can be brought into their true fold of rest, while these are scattered on the hills, as sheep having no shepherd. And do not think your daughters can be trained to the truth of their own human beauty, while the pleasant places, which God made at once for their school-room and their playground, lie desolate and defiled. You cannot baptize them rightly in those inch-deep fonts of yours, unless you baptize them also in the sweet waters which the great Lawgiver strikes forth for ever from the rocks of your native land—waters which a Pagan would have worshipped in their purity, and you worship only with pollution. You cannot lead your children faithfully to those narrow axe-hewn church altars of yours, while the dark azure altars in heaven— the mountains that sustain your island throne,—mountains on which a Pagan would have seen the powers of heaven rest in every wreathed cloud—remain for you without inscription; altars built, not to, but by, an Unknown God.

III. Thus far, then, of the nature, thus far of the teaching, of woman, and thus of her household office, and queenliness. We come now to our last, our widest question,—What is her queenly office with respect to the state?

Generally, we are under an impression that a man's duties are public, and a woman's private. But this is not altogether so. A man has a personal work or duty, relating to his own home, and a public work or duty, which is the expansion of the other, relating to the state. So a woman has a personal work or duty, relating to her own home, and a public work and duty, which is also the expansion of that.

Now the man's work for his own home is, as has been said, to secure its maintenance, progress, and defence ; the woman's to secure its order, comfort, and loveliness.

Expand both these functions. The man's duty, as a member of a commonwealth, is to assist in the maintenance, in the advance, in the defence of the state. The woman's duty, as a member of the commonwealth, is to assist in the ordering, in the comforting, and in the beautiful adornment of the state.

What the man is at his own gate, defending it, if need be, against insult and spoil, that also, not in a less, but in a more devoted measure, he is to be at the gate of his country, leaving his home. if need be, even to the spoiler. to do his more incumbent work there.

And, in like manner, what the woman is to be within her gates, as the centre of order, the balm of distress, and the mirror of beauty ; that she is also to be without her gates, where order is more difficult, distress more imminent, loveliness more rare.

And as within the human heart there is always set an instinct for all its real duties,—an instinct which you cannot quench, but only warp and corrupt if you withdraw it from its true purpose ;—as there is the intense instinct of love, which, rightly disciplined, maintains all the sanctities of life, and, misdirected, undermines them ; and *must* do either the one or the other ;—so there is in the human heart an inextinguishable instinct, the love of power, which, rightly directed, maintains all the majesty of law and life, and misdirected, wrecks them.

Deep rooted in the innermost life of the heart of man, and of the heart of woman, God set it there, and God keeps it there. Vainly, as falsely, you blame or rebuke the desire of power !—For Heaven's sake, and for Man's sake, desire it all you can. But *what* power? That is all the question. Power to destroy? the lion's limb, and the dragon's breath? Not so. Power to heal, to redeem, to guide, and to guard. Power of the sceptre and shield; the power of the royal hand that heals in touching,—that binds the fiend, and looses the captive; the throne that is founded on the rock of Justice, and descended from only by steps of mercy. Will you not covet such power as this, and seek such throne as this, and be no more housewives, but queens?

It is now long since the women of England arrogated, universally, a title which once belonged to nobility only; and, having once been in the habit of accepting the simple title of gentlewoman, as correspondent to that of gentleman, insisted on the privilege of assuming the title of "Lady,"[1] which properly corresponds only to the title of "Lord."

I do not blame them for this; but only for their narrow motive in this. I would have them desire and claim the title of Lady, provided they claim, not merely the title, but the office and duty signified by it. Lady means "bread-giver" or "loaf-giver," and Lord means "maintainer of laws," and both titles have reference, not to the law which is maintained in the house, nor to the bread which is given to the household; but to law maintained for the multitude, and to bread broken among the multitude. So that a Lord has legal claim only to his title in so far as he is the maintainer of the justice of the Lord of Lords; and a Lady has legal claim to her title, only so far as she communicates that help to the poor representatives of her Master, which women once, ministering to Him of their substance, were permitted to extend to that Master Himself; and when she is known, as He Himself once was, in breaking of bread.

---

[1] I wish there were a true order of chivalry instituted for our English youth of certain ranks, in which both boy and girl should receive, at a given age, their knighthood and ladyhood by true title; attainable only by certain probation and trial both of character and accomplishment; and to be forfeited, on conviction, by their peers, of any dishonourable act. Such an institution would be entirely, and with all noble results, possible, in a nation which loved honour. That it would not be possible among us, is not to the discredit of the scheme.

And this beneficent and legal dominion, this power of the Dominus, or House-Lord, and of the Domina, or House-Lady, is great and venerable, not in the number of those through whom it has lineally descended, but in the number of those whom it grasps within its sway; it is always regarded with reverent worship wherever its dynasty is founded on its duty, and its ambition co-relative with its beneficence. Your fancy is pleased with the thought of being noble ladies, with a train of vassals. Be it so; you cannot be too noble, and your train cannot be too great; but see to it that your train is of vassals whom you serve and feed, not merely of slaves who serve and feed *you;* and that the multitude which obeys you is of those whom you have comforted, not oppressed,—whom you have redeemed, not led into captivity.

And this, which is true of the lower or household dominion, is equally true of the queenly dominion;— that highest dignity is open to you, if you will also accept that highest duty. Rex et Regina—Roi et Reine— "*Right*-doers;" they differ but from the Lady and Lord, in that their power is supreme over the mind as over the person—that they not only feed and clothe, but direct and teach. And whether consciously or not, you must be, in many a heart, enthroned: there is no putting by that crown; queens you must always be; queens to your lovers; queens to your husbands and your sons; queens of higher mystery to the world beyond, which bows itself, and will for ever bow, before the myrtle crown, and the stainless sceptre, of womanhood. But, alas! you are too often idle and careless queens, grasping at majesty in the least things, while you abdicate it in the greatest; and leaving misrule and violence to work their will among men, in defiance of the power, which, holding straight in gift from the Prince of all Peace, the wicked among you betray, and the good forget.

"Prince of Peace." Note that name. When kings rule in that name, and nobles, and the judges of the earth, they also, in their narrow place, and mortal measure,

receive the power of it. There are no other rulers
than they: other rule than theirs is but *mis*rule; they
who govern verily "Dei gratiâ" are all princes, yes, or
princesses, of peace. There is not a war in the world, no,
nor an injustice, but you women are answerable for it;
not in that you have provoked, but in that you have not
hindered. Men, by their nature, are prone to fight; they
will fight for any cause, or for none. It is for you to
choose their cause for them, and to forbid them when
there is no cause. There is no suffering, no injustice, no
misery in the earth, but the guilt of it lies lastly with you.
Men can bear the sight of it, but you should not be able
to bear it. Men may tread it down without sympathy
in their own struggle; but men are feeble in sympathy,
and contracted in hope; it is you only who can feel the
depths of pain; and conceive the way of its healing.
Instead of trying to do this, you turn away from it; you
shut yourselves within your park walls and garden gates;
and you are content to know that there is beyond them a
whole world in wilderness—a world of secrets which you
dare not penetrate; and of suffering which you dare not
conceive.

I tell you that this is to me quite the most amazing
among the phenomena of humanity. I am surprised at
no depths to which, when once warped from its honour,
that humanity can be degraded. I do not wonder at the
miser's death, with his hands, as they relax, dropping
gold. I do not wonder at the sensualist's life, with the
shroud wrapped about his feet. I do not wonder at the
single-handed murder of a single victim, done by the
assassin in the darkness of the railway, or reed-shadow of
the marsh. I do not even wonder at the myriad-handed
murder of multitudes, done boastfully in the daylight, by
the frenzy of nations, and the immeasurable, unimagin-
able guilt, heaped up from hell to heaven, of their priests,
and kings. But this is wonderful to me—oh, how
wonderful!—to see the tender and delicate woman
among you, with her child at her breast, and a power, if
she would wield it, over it, and over its father, purer than

the air of heaven, and stronger than the seas of earth—
nay, a magnitude of blessing which her husband would
not part with for all that earth itself, though it were made
of one entire and perfect chrysolite :— to see her abdicate
this majesty to play at precedence with her next-door
neighbour ! This is wonderful—oh, wonderful !—to see
her, with every innocent feeling fresh within her, go out
in the morning into her garden to play with the fringes
of its guarded flowers, and lift their heads when they are
drooping, with her happy smile upon her face, and no
cloud upon her brow, because there is a little wall
around her place of peace : and yet she knows, in her
heart, if she would only look for its knowledge, that,
outside of that little rose-covered wall, the wild grass, to
the horizon, is torn up by the agony of men, and beat
level by the drift of their life-blood.

Have you ever considered what a deep under meaning
there lies, or at least, may be read, if we choose, in our
custom of strewing flowers before those whom we think
most happy ? Do you suppose it is merely to deceive
them into the hope that happiness is always to fall thus
in showers at their feet ?—that wherever they pass they
will tread on herbs of sweet scent, and that the rough
ground will be made smooth for them by depth of roses ?
So surely as they believe that, they will have, instead, to
walk on bitter herbs and thorns ; and the only softness
to their feet will be of snow. But it is not thus intended
they should believe ; there is a better meaning in that
old custom. The path of a good woman is indeed
strewn with flowers ; but they rise behind her steps, not
before them. "Her feet have touched the meadows,
and left the daisies rosy." You think that only a lover's
fancy ;—false and vain ! How if it could be true ? You
think this also, perhaps, only a poet's fancy—

> "Even the light harebell raised its head
> Elastic from her airy tread."

But it is little to say of a woman, that she only does
not destroy where she passes. She should revive ; the

harebells should bloom, not stoop, as she passes.   You
think I am going into wild hyperbole?   Pardon me, not
a whit—I mean what I say in calm English, spoken in
resolute truth.   You have heard it said—(and I believe
there is more than fancy even in that saying, but let it
pass for a fanciful one)—that flowers only flourish rightly
in the garden of some one who loves them.   I know you
would like that to be true; you would think it a pleasant
magic if you could flush your flowers into brighter bloom
by a kind look upon them : nay, more, if your look had
the power, not only to cheer, but to guard them—if you
could bid the black blight turn away, and the knotted
caterpillar spare—if you could bid the dew fall upon
them in the drought, and say to the south wind, in frost
—"Come, thou south, and breathe upon my garden,
that the spices of it may flow out."   This you would
think a great thing?   And do you think it not a greater
thing, that all this, (and how much more than this!) you
can do, for fairer flowers than these—flowers that could
bless you for having blessed them, and will love you for
having loved them ;—flowers that have eyes like yours,
and thoughts like yours, and lives like yours ; which, once
saved, you save for ever?   Is this only a little power?
Far among the moorlands and the rocks,—far in the
darkness of the terrible streets,—these feeble florets are
lying, with all their fresh leaves torn, and their stems
broken—will you never go down to them, nor set them
in order in their little fragrant beds, nor fence them in
their shuddering from the fierce wind?   Shall morning
follow morning, for you, but not for them ; and the dawn
rise to watch, far away, those frantic Dances of Death ; [1]
but no dawn rise to breathe upon these living banks of
wild violet, and woodbine, and rose ; nor call to you,
through your casement,—call, (not giving you the name
of the English poet's lady, but the name of Dante's
great Matilda, who, on the edge of happy Lethe, stood,
wreathing flowers with flowers), saying :—

[1] See note, p. 36.

> " Come into the garden, Maud,
>   For the black bat, night, has flown,
>   And the woodbine spices are wafted abroad
>   And the musk of the roses blown ? "

Will you not go down among them ?—among those sweet living things, whose new courage, sprung from the earth with the deep colour of heaven upon it, is starting up in strength of goodly spire ; and whose purity, washed from the dust, is opening, bud by bud, into the flower of promise ;—and still they turn to you, and for you, "The Larkspur listens—I hear, I hear ! And the Lily whispers—I wait."

Did you notice that I missed two lines when I read you that first stanza ; and think that I had forgotten them ? Hear them now :—

> " Come into the garden, Maud,
>   For the black bat, night, has flown :
>   Come into the garden, Maud,
>   I am here at the gate, alone."

Who is it, think you, who stands at the gate of this sweeter garden, alone, waiting for you ? Did you ever hear, not of a Maude, but a Madeleine, who went down to her garden in the dawn, and found One waiting at the gate, whom she supposed to be the gardener ?   Have you not sought Him often ;—sought Him in vain, all through the night ;—sought Him in vain at the gate of that old garden where the fiery sword is set ? He is never there ; but at the gate of *this* garden He is waiting always— waiting to take your hand—ready to go down to see the fruits of the valley, to see whether the vine has flourished, and the pomegranate budded.   There you shall see with Him the little tendrils of the vines that His hand is guiding—there you shall see the pomegranate springing where His hand cast the sanguine seed ;—more : you shall see the troops of the angel keepers that, with their wings, wave away the hungry birds from the pathsides where He has sown, and call to each other between the vineyard rows, "Take us the foxes, the little foxes, that spoil the vines, for our vines have tender grapes." Oh—you queens—you queens! among the hills and happy green-wood of this land of yours, shall the foxes have holes, and the birds of the air have nests; and, in your cities, shall the stones cry out against you, that they are the only pillows where the Son of Man can lay His head?

THE TWO PATHS

BEING

LECTURES ON ART

AND ITS APPLICATION

TO

DECORATION AND MANUFACTURE

DELIVERED IN 1858-9

By JOHN RUSKIN

PREFACE

THE following addresses, though spoken at different times, are intentionally connected in subject; their aim being to set one or two main principles of art in simple light before the general student, and to indicate their practical bearing on modern design. The law which it has been my effort chiefly to illustrate is the dependence of all noble design, in any kind, on the sculpture or painting of Organic Form.

This is the vital law; lying at the root of all that I have ever tried to teach respecting architecture or any other art. It is also the law most generally disallowed.

I believe this must be so in every subject. We are all of us willing enough to accept dead truths or blunt ones; which can be fitted harmlessly into spare niches, or shrouded and coffined at once out of the way, we holding complacently the cemetery keys, and supposing we have learned something. But a sapling truth, with earth at its root and blossom on its branches; or a trenchant truth, that can cut its way through bars and sods; most men, it seems to me, dislike the sight or entertainment of, if by any means such guest or vision may be avoided. And, indeed, this is no wonder; for one such truth, thoroughly accepted, connects itself strangely with others, and there is no saying what it may lead us to.

And thus the gist of what I have tried to teach about architecture has been throughout denied by my architect readers, even when they thought what I said suggestive in other particulars. "Anything but that. Study Italian Gothic?—perhaps it would be as well: build with pointed arches?—there is no objection: use solid stone and well-burnt brick?—by all means: but—learn to carve or paint organic form ourselves! How can such a thing be asked?

We are above all that. The carvers and painters are our servants—quite subordinate people. They ought to be glad if we leave room for them."

Well : on that it all turns. For those who will not learn to carve or paint, and think themselves greater men because they cannot, it is wholly wasted time to read any words of mine ; in the truest and sternest sense they *can* read no words of mine ; for the most familiar I can use— " form," " proportion," " beauty," " curvature," " colour " —are used in a sense which by no effort I can communicate to such readers ; and in no building that I praise, is the thing that I praise it for, visible to them.

And it is the more necessary for me to state this fully ; because so-called Gothic or Romanesque buildings are now rising every day around us, which might be supposed by the public more or less to embody the principles of those styles, but which embody not one of them, nor any shadow or fragment of them ; but merely serve to caricature the noble buildings of past ages, and to bring their form into dishonour by leaving out their soul.

The following addresses are therefore arranged, as I have just stated, to put this great law, and one or two collateral ones, in less mistakeable light, securing even in this irregular form at least clearness of assertion. For the rest, the question at issue is not one to be decided by argument, but by experiment, which if the reader is disinclined to make, all demonstration must be useless to him.

The lectures are for the most part printed as they were read, mending only obscure sentences here and there. The parts which were trusted to extempore speaking are supplied, as well as I can remember (only with an addition here and there of things I forgot to say), in the words, or at least the kind of words, used at the time ; and they contain, at all events, the substance of what I said more accurately than hurried journal reports. I must beg my readers not in general to trust to such, for even in fast speaking I try to use words carefully ; and any alteration of expression will sometimes involve a great alteration in

meaning. A little while ago I had to speak of an architectural design, and called it "elegant," meaning, founded
on good and well "elected" models; the printed report
gave "excellent" design (that is to say, design *excellingly*
good), which I did not mean, and should, even in the
most hurried speaking, never have said.

The illustrations of the lecture on iron were sketches
made too roughly to be engraved, and yet of too elaborate
subjects to allow of my drawing them completely. Those
now substituted will, however, answer the purpose nearly
as well, and are more directly connected with the subjects
of the preceding lectures; so that I hope throughout the
volume the student will perceive an insistance upon one
main truth, nor lose in any minor direction of inquiry the
sense of the responsibility which the acceptance of that
truth fastens upon him; responsibility for choice, decisive
and conclusive, between two modes of study, which involve
ultimately the development, or deadening, of every power
he possesses. I have tried to hold that choice clearly
out to him, and to unveil for him to its farthest the issue
of his turning to the right hand or the left. Guides he
may find many, and aids many; but all these will be in
vain unless he has first recognised the hour and the
point of life when the way divides itself, one way leading
to the Olive mountains—one to the vale of the Salt Sea.
There are few cross roads, that I know of, from one to
the other. Let him pause at the parting of THE TWO
PATHS.

LECTURE I

THE DETERIORATIVE POWER OF CONVENTIONAL ART OVER NATIONS

AN INAUGURAL LECTURE

Delivered at the Kensington Museum,[1] January, 1858.

As I passed, last summer, for the first time, through the north of Scotland, it seemed to me that there was a peculiar painfulness in its scenery, caused by the non-manifestation of the powers of human art. I had never travelled in, nor even heard or conceived of such a country before ; nor, though I had passed much of my life amidst mountain scenery in the south, was I before aware how much of its charm depended on the little graceful-nesses and tendernesses of human work, which are mingled with the beauty of the Alps, or spared by their desolation. It is true that the art which carves and colours the front of a Swiss cottage is not of any very exalted kind ; yet it testifies to the completeness and the delicacy of the faculties of the mountaineer : it is true that the remnants of tower and battlement, which afford footing to the wild vine on the Alpine promontory, form but a small part of the great serration of its rocks ; and yet it is just that fragment of their broken outline which gives them their

[1] A few introductory words, in which, at the opening of this lecture, I thanked the Chairman (Mr. Cockerell), for his support on the occasion, and asked his pardon for any hasty expressions in my writings, which might have seemed discourteous towards him, or other architects whose general opinions were opposed to mine, may be found by those who care for preambles, not much misreported, in the *Building Chronicle ;* with such comments as the genius of that journal was likely to suggest to it.

pathetic power, and historical majesty.   And this element among the wilds of our own country I found wholly wanting.   The Highland cottage is literally a heap of gray stones, choked up, rather than roofed over, with black peat and withered heather ; the only approach to an effort at decoration consists in the placing of the clods of protective peat obliquely on its roof, so as to give a diagonal arrangement of lines, looking somewhat as if the surface had been scored over by a gigantic claymore.

And, at least among the northern hills of Scotland, elements of more ancient architectural interest are equally absent.   The solitary peel-house is hardly discernible by the windings of the stream ; the roofless aisle of the priory is lost among the enclosures of the village ; and the capital city of the Highlands, Inverness, placed where it might ennoble one of the sweetest landscapes, and by the shore of one of the loveliest estuaries in the world ;— placed between the crests of the Grampians and the flowing of the Moray Firth, as if it were a jewel clasping the folds of the mountains to the blue zone of the sea,—is only distinguishable from a distance by one architectural feature, and exalts all the surrounding landscape by no other associations than those which can be connected with its modern castellated gaol.

While these conditions of Scottish scenery affected me very painfully, it being the first time in my life that I had been in any country possessing no valuable monuments or examples of art, they also forced me into the consideration of one or two difficult questions respecting the effect of art on the human mind ; and they forced these questions upon me eminently for this reason, that while I was wandering disconsolately among the moors of the Grampians, where there was no art to be found, news of peculiar interest were every day arriving from a country where there was a great deal of art, and art of a delicate kind, to be found.   Among the models set before you in this institution, and in the others established throughout the kingdom for the teaching of design, there are, I suppose, none in their kind more admirable than the decorated works of India. They are, indeed, in all materials capable of colour, wool, marble, or metal, almost inimitable in their delicate application of divided hue, and fine arrangement of fantastic line. Nor is this power of theirs exerted by the people rarely, or without enjoyment; the love of subtle design seems universal in the race, and is developed in every implement that they shape, and every building that they raise; it attaches itself with the same intensity, and with the same success, to the service of superstition, of pleasure or of cruelty; and enriches alike, with one profusion of enchanted iridescence, the dome of the pagoda, the fringe of the girdle, and the edge of the sword.

So then you have, in these two great populations, Indian and Highland—in the races of the jungle and of the moor—two national capacities distinctly and accurately opposed. On the one side you have a race rejoicing in art, and eminently and universally endowed with the gift of it; on the other you have a people careless of art, and apparently incapable of it, their utmost efforts hitherto reaching no farther than to the variation of the positions of the bars of colour in square chequers. And we are thus urged naturally to inquire what is the effect on the moral character, in each nation, of this vast difference in their pursuits and apparent capacities? and whether those rude chequers of the tartan, or the exquisitely fancied involutions of the Cashmere, fold habitually over the noblest hearts? We have had our answer. Since the race of man began its course of sin on this earth, nothing has ever been done by it so significative of all bestial, and lower than bestial degradation, as the acts of the Indian race in the year that has just passed by. Cruelty as fierce may indeed have been wreaked, and brutality as abominable been practised before, but never under like circumstances; rage of prolonged war, and resentment of prolonged oppression, have made men as cruel before now; and gradual decline into barbarism, where no examples of decency or civilization existed around them, has sunk, before now, isolated populations

*D 2

to the lowest level of possible humanity. But cruelty stretched to its fiercest against the gentle and unoffending, and corruption festered to its loathsomest in the midst of the witnessing presence of a disciplined civilization,—these we could not have known to be within the practicable compass of human guilt, but for the acts of the Indian mutineer. And, as thus, on the one hand, you have an extreme energy of baseness displayed by these lovers of art ; on the other,—as if to put the question into the narrowest compass—you have had an extreme energy of virtue displayed by the despisers of art. Among all the soldiers to whom you owe your victories in the Crimea, and your avenging in the Indies, to none are you bound by closer bonds of gratitude than to the men who have been born and bred among those desolate Highland moors. And thus you have the differences in capacity and circumstance between the two nations, and the differences in result on the moral habits of two nations, put into the most significant—the most palpable—the most brief opposition. Out of the peat cottage come faith, courage, self-sacrifice, purity, and piety, and whatever else is fruitful in the work of Heaven ; out of the ivory palace come treachery, cruelty, cowardice, idolatry, bestiality,—whatever else is fruitful in the work of Hell.

But the difficulty does not close here. From one instance, of however great apparent force, it would be wholly unfair to gather any general conclusion—wholly illogical to assert that because we had once found love of art connected with moral baseness, the love of art must be the general root of moral baseness ; and equally unfair to assert that, because we had once found neglect of art coincident with nobleness of disposition, neglect of art must be always the source or sign of that nobleness. But if we pass from the Indian peninsula into other countries of the globe ; and from our own recent experience, to the records of history, we shall still find one great fact fronting us, in stern universality—namely, the apparent connection of great success in art with subsequent national degradation. You find, in the first place, that the nations which possessed a refined art were always subdued by those who possessed none : you find the Lydian subdued by the Mede ; the Athenian by the Spartan ; the Greek by the Roman ; the Roman by the Goth ; the Burgundian by the Switzer: but you find, beyond this—that even where no attack by any external power has accelerated the catastrophe of the state, the period in which any given people reach their highest power in art is precisely that in which they appear to sign the warrant of their own ruin ; and that, from the moment in which a perfect statue appears in Florence, a perfect picture in Venice, or a perfect fresco in Rome, from that hour forward, probity, industry, and courage seem to be exiled from their walls, and they perish in a sculpturesque paralysis, or a many-coloured corruption.

But even this is not all. As art seems thus, in its delicate form, to be one of the chief promoters of indolence and sensuality,—so, I need hardly remind you, it hitherto has appeared only in energetic manifestation when it was in the service of superstition. The four great manifestations of human intellect which founded the four principal kingdoms of art, Egyptian, Babylonian, Greek, and Italian, were developed by the strong excitement of active superstition in the worship of Osiris, Belus, Minerva, and the Queen of Heaven. Therefore, to speak briefly, it may appear very difficult to show that art has ever yet existed in a consistent and thoroughly energetic school, unless it was engaged in the propagation of falsehood, or the encouragement of vice.

And finally, while art has thus shown itself always active in the service of luxury and idolatry, it has also been strongly directed to the exaltation of cruelty. A nation which lives a pastoral and innocent life never decorates the shepherd's staff or the plough-handle, but races who live by depredation and slaughter nearly always bestow exquisite ornaments on the quiver, the helmet, and the spear.

Does it not seem to you, then, on all these three

counts, more than questionable whether we are assembled here in Kensington museum to any good purpose? Might we not justly be looked upon with suspicion and fear, rather than with sympathy, by the innocent and un-artistical public? Are we even sure of ourselves? Do we know what we are about? Are we met here as honest people? or are we not rather so many Catilines assembled to devise the hasty degradation of our country, or, like a conclave of midnight witches, to summon and send forth, on new and unsuspected missions, the demons of luxury, cruelty, and superstition?

I trust, upon the whole, that it is not so: I am sure that Mr. Redgrave and Mr. Cole do not at all include results of this kind in their conception of the ultimate objects of the institution which owes so much to their strenuous and well-directed exertions. And I have put this painful question before you, only that we may face it thoroughly, and, as I hope, out-face it. If you will give it a little sincere attention this evening, I trust we may find sufficiently good reasons for our work, and pro-ceed to it hereafter, as all good workmen should do, with clear heads, and calm consciences.

To return, then, to the first point of difficulty, the re-lations between art and mental disposition in India and Scotland. It is quite true that the art of India is delicate and refined. But it has one curious character distin-guishing it from all other art of equal merit in design—*it never represents a natural fact.* It either forms its compositions out of meaningless fragments of colour and flowings of line; or, if it represents any living creature, it represents that creature under some distorted and monstrous form. To all the facts and forms of nature it wilfully and resolutely opposes itself; it will not draw a man, but an eight-armed monster; it will not draw a flower, but only a spiral or a zigzag.

It thus indicates that the people who practise it are cut off from all possible sources of healthy knowledge or natural delight; that they have wilfully sealed up and put aside the entire volume of the world, and have got nothing to read, nothing to dwell upon, but that imagination of the thoughts of their hearts, of which we are told that " it is only evil continually." Over the whole spectacle of creation they have thrown a veil in which there is no rent. For them no star peeps through the blanket of the dark—for them neither their heaven shines nor their mountains rise—for them the flowers do not blossom—for them the creatures of field and forest do not live. They lie bound in the dungeon of their own corruption, encompassed only by doleful phantoms, or by spectral vacancy.

Need I remind you what an exact reverse of this condition of mind, as respects the observance of nature, is presented by the people whom we have just been led to contemplate in contrast with the Indian race? You will find upon reflection, that all the highest points of the Scottish character are connected with impressions derived straight from the natural scenery of their country. No nation has ever before shown, in the general tone of its language,—in the general current of its literature,— so constant a habit of hallowing its passions and confirming its principles by direct association with the charm, or power, of nature. The writings of Scott and Burns—and yet more, of the far greater poets than Burns who gave Scotland her traditional ballads,—furnish you in every stanza—almost in every line,—with examples of this association of natural scenery with the passions ; [1] but an instance of its farther connection with moral principle struck me forcibly just at the time

[1] The great poets of Scotland, like the great poets of all other countries, never write dissolutely, either in matter or method ; but with stern and measured meaning in every syllable. Here's a bit of first-rate work for example :—

> " Tweed said to Till,
> ' What gars ye rin sae still?'
> Till said to Tweed,
> ' Though ye rin wi' speed,
> And I rin slaw,
> Whar ye droon ae man,
> I droon twa.'"

when I was most lamenting the absence of art among the people. In one of the loneliest districts of Scotland, where the peat cottages are darkest, just at the western foot of that great mass of the Grampians which encircles the sources of the Spey and the Dee, the main road which traverses the chain winds round the foot of a broken rock called Crag, or Craig Ellachie. There is nothing remarkable in either its height or form; it is darkened with a few scattered pines, and touched along its summit with a flush of heather; but it constitutes a kind of headland, or leading promontory, in the group of hills to which it belongs—a sort of initial letter of the mountains; and thus stands in the mind of the inhabitants of the district, the Clan Grant, for a type of their country, and of the influence of that country upon themselves. Their sense of this is beautifully indicated in the war-cry of the clan, "Stand fast, Craig Ellachie." You may think long over those few words without exhausting the deep wells of feeling and thought contained in them—the love of the native land, the assurance of their faithfulness to it; the subdued and gentle assertion of indomitable courage—I *may* need to be told to stand, but, if I do, Craig Ellachie does. You could not but have felt, had you passed beneath it at the time when so many of England's dearest children were being defended by the strength of heart of men born at its foot, how often among the delicate Indian palaces, whose marble was pallid with horror, and whose vermilion was darkened with blood, the remembrance of its rough gray rocks and purple heaths must have risen before the sight of the Highland soldier; how often the hailing of the shot and the shriek of battle would pass away from his hearing, and leave only the whisper of the old pine branches, —"Stand fast, Craig Ellachie!"

You have, in these two nations, seen in direct opposition the effects on moral sentiment of art without nature, and of nature without art. And you see enough to justify you in suspecting—while, if you choose to investigate the subject more deeply and with other examples, you will find enough to justify you in *concluding*—that art, followed as such, and for its own sake, irrespective of the interpretation of nature by it, is destructive of whatever is best and noblest in humanity; but that nature, however simply observed, or imperfectly known, is, in the degree of the affection felt for it, protective and helpful to all that is noblest in humanity.

You might then conclude farther, that art, so far as it was devoted to the record or the interpretation of nature, would be helpful and ennobling also.

And you would conclude this with perfect truth. Let me repeat the assertion distinctly and solemnly, as the first that I am permitted to make in this building, devoted in a way so new and so admirable to the service of the art-students of England—Wherever art is practised for its own sake, and the delight of the workman is in what he *does* and *produces*, instead of in what he *interprets* or *exhibits*,—there art has an influence of the most fatal kind on brain and heart, and it issues, if long so pursued, in the *destruction both of intellectual power* and *moral principle*; whereas art, devoted humbly and self-forgetfully to the clear statement and record of the facts of the universe, is always helpful and beneficent to mankind, full of comfort, strength, and salvation.

Now, when you were once well assured of this, you might logically infer another thing, namely, that when Art was occupied in the function in which she was serviceable, she would herself be strengthened by the service; and when she was doing what Providence without doubt intended her to do, she would gain in vitality and dignity just as she advanced in usefulness. On the other hand, you might gather, that when her agency was distorted to the deception or degradation of mankind, she would herself be equally misled and degraded—that she would be checked in advance, or precipitated in decline.

And this is the truth also; and holding this clue you will easily and justly interpret the phenomena of history. So long as Art is steady in the contemplation and exhibition of natural facts, so long she herself lives and grows; and in her own life and growth partly implies, partly secures, that of the nation in the midst of which she is practised. But a time has always hitherto come, in which, having thus reached a singular perfection, she begins to contemplate that perfection, and to imitate it, and deduce rules and forms from it; and thus to forget her duty and ministry as the interpreter and discoverer of Truth. And in the very instant when this diversion of her purpose and forgetfulness of her function take place—forgetfulness generally coincident with her apparent perfection — in that instant, I say, begins her actual catastrophe; and by her own fall—so far as she has influence—she accelerates the ruin of the nation by which she is practised.

The study, however, of the effect of art on the mind of nations is one rather for the historian than for us; at all events it is one for the discussion of which we have no more time this evening. But I will ask your patience with me while I try to illustrate, in some farther particulars, the dependence of the healthy state and power of art itself upon the exercise of its appointed function in the interpretation of fact.

You observe that I always say *interpretation*, never *imitation*. My reason for doing so is, first, that good art rarely imitates; it usually only describes or explains. But my second and chief reason is that good art always consists of two things: First, the observation of fact; secondly, the manifesting of human design and authority in the way that fact is told. Great and good art must unite the two; it cannot exist for a moment but in their unity; it consists of the two as essentially as water consists of oxygen and hydrogen, or marble of lime and carbonic acid.

Let us inquire a little into the nature of each of the elements. The first element, we say, is the love of Nature, leading to the effort to observe and report her truly. And this is the first and leading element. Review for yourselves the history of art, and you will find this to be a manifest certainty, that *no great school ever yet existed which had not for primal aim the representation of some natural fact as truly as possible.* There have only yet appeared in the world three schools of perfect art—schools, that is to say, which did their work as well as it seems possible to do it. These are the Athenian,[1] Florentine, and Venetian. The Athenian proposed to itself the perfect representation of the form of the human body. It strove to do that as well as it could; it did that as well as it can be done; and all its greatness was founded upon and involved in that single and honest effort. The Florentine school proposed to itself the perfect expression of human emotion—the showing of the effects of passion in the human face and gesture. I call this the Florentine school, because, whether you take Raphael for the culminating master of expressional art in Italy, or Leonardo, or Michael Angelo, you will find that the whole energy of the national effort which produced those masters had its root in Florence; not at Urbino or Milan. I say, then, this Florentine or leading Italian school proposed to itself human expression for its aim in natural truth; it strove to do that as well as it could—did it as well as it can be done—and all its greatness is rooted in that single and honest effort. Thirdly, the Venetian school proposed to itself the representation of the effect of colour and shade on all things; chiefly on the human form. It tried to do that as well as it could—did it as well as it can be done—and all its greatness is founded on that single and honest effort.

Pray, do not leave this room without a perfectly clear holding of these three ideas. You may try them, and toss them about, afterwards, as much as you like, to see if they'll bear shaking; but do let me put them well and plainly into your possession. Attach them to three works of art which you all have either seen or continually heard of. There's the (so-called) "Theseus" of the Elgin marbles. That represents the whole end and aim

---

[1] See below, the farther notice of the real spirit of Greek work, in the address at Bradford.

of the Athenian school—the natural form of the human body. All their conventional architecture—their graceful shaping and painting of pottery—whatsoever other art they practised—was dependent for its greatness on this sheet-anchor of central aim : true shape of living man. Then take, for your type of the Italian school, Raphael's "Disputa del Sacramento;" that will be an accepted type by everybody, and will involve no possibly questionable points: the Germans will admit it; the English academicians will admit it; and the English purists and pre-Raphaelites will admit it. Well, there you have the truth of human expression proposed as an aim. That is the way people look when they feel this or that—when they have this or that other mental character : are they devotional, thoughtful, affectionate, indignant, or inspired ? are they prophets, saints, priests, or kings ? then—whatsoever is truly thoughtful, affectionate, prophetic, priestly, kingly—*that* the Florentine school tried to discern, and show; *that* they have discerned and shown ; and all their greatness is first fastened in their aim at this central truth—the open expression of the living human soul.

Lastly, take Veronese's " Marriage in Cana " in the Louvre. There you have the most perfect representation possible of colour, and light, and shade, as they affect the external aspect of the human form, and its immediate accessories, architecture, furniture, and dress. This external aspect of noblest nature was the first aim of the Venetians, and all their greatness depended on their resolution to achieve, and their patience in achieving it.

Here, then, are the three greatest schools of the former world exemplified for you in three well-known works. The Phidian "Theseus" represents the Greek school pursuing truth of form ; the " Disputa " of Raphael, the Florentine school pursuing truth of mental expression ; the " Marriage in Cana," the Venetian school pursuing truth of colour and light. But do not suppose that the law which I am stating to you—the great law of art-life—can only be seen in these, the most powerful of all art schools. It is just as manifest in each and every school that ever has had life in it at all. Wheresoever the search after truth begins, there life begins; wheresoever that search ceases, there life ceases. As long as a school of art holds any chain of natural facts, trying to discover more of them and express them better daily, it may play hither and thither as it likes on this side of the chain or that; it may design grotesques and conventionalisms, build the simplest buildings, serve the most practical utilities, yet all it does will be gloriously designed and gloriously done; but let it once quit hold of the chain of natural fact, cease to pursue that as the clue to its work; let it propose to itself any other end than preaching this living word, and think first of showing its own skill or its own fancy, and from that hour its fall is precipitate—its destruction sure; nothing that it does or designs will ever have life or loveliness in it more; its hour has come, and there is no work, nor device, nor knowledge, nor wisdom in the grave whither it goeth.

Let us take for example that school of art over which many of you would perhaps think this law had little power—the school of Gothic architecture. Many of us may have been in the habit of thinking of that school rather as of one of forms than of facts—a school of pinnacles, and buttresses, and conventional mouldings, and disguise of nature by monstrous imaginings—not a school of truth at all. I think I shall be able, even in the little time we have to-night, to show that this is not so; and that our great law holds just as good at Amiens and Salisbury as it does at Athens and Florence.

I will go back then first to the very beginnings of Gothic art, and before you, the students of Kensington, as an impannelled jury, I will bring two examples of the barbarism out of which Gothic art emerges, approximately contemporary in date and parallel in executive skill; but, the one, a barbarism that did not get on, and could not get on; the other, a barbarism that could get on, and did get on; and you, the impannelled jury, shall judge what is the essential difference between the two barbarisms, and decide for yourselves what is the seed of life in the one, and the sign of death in the other.

The first,—that which has in it the sign of death,—furnishes us at the same time with an illustration far too interesting to be passed by, of certain principles much depended on by our common modern designers. Taking up one of our architectural publications the other day, and opening it at random, I chanced upon this piece of information, put in rather curious English; but you shall have it as it stands—

"Aristotle asserts, that the greatest species of the beautiful are Order, Symmetry, and the Definite."

I should tell you, however, that this statement is not given as authoritative; it is one example of various Architectural teachings, given in a report in the *Building Chronicle* for May, 1857, of a lecture on Proportion; in which the only thing the lecturer appears to have proved was that,—

"The system of dividing the diameter of the shaft of a column into parts for copying the ancient architectural remains of Greece and Rome, adopted by architects from Vitruvius (circa B.C. 25) to the present period, as a method for producing ancient architecture, *is entirely useless*, for the several parts of Grecian architecture cannot be reduced or subdivided by this system; neither does it apply to the architecture of Rome."

Still, as far as I can make it out, the lecture appears to have been just one of those of which you will at present hear so many, the protests of architects who have no knowledge of sculpture—or of any other mode of expressing natural beauty—*against* natural beauty; and their endeavour to substitute mathematical proportions for the knowledge of life they do not possess, and the representation of life of which they are incapable. Now, this substitution of obedience to mathematical law for sympathy with observed life, is the first characteristic of the hopeless work of all ages; as such, you will find it eminently manifested in the specimen I have to give you of the hopeless Gothic barbarism; the barbarism from which nothing could emerge—for which no future was possible but extinction. The Aristotelian principles of the Beautiful are, you remember, Order, Symmetry, and the Definite. Here you have the three, in perfection, applied to the ideal of an angel, in a psalter of the eighth century, existing in the library of St. John's College, Cambridge.[1]

Now, you see the characteristics of this utterly dead school are, first the wilful closing of its eyes to natural facts; —for, however ignorant a person may be, he need only look at a human being to see that it has a mouth as well as eyes; and secondly, the endeavour to adorn or idealize natural fact according to its own notions: it puts red spots in the middle of the hands, and sharpens the thumbs, thinking to improve them. Here you have the most pure type possible of the principles of idealism in all ages; whenever people don't look at Nature, they always think they can improve her. You will also admire, doubtless, the exquisite result of the application of our great modern architectural principle of beauty—symmetry, or equal balance of part by part; you see even the eyes are made symmetrical, instead of irregularly oval; and the iris is set properly in the middle, instead of—as nature has absurdly put it—rather under the upper lid. You will also observe the "principle of the pyramid" in the general arrangement of the figure, and the value of "series" in the placing of the dots.

From this dead barbarism we pass to living barbarism —to work done by hands quite as rude, if not ruder, and

---

[1] I copy this woodcut from Westwood's "Palæographia Sacra."

by minds as uninformed ; and yet work which in every line of it is prophetic of power, and has in it the sure dawn of day. You have often heard it said that Giotto was the founder of art in Italy. He was not : neither he, nor Giunta Pisano, nor Niccolo Pisano. They all laid strong hands to the work, and brought it first into aspect above ground ; but the foundation had been laid for them by the builders of the Lombardic churches in the valleys of the Adda and the Arno. It is in the sculpture of the round arched churches of North Italy, bearing disputable dates, ranging from the eighth to the twelfth century, that you will find the lowest struck roots of the art of Titian and Raphael.[1] I go, therefore, to the church which is certainly the earliest of these, St. Ambrogio, of Milan, said still to retain some portions of the actual structure from which St. Ambrose excluded Theodosius, and at all events furnishing the most archaic examples of Lombardic sculpture in North Italy. I do not venture to guess their date ; they are barbarous enough for any date.

We find the pulpit of this church covered with in-terlacing patterns, closely resembling those of the manuscript at Cambridge, but among them is figure sculpture of a very different kind. It is wrought with mere incisions in the stone, of which the effect may be tolerably given by single lines in a drawing. Remember, therefore, for a moment—as characteristic of culminating Italian art—Michael Angelo's fresco of the "Temptation of Eve," in the Sistine chapel, and you will be more interested in seeing the birth of Italian art, illustrated by the same subject, from St. Ambrogio, of Milan, the "Serpent beguiling Eve." [2]

Yet, in that sketch, rude and ludicrous as it is, you

[1] I have said elsewhere, "the root of *all* art is struck in the thirteenth century." This is quite true : but of course some of the smallest fibres run lower, as in this instance.

[2] This cut is ruder than it should be ; the incisions in the marble have a lighter effect than these rough black lines ; but it is not worth while to do it better.

have the elements of life in their first form. The people who could do that were sure to get on. For, observe, the workman's whole aim is straight at the facts, as well as he can get them ; and not merely at the facts, but at the very heart of the facts. A common workman might have looked at nature for his serpent, but he would have thought only of its scales. But this fellow does not want scales, nor coils ; he can do without them ; he wants the serpent's heart—malice and insinuation ;—and he has

actually got them to some extent. So also a common workman, even in this barbarous stage of art, might have carved Eve's arms and body a good deal better ; but this man does not care about arms and body, if he can only get at Eve's mind—show that she is pleased at being flattered, and yet in a state of uncomfortable hesitation. And some look of listening, of complacency, and of embarrassment he has verily got :—note the eyes slightly askance, the lips compressed, and the right hand nervously grasping the left arm : nothing can be declared impossible to the people who could begin thus—the world is open to them, and all that is in it ; while, on the contrary, nothing is possible to the man who did the symmetrical angel—the world is keyless to him ; he has built a cell for himself in which he must abide, barred up for ever—there is no more hope for him than for a sponge or a madrepore.

I snail not trace from this embryo the progress of Gothic art in Italy, because it is much complicated and involved with traditions of other schools, and because most of the students will be less familiar with its results than with their own northern buildings. So, these two designs indicating Death and Life in the beginnings of mediæval art, we will take an example of the *progress* of that art from our northern work. Now, many of you, doubtless, have been interested by the mass, grandeur, and gloom of Norman architecture, as much as by Gothic traceries; and when you hear me say that the root of all good work lies in natural facts, you doubtless think instantly of your round arches, with their rude cushion capitals, and of the billet or zigzag work by which they are surrounded, and you cannot see what the knowledge of nature has to do with either the simple plan or the rude mouldings. But all those simple conditions of Norman art are merely the expiring of it towards the extreme north. Do not study Norman architecture in Northumberland, but in Normandy, and then you will find that it is just a peculiarly manly, and practically useful, form of the whole great French school of rounded architecture. And where has that French school its origin? Wholly in the rich conditions of sculpture, which, rising first out of imitations of the Roman bas-reliefs, covered all the façades of the French early churches with one continuous arabesque of floral or animal life. If you want to study round-arched buildings, do not go to Durham, but go to Poictiers, and there you will see how all the simple decorations which give you so much pleasure even in their isolated application were invented by persons practised in carving men, monsters, wild animals, birds, and flowers, in overwhelming redundance; and then trace this architecture forward in central France, and you will find it loses nothing of its richness—it only gains in truth, and therefore in grace, until just at the moment of transition into the pointed style, you have the consummate type of the sculpture of the school given you in the west front of the Cathedral of Chartres. From that front I have chosen two fragments to illustrate it.[1]

These statues have been long, and justly, considered as representative of the highest skill of the twelfth or earliest part of the thirteenth century in France; and they indeed possess a dignity and delicate charm, which are for the most part wanting in later works. It is owing partly to real nobleness of feature, but chiefly to the grace, mingled with severity, of the falling lines of excessively *thin* drapery; as well as to a most studied finish in composition, every part of the ornamentation tenderly harmonizing with the rest. So far as their power over certain tones of religious mind is owing to a palpable degree of non-naturalism in them, I do not praise it—the exaggerated thinness of body and stiffness of attitude are faults; but they are noble faults, and give the statues a strange look of forming part of the very building itself, and sustaining it—not like the Greek caryatid, without effort—nor like the Renaissance caryatid, by painful or impossible effort—but as if all that was silent, and stern, and withdrawn apart, and stiffened in chill of heart against the terror of earth, had passed into a shape of eternal marble; and thus the Ghost had given, to bear up the pillars of the church on earth, all the patient and expectant nature that it needed no more in heaven. This is the transcendental view of the meaning of those sculptures. I do not dwell upon it. What I do lean upon is their purely naturalistic and vital power. They are all portraits—unknown, most of them, I believe,—but palpably and unmistakeably portraits, if not taken from the actual person for whom the

[1] This part of the lecture was illustrated by two drawings, made admirably by Mr. J. T. Laing, with the help of photographs, from statues at Chartres. The drawings may be seen at present at the Kensington Museum; but any large photograph of the west front of Chartres will enable the reader to follow what is stated in the lecture, as far as is needful.

statue stands, at all events studied from some living person whose features might fairly represent those of the king or saint intended. Several of them I suppose to be authentic: there is one of a queen, who has evidently, while she lived, been notable for her bright black eyes. The sculptor has cut the iris deep into the stone, and her dark eyes are still suggested with her smile.

There is another thing I wish you to notice specially in these statues—the way in which the floral moulding is associated with the vertical lines of the figure. You have thus the utmost complexity and richness of curvature set side by side with the pure and delicate parallel lines, and both the characters gain in interest and beauty; but there is deeper significance in the thing than that of mere effect in composition;—significance not intended on the part of the sculptor, but all the more valuable because unintentional. I mean the close association of the beauty of lower nature in animals and flowers, with the beauty of higher nature in human form. You never get this in Greek work. Greek statues are always isolated; blank fields of stone, or depths of shadow, relieving the form of the statue, as the world of lower nature which they despised retired in darkness from their hearts. Here, the clothed figure seems the type of the Christian spirit—in many respects feebler and more contracted—but purer; clothed in its white robes and crown, and with the riches of all creation at its side.

The next step in the change will be set before you in a moment, merely by comparing this statue from the west front of Chartres with that of the Madonna, from the south transept door of Amiens.[1]

This Madonna, with the sculpture round her, represents the culminating power of Gothic art in the thirteenth century. Sculpture has been gaining continually in the interval; gaining, simply because becoming every day

[1] There are many photographs of this door and of its central statue. Its sculpture in the tympanum is farther described in the Fourth Lecture.

more truthful, more tender, and more suggestive. By the way, the old Douglas motto, "Tender and true," may wisely be taken up again by all of us, for our own, in art no less than in other things. Depend upon it, the first universal characteristic of all great art is Tenderness, as the second is Truth. I find this more and more every day: an infinitude of tenderness is the chief gift and inheritance of all the truly great men. It is sure to involve a relative intensity of disdain towards base things, and an appearance of sternness and arrogance in the eyes of all hard, stupid, and vulgar people—quite terrific to such, if they are capable of terror, and hateful to them, if they are capable of nothing higher than hatred. Dante's is the great type of this class of mind. I say the *first* inheritance is Tenderness—the *second* Truth, because the Tenderness is in the make of the creature, the Truth in his acquired habits and knowledge; besides, the love comes first in dignity as well as in time, and that is always pure and complete: the truth, at best, imperfect.

To come back to our statue. You will observe that the arrangement of this sculpture is exactly the same as at Chartres—severe falling drapery, set off by rich floral ornament at the side; but the statue is now completely animated: it is no longer fixed as an upright pillar, but bends aside out of its niche, and the floral ornament, instead of being a conventional wreath, is of exquisitely arranged hawthorn. The work, however, as a whole, though perfectly characteristic of the advance of the age in style and purpose, is in some subtler qualities inferior to that of Chartres. The individual sculptor, though trained in a more advanced school, has been himself a man of inferior order of mind compared to the one who worked at Chartres. But I have not time to point out to you the subtler characters by which I know this.

This statue, then, marks the culminating point of Gothic art, because, up to this time, the eyes of its designers had been steadily fixed on natural truth—they had been advancing from flower to flower, from form to form, from face to face,—gaining perpetually in knowledge and veracity—therefore, perpetually in power and in grace. But at this point a fatal change came over their aim. From the statue they now began to turn the attention chiefly to the niche of the statue, and from the floral ornament to the mouldings that enclosed the floral ornament. The first result of this was, however, though not the grandest, yet the most finished of northern genius. You have, in the earlier Gothic, less wonderful construction, less careful masonry, far less expression of harmony of parts in the balance of the building. Earlier work always has more or less of the character of a good solid wall with irregular holes in it, well carved wherever there was room. But the last phase of good Gothic has no room to spare; it rises as high as it can on narrowest foundation, stands in perfect strength with the least possible substance in its bars; connects niche with niche, and line with line, in an exquisite harmony, from which no stone can be removed, and to which you can add not a pinnacle: and yet introduces in rich, though now more calculated profusion, the living element of its sculpture: sculpture in the quatrefoils—sculpture in the brackets—sculpture in the gargoyles—sculpture in the niches—sculpture in the ridges and hollows of its mouldings,—not a shadow without meaning, and not a light without life.[1] But with this very perfection of his work came the unhappy pride of the builder in what he had done. As long as he had been merely raising clumsy walls and carving them, like a child, in waywardness of fancy, his delight was in the things he thought of as he carved; but when he had once reached this pitch of constructive science, he began to think only how cleverly he could put the stones together. The question was

---

[1] The two *transepts* of Rouen Cathedral illustrate this style. There are plenty of photographs of them. I take this opportunity of repeating what I have several times before stated, for the sake of travellers, that St. Ouen, impressive as it is, is entirely inferior to the transepts of Rouen Cathedral.

not now with him, What can I represent? but, How high can I build—how wonderfully can I hang this arch in air, or weave this tracery across the clouds? And the catastrophe was instant and irrevocable. Architecture became in France a mere web of waving lines,—in England a mere grating of perpendicular ones. Redundance was substituted for invention, and geometry for passion; the Gothic art became a mere expression of wanton expenditure, and vulgar mathematics; and was swept away, as it then deserved to be swept away, by the severer pride, and purer learning, of the schools founded on classical traditions.

You cannot now fail to see how, throughout the history of this wonderful art—from its earliest dawn in Lombardy to its last catastrophe in France and England—*sculpture,* founded on love of nature, was the talisman of its existence; wherever sculpture was practised, architecture arose—wherever that was neglected, architecture expired; and, believe me, all you students who love this mediæval art, there is no hope of your ever doing any good with it, but on this everlasting principle. Your patriotic associations with it are of no use; your romantic associations with it—either of chivalry or religion—are of no use; they are worse than useless, they are false. Gothic is not an art for knights and nobles; it is an art for the people: it is not an art for churches or sanctuaries; it is an art for houses and homes: it is not an art for England only, but an art for the world: above all, it is not an art of form or tradition only, but an art of vital practice and perpetual renewal. And whosoever pleads for it as an ancient or a formal thing, and tries to teach it you as an ecclesiastical tradition or a geometrical science, knows nothing of its essence, less than nothing of its power.

Leave, therefore, boldly, though not irreverently, mysticism and symbolism on the one side; cast away with utter scorn geometry and legalism on the other; seize hold of God's hand, and look full in the face of His creation, and there is nothing He will not enable you to achieve.

Thus, then, you will find—and the more profound and accurate your knowledge of the history of art the more assuredly you will find—that the living power in all the real schools, be they great or small, is love of nature. But do not mistake me by supposing that I mean this law to be all that is necessary to form a school. There needs to be much superadded to it, though there never must be anything superseding it. The main thing which needs to be superadded is the gift of design.

It is always dangerous, and liable to diminish the clearness of impression, to go over much ground in the course of one lecture. But I dare not present you with a maimed view of this important subject : I dare not put off to another time, when the same persons would not be again assembled, the statement of the great collateral necessity which, as well as the necessity of truth, governs all noble art.

That collateral necessity is *the visible operation of human intellect in the presentation of truth*, the evidence of what is properly called design or plan in the work, no less than of veracity. A looking-glass does not design—it receives and communicates indiscriminately all that passes before it ; a painter designs when he chooses some things, refuses others, and arranges all.

This selection and arrangement must have influence over everything that the art is concerned with, great or small—over lines, over colours, and over ideas. Given a certain group of colours, by adding another colour at the side of them, you will either improve the group and render it more delightful, or injure it, and render it discordant and unintelligible. " Design " is the choosing and placing the colour so as to help and enhance all the other colours it is set beside. So of thoughts : in a good composition, every idea is presented in just that order, and with just that force, which will perfectly connect it with all the other thoughts in the work, and will illustrate the others as well as receive illustration from them ; so that the entire chain of thoughts offered to the beholder's mind shall be received by him with as much delight and with as little effort as is possible. And thus you see design, properly so called, is human invention, consulting human capacity. Out of the infinite heap of things around us in the world, it chooses a certain number which it can thoroughly grasp, and presents this group to the spectator in the form best calculated to enable him to grasp it also, and to grasp it with delight.

And accordingly, the capacities of both gatherer and receiver being limited, the object is to make *everything that you offer helpful* and precious. If you give one grain of weight too much, so as to increase fatigue without profit, or bulk without value—that added grain is hurtful : if you put one spot or one syllable out of its proper place, that spot or syllable will be destructive— how far destructive it is almost impossible to tell : a misplaced touch may sometimes annihilate the labour of hours. Nor are any of us prepared to understand the work of any great master, till we feel this, and feel it as distinctly as we do the value of arrangement in the notes of music. Take any noble musical air, and you find, on examining it, that not one even of the faintest or shortest notes can be removed without destruction to the whole passage in which it occurs ; and that every note in the passage is twenty times more beautiful so introduced, than it would have been if played singly on the instrument. Precisely this degree of arrangement and relation must exist between every touch [1] and line in a great picture. You may consider the whole as a prolonged musical composition : its parts, as separate airs connected in the story ; its little bits and fragments of colour and line, as separate passages or bars in melodies ; and down to the minutest note of the whole —down to the minutest *touch*,—if there is one that can be spared—that one is doing mischief.

Remember therefore always, you have two characters in which all greatness of art consists :—First, the earnest

---

[1] Literally. I know how exaggerated this statement sounds ; but I mean it,—every syllable of it.—See Appendix IV.

and intense seizing of natural facts; then the ordering those facts by strength of human intellect, so as to make them, for all who look upon them, to the utmost serviceable, memorable, and beautiful. And thus great art is nothing else than the type of strong and noble life; for, as the ignoble person, in his dealings with all that occurs in the world about him, first sees nothing clearly,—looks nothing fairly in the face, and then allows himself to be swept away by the trampling torrent, and unescapable force, of the things that he would not foresee, and could not understand: so the noble person, looking the facts of the world full in the face, and fathoming them with deep faculty, then deals with them in unalarmed intelligence and unhurried strength, and becomes, with his human intellect and will, no unconscious nor insignificant agent in consummating their good, and restraining their evil.

Thus in human life you have the two fields of rightful toil for ever distinguished, yet for ever associated; Truth first—plan, or design, founded thereon: so in art, you have the same two fields for ever distinguished, for ever associated; Truth first—plan, or design, founded thereon.

Now hitherto there is not the least difficulty in the subject; none of you can look for a moment at any great sculptor or painter without seeing the full bearing of these principles. But a difficulty arises when you come to examine the art of a lower order, concerned with furniture and manufacture, for in that art the element of design enters without, apparently, the element of truth. You have often to obtain beauty and display invention without direct representation of nature. Yet, respecting all these things also, the principle is perfectly simple. If the designer of furniture, of cups and vases, of dress patterns, and the like, exercises himself continually in the imitation of natural form in some leading division of his work; then, holding by this stem of life, he may pass down into all kinds of merely geometrical or formal design with perfect safety, and with noble results.[1] Thus Giotto, being primarily a figure painter and sculptor, is, secondarily, the richest of all designers in mere mosaic of coloured bars and triangles; thus Benvenuto Cellini, being in all the higher branches of metal work a perfect imitator of nature, is in all its lower branches the best designer of curve for lips of cups and handles of vases; thus Holbein, exercised primarily in the noble art of truthful portraiture, becomes, secondarily, the most exquisite designer of embroideries of robe, and blazonries on wall; and thus Michael Angelo, exercised primarily in the drawing of body and limb, distributes in the mightiest masses the order of his pillars, and in the loftiest shadow the hollows of his dome. But once quit hold of this living stem, and set yourself to the designing of ornamentation, either in the ignorant play of your own heartless fancy, as the Indian does, or according to received application of heartless laws, as the modern European does, and there is but one word for you—Death:—death of every healthy faculty, and of every noble intelligence, incapacity of understanding one great work that man has ever done, or of doing anything that it shall be helpful for him to behold. You have cut yourselves off voluntarily, presumptuously, insolently, from the whole teaching of your Maker in His universe; you have cut yourselves off from it, not because you were forced to mechanical labour for your bread—not because your fate had appointed you to wear away your life in walled chambers, or dig your life out of dusty furrows; but, when your whole profession, your whole occupation—all the necessities and chances of your existence, led you straight to the feet of the great Teacher, and thrust you into the treasury of His works; where you have nothing to do but to live by gazing, and to grow by wondering;—wilfully you bind up your eyes from the splendour—wilfully bind up your life-blood from its beating—wilfully turn your backs upon all the majesties

---

[1] This principle, here cursorily stated, is one of the chief subjects of inquiry in the following Lectures.

of Omnipotence—wilfully snatch your hands from all
the aids of love ; and what can remain for you, but
helplessness and blindness,—except the worse fate than
the being blind yourselves—that of becoming Leaders
of the blind ?

Do not think that I am speaking under excited feeling, or in any exaggerated terms. I have *written* the
words I use, that I may know what I say, and that you,
if you choose, may see what I have said. For, indeed,
I have set before you to-night, to the best of my power,
the sum and substance of the system of art to the
promulgation of which I have devoted my life hitherto,
and intend to devote what of life may still be spared to
me. I have had but one steady aim in all that I have
ever tried to teach, namely—to declare that whatever
was great in human art was the expression of man's
delight in God's work.

And at this time I have endeavoured to prove to you
—if you investigate the subject you may more entirely
prove to yourselves—that no school ever advanced far
which had not the love of natural fact as a primal
energy. But it is still more important for you to be
assured that the conditions of life and death in the art
of nations are also the conditions of life and death in
your own ; and that you have it, each in his power at this
very instant, to determine in which direction his steps
are turning. It seems almost a terrible thing to tell
you, that all here have all the power of knowing at once
what hope there is for them as artists ; you would,
perhaps, like better that there was some unremovable
doubt about the chances of the future—some possibility
that you might be advancing, in unconscious ways, towards unexpected successes—some excuse or reason for
going about, as students do so often, to this master or
the other, asking him if they have genius, and whether
they are doing right, and gathering, from his careless
or formal replies, vague flashes of encouragement, or
fitfulnesses of despair. There is no need for this—no
excuse for it. All of you have the trial of yourselves

in your own power ; each may undergo at this instant, before his own judgment seat, the ordeal by fire. Ask yourselves what is the leading motive which actuates you while you are at work. I do not ask you what your leading motive is for working—that is a different thing ; you may have families to support—parents to help—brides to win ; you may have all these, or other such sacred and pre-eminent motives, to press the morning's labour and prompt the twilight thought. But when you are fairly *at* the work, what is the motive then which tells upon every touch of it ? If it is the love of that which your work represents—if, being a landscape painter, it is love of hills and trees that moves you—if, being a figure painter, it is love of human beauty and human soul that moves you—if, being a flower or animal painter, it is love, and wonder, and delight in petal and in limb that move you, then the Spirit is upon you, and the earth is yours, and the fulness thereof. But if, on the other hand, it is petty self-complacency in your own skill, trust in precepts and laws, hope for academical or popular approbation, or avarice of wealth,—it is quite possible that by steady industry, or even by fortunate chance, you may win the applause, the position, the fortune, that you desire ;—but one touch of true art you will never lay on canvas or on stone as long as you live.

Make, then, your choice, boldly and consciously, for one way or other it *must* be made. On the dark and dangerous side are set, the pride which delights in self-contemplation — the indolence which rests in un-questioned forms—the ignorance that despises what is fairest among God's creatures, and the dulness that denies what is marvellous in His working : there is a life of monotony for your own souls, and of misguiding for those of others. And, on the other side, is open to your choice the life of the crowned spirit, moving as a light in creation — discovering always — illuminating always, gaining every hour in strength, yet bowed down every hour into deeper humility ; sure of being right in its aim, sure of being irresistible in its progress ; happy in what it has securely done—happier in what, day by day, it may as securely hope ; happiest at the close of life, when the right hand begins to forget its cunning, to remember, that there was never a touch of the chisel or the pencil it wielded, but has added to the knowledge and quickened the happiness of mankind.

LECTURE II

THE UNITY OF ART

Part of an Address[1] delivered at Manchester, 14th March, 1859.

IT is sometimes my pleasant duty to visit other cities, in the hope of being able to encourage their art students; but here it is my pleasanter privilege to come for encouragement myself. I do not know when I have received so much as from the report read this evening by Mr. Hammersley, bearing upon a subject which has caused me great anxiety. For I have always felt in my own pursuit of art, and in my endeavours to urge the pursuit of art on others, that while there are many advantages now that never existed before, there are certain grievous difficulties existing, just in the very cause that is giving the stimulus to art—in the immense spread of the manufactures of every country which is now attending vigorously to art. We find that manufacture and art are now going on always together; that where there is no manufacture there is no art. I know how much there is of pretended art where there is no manufacture : there is much in Italy, for instance; no country makes so bold pretence to the production of new art as Italy at this moment; yet no country produces so little. If you glance over the map of Europe,

---

[1] I was prevented, by press of other engagements, from preparing this address with the care I wished; and forced to trust to such expression as I could give at the moment to the points of principal importance; reading, however, the close of the preceding lecture, which I thought contained some truths that would bear repetition. The whole was reported, better than it deserved, by Mr. Pitman, of the *Manchester Courier*, and published nearly verbatim. I have here extracted, from the published report, the facts which I wish especially to enforce; and have a little cleared their expression; its loose and colloquial character I cannot now help, unless by re-writing the whole, which it seems not worth while to do.

you will find that where the manufactures are strongest, there art also is strongest. And yet I always felt that there was an immense difficulty to be encountered by the students who were in these centres of modern movement. They had to avoid the notion that art and manufacture were in any respect one. Art may be healthily associated with manufacture, and probably in future will always be so ; but the student must be strenuously warned against supposing that they can ever be one and the same thing, that art can ever be followed on the principles of manufacture. Each must be followed separately ; the one must influence the other, but each must be kept distinctly separate from the other.

It would be well if all students would keep clearly in their mind the real distinction between those words which we use so often, "Manufacture," "Art," and "Fine Art." "MANUFACTURE" is, according to the etymology and right use of the word, "the making of anything by hands,"—directly or indirectly, with or without the help of instruments or machines. Anything proceeding from the hand of man is manufacture ; but it must have proceeded from his hand only, acting mechanically, and uninfluenced at the moment by direct intelligence.

Then, secondly, ART is the operation of the hand and the intelligence of man together : there is an art of making machinery ; there is an art of building ships ; an art of making carriages ; and so on. All these, properly called Arts, but not Fine Arts, are pursuits in which the hand of man and his head go together, working at the same instant.

Then FINE ART is that in which the hand, the head, and the *heart* of man go together.

Recollect this triple group ; it will help you to solve many difficult problems. And remember that though the hand must be at the bottom of everything, it must also go to the top of everything ; for Fine Art must be produced by the hand of man in a much greater and clearer sense than manufacture is. Fine Art must always

be produced by the subtlest of all machines, which is
the human hand. No machine yet contrived, or hereafter contrivable, will ever equal the fine machinery of
the human fingers. Thoroughly perfect art is that which
proceeds from the heart, which involves all the noble
emotions ;—associates with these the head, yet as inferior
to the heart; and the hand, yet as inferior to the heart
and head ; and thus brings out the whole man.

Hence it follows that since Manufacture is simply the
operation of the hand of man in producing that which
is useful to him, it essentially separates itself from the
emotions ; when emotions interfere with machinery they
spoil it : machinery must go evenly, without emotion.
But the Fine Arts cannot go evenly ; they always must
have emotion ruling their mechanism, and until the
pupil begins to feel, and until all he does associates
itself with the current of his feeling, he is not an artist.
But pupils in all the schools in this country are now
exposed to all kinds of temptations which blunt their
feelings. I constantly feel discouraged in addressing them
because I know not how to tell them boldly what they
ought to do, when I feel how practically difficult it is for
them to do it. There are all sorts of demands made
upon them in every direction, and money is to be made
in every conceivable way but the right way. If you paint
as you ought, and study as you ought, depend upon it the
public will take no notice of you for a long while. If you
study wrongly, and try to draw the attention of the public
upon you,—supposing you to be clever students—you
will get swift reward ; but the reward does not come
fast when it is sought wisely ; it is always held aloof for
a little while ; the right roads of early life are very quiet
ones, hedged in from nearly all help or praise. But the
wrong roads are noisy,—vociferous everywhere with all
kinds of demand upon you for art which is not properly
art at all ; and in the various meetings of modern interests,
money is to be made in every way ; but art is to be
followed only in *one* way. That is what I want mainly
to say to you, or if not to you yourselves (for, from what

I have heard from your excellent master to-night, I know you are going on all rightly), you must let me say it through you to others. Our Schools of Art are confused by the various teaching and various interests that are now abroad among us. Everybody is talking about art, and writing about it, and more or less interested in it; everybody wants art, and there is not art for everybody, and few who talk know what they are talking about; thus students are led in all variable ways, while there is only one way in which they can make steady progress, for true art is always and will be always one. Whatever changes may be made in the customs of society, whatever new machines we may invent, whatever new manufactures we may supply, Fine Art must remain what it was two thousand years ago, in the days of Phidias; two thousand years hence, it will be, in all its principles, and in all its great effects upon the mind of man, just the same. Observe this that I say, please, carefully, for I mean it to the very utmost. *There is but one right way of doing any given thing required of an artist;* there may be a hundred wrong, deficient, or mannered ways, but there is only one complete and right way. Whenever two artists are trying to do the same thing with the same materials, and do it in different ways, one of them is wrong; he may be charmingly wrong, or impressively wrong— various circumstances in his temper may make his wrong pleasanter than any person's right; it may for him, under his given limitations of knowledge or temper, be better perhaps that he should err in his own way than try for anybody else's—but for all that his way *is* wrong, and it is essential for all masters of schools to know what the right way is, and what right art is, and to see how simple and how single all right art has been, since the beginning of it.

But farther, not only is there but one way of *doing* things rightly, but there is only one way of *seeing* them, and that is, seeing the whole of them, without any choice, or more intense perception of one point than another, owing to our special idiosyncrasies. Thus.

when Titian or Tintoret look at a human being, they
see at a glance the whole of its nature, outside and in ;
all that it has of form, of colour, of passion, or of
thought ; saintliness, and loveliness ; fleshly body, and
spiritual power ; grace, or strength, or softness, or whatsoever other quality, those men will see to the full, and
so paint, that, when narrower people come to look at
what they have done, every one may, if he chooses, find
his own special pleasure in the work. The sensualist
will find sensuality in Titian ; the thinker will find
thought ; the saint, sanctity ; the colourist, colour ; the
anatomist, form ; and yet the picture will never be a
popular one in the full sense, for none of these narrower
people will find their special taste so alone consulted,
as that the qualities which would ensure their gratification shall be sifted or separated from others ; they are
checked by the presence of the other qualities which
ensure the gratification of other men. Thus, Titian
is not soft enough for the sensualist, Correggio suits
him better ; Titian is not defined enough for the
formalist,—Leonardo suits him better ; Titian is not
pure enough for the religionist,—Raphael suits him
better ; Titian is not polite enough for the man of
the world,—Vandyke suits him better ; Titian is not
forcible enough for the lover of the picturesque,—
Rembrandt suits him better. So Correggio is popular
with a certain set, and Vandyke with a certain set, and
Rembrandt with a certain set. All are great men,
but of inferior stamp, and therefore Vandyke is popular,
and Rembrandt is popular,[1] but nobody cares much
at heart about Titian ; only there is a strange under-
current of everlasting murmur about his name, which
means the deep consent of all great men that he is
greater than they—the consent of those who, having
sat long enough at his feet, have found in that restrained
harmony of his strength there are indeed depths of each
balanced power more wonderful than all those separate

---

[1] And Murillo, of all true painters the narrowest, feeblest, and
most superficial, for those reasons the most popular.

manifestations in inferior painters: that there is a softness more exquisite than Correggio's, a purity loftier
than Leonardo's, a force mightier than Rembrandt's, a
sanctity more solemn even than Raffaelle's.

Do not suppose that in saying this of Titian, I am
returning to the old eclectic theories of Bologna; for
all those eclectic theories, observe, were based, not
upon an endeavour to unite the various characters of
nature (which it is possible to do), but the various
narrownesses of taste, which it is impossible to do.
Rubens is not more vigorous than Titian, but less
vigorous; but because he is so narrow-minded as to enjoy
vigour only, he refuses to give the other qualities of
nature, which would interfere with that vigour and with
our perception of it. Again, Rembrandt is not a greater
master of chiaroscuro than Titian;—he is a less master,
but because he is so narrow-minded as to enjoy chiaroscuro only, he withdraws from you the splendour of
hue which would interfere with this, and gives you only
the shadow in which you can at once feel it. Now all
these specialties have their own charm in their own way;
and there are times when the particular humour of each
man is refreshing to us from its very distinctness; but
the effort to add any other qualities to this refreshing
one instantly takes away the distinctiveness, and therefore the exact character to be enjoyed in its appeal to a
particular humour in us. Our enjoyment arose from a
weakness meeting a weakness, from a partiality in the
painter fitting to a partiality in us, and giving us sugar
when we wanted sugar, and myrrh when we wanted
myrrh; but sugar and myrrh are not meat: and when
we want meat and bread, we must go to better men.

The eclectic schools endeavoured to unite these
opposite partialities and weaknesses. They trained
themselves under masters of exaggeration, and tried
to unite opposite exaggerations. That was impossible.
They did not see that the only possible eclecticism had
been already accomplished;—the eclecticism of temperance, which, by the restraint of force, gains higher force;

and by the self-denial of delight, gains higher delight. This you will find is ultimately the case with every true and right master ; at first, while we are tyros in art, or before we have earnestly studied the man in question, we shall see little in him ; or perhaps see, as we think, defici- encies ; we shall fancy he is inferior to this man in that, and to the other man in the other ; but as we go on studying him we shall find that he has got both that and the other ; and both in a far higher sense than the man who seemed to possess those qualities in excess. Thus in Turner's lifetime, when people first looked at him, those who liked rainy weather, said he was not equal to Copley Fielding ; but those who looked at Turner long enough found that he could be much more wet than Copley Fielding, when he chose. The people who liked force, said that "Turner was not strong enough for them ; he was effeminate ; they liked De Wint,—nice strong tone ;—or Cox—great, greeny, dark masses of colour— solemn feeling of the freshness and depth of nature ;— they liked Cox—Turner was too hot for them." Had they looked long enough they would have found that he had far more force than De Wint, far more freshness than Cox when he chose,—only united with other elements ; and that he didn't choose to be cool, if nature had appointed the weather to be hot. The people who liked Prout said "Turner had not firmness of hand— he did not know enough about architecture—he was not picturesque enough." Had they looked at his architec- ture long, they would have found that it contained subtle picturesquenesses, infinitely more picturesque than any- thing of Prout's. People who liked Callcott said that "Turner was not correct or pure enough—had no classical taste." Had they looked at Turner long enough they would have found him as severe, when he chose, as the greater Poussin ;—Callcott, a mere vulgar imitator of other men's high breeding. And so through- out with all thoroughly great men, their strength is not seen at first, precisely because they unite, in due place and measure, every great quality.

Now the question is, whether, as students, we are to study only these mightiest men, who unite all greatness, or whether we are to study the works of inferior men, who present us with the greatness which we particularly like? That question often comes before me when I see a strong idiosyncrasy in a student, and he asks me what he should study. Shall I send him to a true master, who does not present the quality in a prominent way in which that student delights, or send him to a man with whom he has direct sympathy? It is a hard question. For very curious results have sometimes been brought out, especially in late years, not only by students following their own bent, but by their being withdrawn from teaching altogether. I have just named a very great man in his own field—Prout. We all know his drawings, and love them : they have a peculiar character which no other architectural drawings ever possessed, and which no others ever can possess, because all Prout's subjects are being knocked down, or restored. (Prout did not like restored buildings any more than I do.) There will never be any more Prout drawings. Nor could he have been what he was, or expressed with that mysteriously effective touch that peculiar delight in broken and old buildings, unless he had been withdrawn from all high art influence. You know that Prout was born of poor parents—that he was educated down in Cornwall ;—and that, for many years, all the art-teaching he had was his own, or the fishermen's. Under the keels of the fishing-boats, on the sands of our southern coasts, Prout learned all he needed to learn about art. Entirely by himself, he felt his way to this particular style, and became the painter of pictures which I think we should all regret to lose. It becomes a very difficult question what that man would have been, had he been brought under some entirely wholesome artistic influence. He had immense gifts of composition. I do not know any man who had more power of invention than Prout, or who had a sublimer instinct in his treat-ment of things ; but being entirely withdrawn from all artistical help, he blunders his way to that short-coming representation, which, by the very reason of its short-coming, has a certain charm we should all be sorry to lose. And therefore I feel embarrassed when a student comes to me, in whom I see a strong instinct of that kind : and cannot tell whether I ought to say to him, " Give up all your studies of old boats, and keep away from the sea-shore, and come up to the Royal Academy in London, and look at nothing but Titian." It is a difficult thing to make up one's mind to say that. However, I believe, on the whole, we may wisely leave such matters in the hands of Providence ; that if we have the power of teaching the right to anybody, we should teach them the right ; if we have the power of showing them the best thing, we should show them the best thing ; there will always, I fear, be enough want of teaching, and enough bad teaching, to bring out very curious erratical results if we want them. So, if we are to teach at all, let us teach the right thing, and ever the right thing. There are many attractive qualities inconsistent with rightness ;—do not let us teach them,—let us be content to waive them. There are attractive qualities in Burns, and attractive qualities in Dickens, which neither of those writers would have possessed if the one had been educated, and the other had been studying higher nature than that of cockney London ; but those attractive qualities are not such as we should seek in a school of literature. If we want to teach young men a good manner of writing, we should teach it from Shakspeare,—not from Burns ; from Walter Scott,—and not from Dickens. And I believe that our schools of painting are at present inefficient in their action, because they have not fixed on this high principle what are the painters to whom to point ; nor boldly resolved to point to the best, if determinable. It is becoming a matter of stern necessity that they should give a simple direction to the attention of the student, and that they should say, " This is the mark you are to aim at ; and you are not to go about to the print-shops, and peep in, to see how this engraver does that, and the other engraver does the other, and how a nice bit of character has been caught by a new man, and why this odd picture has caught the popular attention. You are to have nothing to do with all that; you are not to mind about popular attention just now; but here is a thing which is eternally right and good: you are to look at that, and see if you cannot do something eternally right and good too."

But suppose you accept this principle; and resolve to look to some great man, Titian, or Turner, or whomsoever it may be, as the model of perfection in art;—then the question is, since this great man pursued his art in Venice, or in the fields of England, under totally different conditions from those possible to us now—how are you to make your study of him effective here in Manchester? how bring it down into patterns, and all that you are called upon as operatives to produce? how make it the means of your livelihood, and associate inferior branches of art with this great art? That may become a serious doubt to you. You may think there is some other way of producing clever, and pretty, and saleable patterns than going to look at Titian, or any other great man. And that brings me to the question, perhaps the most vexed question of all amongst us just now, between conventional and perfect art. You know that among architects and artists there are, and have been almost always, since art became a subject of much discussion, two parties, one maintaining that nature should be always altered and modified, and that the artist is greater than nature; they do not maintain, indeed, in words, but they maintain in idea, that the artist is greater than the Divine Maker of these things, and can improve them; while the other party say that he cannot improve nature, and that nature on the whole should improve him. That is the real meaning of the two parties, the essence of them; the practical result of their several theories being that the Idealists are always producing more or less formal conditions of art, and the Realists striving to produce in all their art either some image of nature, or record of nature; these, observe, being quite different things, the image being a resemblance, and the record, something which will give information about nature, but not necessarily imitate it.[1]

* * * * * * *

You may separate these two groups of artists more distinctly in your mind as those who seek for the pleasure of art, in the relations of its colours and lines, without caring to convey any truth with it; and those who seek for the truth first, and then go down from the truth to the pleasure of colour and line. Marking those two bodies distinctly as separate, and thinking over them, you may come to some rather notable conclusions respecting the mental dispositions which are involved in each mode of study. You will find that large masses of the art of the world fall definitely under one or the other of these heads. Observe, pleasure first and truth afterwards, (or not at all,) as with the Arabians and Indians; or, truth first and pleasure afterwards, as with Angelico and all other great European painters. You will find that the art whose end is pleasure only is pre-eminently the gift of cruel and savage nations, cruel in temper, savage in habits and conception; but that the art which is especially dedicated to natural fact always indicates a peculiar gentleness and tenderness of mind, and that all great and successful work of that kind will assuredly be the production of thoughtful, sensitive, earnest, kind men, large in their views of life, and full of various intellectual power. And farther, when you examine the men in whom the gifts of art are variously mingled, or universally mingled, you will discern that the ornamental, or pleasurable power, though it may be possessed by good men, is not in itself an indication of their goodness, but is rather, unless balanced by other faculties, indicative of violence of temper, inclining to cruelty and to irreligion. On the other hand, so sure as you find any man endowed with a keen and separate faculty of representing natural

---

[1] The portion of the lecture here omitted was a recapitulation of that part of the previous one which opposed conventional art to natural art.

fact, so surely you will find that man gentle and upright, full of nobleness and breadth of thought. I will give you two instances, the first peculiarly English, and another peculiarly interesting because it occurs among a nation not generally very kind or gentle.

I am inclined to think that, considering all the disadvantages of circumstances and education under which his genius was developed, there was perhaps hardly ever born a man with a more intense and innate gift of insight into nature than our own Sir Joshua Reynolds. Considered as a painter of individuality in the human form and mind, I think him, even as it is, the prince of portrait painters. Titian paints nobler pictures, and Vandyke had nobler subjects, but neither of them entered so subtly as Sir Joshua did into the minor varieties of human heart and temper; and when you consider that, with a frightful conventionality of social habitude all around him, he yet conceived the simplest types of all feminine and childish loveliness;—that in a northern climate, and with gray, and white, and black, as the principal colours around him, he yet became a colourist who can be crushed by none, even of the Venetians;—and that with Dutch painting and Dresden china for the prevailing types of art in the saloons of his day, he threw himself at once at the feet of the great masters of Italy, and arose from their feet to share their throne—I know not that in the whole history of art you can produce another instance of so strong, so unaided, so unerring an instinct for all that was true, pure, and noble.

Now, do you recollect the evidence respecting the character of this man,—the two points of bright peculiar evidence given by the sayings of the two greatest literary men of his day, Johnson and Goldsmith ? Johnson, who, as you know, was always Reynolds' attached friend, had but one complaint to make against him, that he hated nobody:—"Reynolds," he said, "you hate no one living; I like a good hater !" Still more significant is the little touch in Goldsmith's "Retaliation." You recollect how in that poem he describes the various persons who met at one of their dinners at St. James's Coffee-house, each person being described under the name of some appropriate dish. You will often hear the concluding lines about Reynolds quoted—

> " He shifted his trumpet," &c. ;—

less often, or at least less attentively, the preceding ones, far more important—

> " Still born to improve us in every part—
> His pencil our faces, his *manners our heart;*"

and never, the most characteristic touch of all, near the beginning :—

> " Our dean shall be venison, just fresh from the plains ;
> Our Burke shall be tongue, with a garnish of brains ;
> To make out the dinner, full certain I am,
> That Rich is anchovy, and Reynolds is *lamb.*"

The other painter whom I would give you as an instance of this gentleness is a man of another nation, on the whole I suppose one of the most cruel civilized nations in the world,—the Spaniards. They produced but one great painter, only one ; but he among the very greatest of painters, Velasquez. You would not suppose, from looking at Velasquez' portraits generally, that he was an especially kind or good man ; you perceive a peculiar sternness about them ; for they were as true as steel, and the persons whom he had to paint being not generally kind or good people, they were stern in expression, and Velasquez gave the sternness ; but he had precisely the same intense perception of truth, the same marvellous instinct for the rendering of all natural soul and all natural form that our Reynolds had. Let me, then, read you his character as it is given by Mr Stirling, of Kier :—

" Certain charges, of what nature we are not informed, brought against him after his death, made it necessary for his executor, Fuensalida, to refute them at a private audience granted to him by the king for that purpose. After listening to the defence of his friend, Philip immediately made answer :

' I can believe all you say of the excellent disposition of Diego Velasquez.' Having lived for half his life in courts, he was yet capable both of gratitude and generosity, and in the misfortunes, he could remember the early kindness of Olivares. The friend of the exile of Loeches, it is just to believe that he was also the friend of the all-powerful favourite at Buen-retiro. No mean jealousy ever influenced his conduct to his brother artists ; he could afford not only to acknowledge the merits, but to forgive the malice, of his rivals. His character was of *that rare and happy kind, in which high intellectual power is combined with indomitable strength of will, and a winning sweetness of temper*, and which seldom fails to raise the possessor above his fellow-men, making his life a

> ' laurelled victory, and smooth success
> Be strewed before his feet.' "

I am sometimes accused of trying to make art too moral ; yet, observe, I do not say in the least that in order to be a good painter you must be a good man ; but I do say that in order to be a good natural painter there must be strong elements of good in the mind, however warped by other parts of the character. There are hundreds of other gifts of painting which are not at all involved with moral conditions, but this one, the perception of nature, is never given but under certain moral conditions. Therefore, now you have it in your choice ; here are your two paths for you : it is required of you to produce conventional ornament, and you may approach the task as the Hindoo does, and as the Arab did, without nature at all, with the chance of approximat-ing your disposition somewhat to that of the Hindoos and Arabs ; or as Sir Joshua and Velasquez did, with, not the chance, but the certainty, of approximating your disposition, according to the sincerity of your effort—to the disposition of those great and good men.

And do you suppose you will lose anything by ap-proaching your conventional art from this higher side ? Not so. I called, with deliberate measurement of my expression, long ago, the decoration of the Alhambra "detestable," not merely because indicative of base conditions of moral being, but because merely as decorative work, however captivating in some respects, it is wholly wanting in the real, deep, and intense qualities of ornamental art. Noble conventional decoration belongs only to three periods. First, there is the conventional decoration of the Greeks, used in subordination to their sculpture. There are then the noble conventional decoration of the early Gothic schools, and the noble conventional arabesque of the great Italian schools. All these were reached from above, all reached by stooping from a knowledge of the human form. Depend upon it you will find, as you look more and more into the matter, that good subordinate ornament has ever been rooted in a higher knowledge; and if you are again to produce anything that is noble, you must have the higher knowledge first, and descend to all lower service; condescend as much as you like,—condescension never does any man any harm,—but get your noble standing first. So, then, without any scruple, whatever branch of art you may be inclined as a student here to follow,—whatever you are to make your bread by, I say, so far as you have time and power, make yourself first a noble and accomplished artist; understand at least what noble and accomplished art is, and then you will be able to apply your knowledge to all service whatsoever.

I am now going to ask your permission to name the masters whom I think it would be well if we could agree, in our Schools of Art in England, to consider our leaders. The first and chief I will not myself presume to name; he shall be distinguished for you by the authority of those two great painters of whom we have just been speaking— Reynolds and Velasquez. You may remember that in your Manchester Art Treasures Exhibition the most impressive things were the works of those two men— nothing told upon the eye so much; no other pictures retained it with such a persistent power. Now, I have the testimony, first of Reynolds to Velasquez, and then of Velasquez to the man whom I want you to take as the master of all your English schools. The testimony of

Reynolds to Velasquez is very striking. I take it from some fragments which have just been published by Mr. William Cotton—precious fragments—of Reynolds' diaries, which I chanced upon luckily as I was coming down here : for I was going to take Velasquez' testimony alone, and then fell upon this testimony of Reynolds to Velasquez, written most fortunately in Reynolds' own hand—you may see the manuscript. "What *we* are all," said Reynolds, "attempting to do with great labour, *Velasquez does at once*." Just think what is implied when a man of the enormous power and facility that Reynolds had, says he was "trying to do with great labour" what Velasquez "did at once."

Having thus Reynolds' testimony to Velasquez, I will take Velasquez' testimony to somebody else. You know that Velasquez was sent by Philip of Spain, to Italy, to buy pictures for him. He went all over Italy, saw the living artists there, and all their best pictures when freshly painted, so that he had every opportunity of judging ; and never was a man so capable of judging. He went to Rome and ordered various works of living artists ; and while there, he was one day asked by Salvator Rosa what he thought of Raphael. His reply, and the ensuing conversation, are thus reported by Boschini, in curious Italian verse, which, thus translated by Dr. Donaldson, is quoted in Mr. Stirling's Life of Velasquez :—

> "The master" [Velasquez] "stiffly bowed his figure tall
>   And said, 'For Rafael, to speak the truth—
>   I always was plain-spoken from my youth—
> I cannot say I like his works at all.'
>
> "'Well,' said the other" [Salvator], "'if you can run down
>   So great a man, I really cannot see
>   What you can find to like in Italy ;
> To him we all agree to give the crown.'
>
> "Diego answered thus : 'I saw in Venice
>   The true test of the good and beautiful ;
>   First, in my judgment, ever stands that school,
> And Titian first of all Italian men is.'"
>
> "*Tizian ze quel che porta la bandiera.*"

Learn that line by heart, and act, at all events for some time to come, upon Velasquez' opinion in that matter. Titian is much the safest master for you. Raphael's power, such as it was, and great as it was, depended wholly upon transcendental characters in his mind ; it is "Raphaelesque," properly so called ; but Titian's power is simply the power of doing right. Whatever came before Titian, he did wholly as it *ought* to be done. Do not suppose that now in recommending Titian to you so strongly, and speaking of nobody else to-night, I am re-treating in anywise from what some of you may perhaps recollect in my works, the enthusiasm with which I have always spoken of another Venetian painter. There are three Venetians who are never separated in my mind— Titian, Veronese, and Tintoret. They all have their own unequalled gifts, and Tintoret especially has imagination and depth of soul which I think renders him indisputably the greatest *man ;* but, equally indisputably, Titian is the greatest painter ; and therefore the greatest painter who ever lived. You may be led wrong by Tintoret[1] in many respects, wrong by Raphael in more ; all that you learn from Titian will be right. Then, with Titian, take Leonardo, Rembrandt, and Albert Durer. I name those three masters for this reason : Leonardo has powers of subtle drawing which are peculiarly applicable in many ways to the drawing of fine ornament, and are very useful for all students. Rembrandt and Durer are the only men whose actual work of hand you can have to look at; you can have Rembrandt's etchings, or Durer's engravings actually hung in your schools ; and it is a main point for the student to see the real thing, and avoid judging of masters at second-hand. As, however, in obeying this principle, you cannot often have oppor-tunities of studying Venetian painting, it is desirable that you should have a useful standard of colour, and I think it is possible for you to obtain this. I cannot, indeed, without entering upon ground which might involve the

See Appendix I.—" Right and Wrong."

hurting the feelings of living artists, state exactly what I believe to be the relative position of various painters in England at present with respect to power of colour. But I may say this, that in the peculiar gifts of colour which will be useful to you as students, there are only one or two of the pre-Raphaelites, and William Hunt, of the old Water Colour Society, who would be safe guides for you; and as quite a safe guide, there is nobody but William Hunt, because the pre-Raphaelites are all more or less affected by enthusiasm and by various morbid conditions of intellect and temper; but old William Hunt—I am sorry to say "old," but I say it in a loving way, for every year that has added to his life has added also to his skill —William Hunt is as right as the Venetians, as far as he goes, and what is more, nearly as inimitable as they. And I think if we manage to put in the principal schools of England a little bit of Hunt's work, and make that somewhat of a standard of colour, that we can apply his principles of colouring to subjects of all kinds. Until you have had a work of his long near you; nay, unless you have been labouring at it, and trying to copy it, you do not know the thoroughly grand qualities that are concentrated in it. Simplicity, and intensity, both of the highest character;—simplicity of aim, and intensity of power and success, are involved in that man's unpretending labour.

Finally, you cannot believe that I would omit my own favourite, Turner. I fear from the very number of his works left to the nation, that there is a disposition now rising to look upon his vast bequest with some contempt. I beg of you, if in nothing else, to believe me in this, that you cannot further the art of England in any way more distinctly than by giving attention to every fragment that has been left by that man. The time will come when his full power and right place will be acknowledged; that time will not be for many a day yet: nevertheless, be assured—as far as you are inclined to give the least faith to anything I may say to you, be assured—that you can act for the good of art in England

in no better way than by using whatever influence any of
you have in any direction to urge the reverent study and
yet more reverent preservation of the works of Turner.
I do not say "the exhibition" of his works, for we are
not altogether ripe for it : they are still too far above us ;
uniting, as I was telling you, too many qualities for us
yet to feel fully their range and their influence ;—but let
us only try to keep them safe from harm, and show
thoroughly and conveniently what we show of them at
all, and day by day their greatness will dawn upon us
more and more, and be the root of a school of art in
England, which I do not doubt may be as bright, as just,
and as refined as even that of Venice herself. The
dominion of the sea seems to have been associated, in
past time, with dominion in the arts also : Athens had
them together; Venice had them together; but by so
much as our authority over the ocean is wider than theirs
over the Ægean or Adriatic, let us strive to make our
art more widely beneficent than theirs, though it cannot
be more exalted ; so working out the fulfilment, in their
wakening as well as their warning sense, of those great
words of the aged Tintoret :

"Sempre si fa il Mare Maggiore."

LECTURE III

MODERN MANUFACTURE AND DESIGN

A LECTURE

Delivered at Bradford, March, 1859.

It is with a deep sense of necessity for your indulgence that I venture to address you to-night, or that I venture at any time to address the pupils of schools of design intended for the advancement of taste in special branches of manufacture. No person is able to give useful and definite help towards such special applications of art, unless he is entirely familiar with the conditions of labour and natures of material involved in the work; and *in*definite help is little better than no help at all. Nay, the few remarks which I propose to lay before you this evening will, I fear, be rather suggestive of difficulties than helpful in conquering them: nevertheless, it may not be altogether unserviceable to define clearly for you (and this, at least, I am able to do) one or two of the more stern general obstacles which stand at present in the way of our success in design; and to warn you against exertion of effort in any vain or wasteful way, till these main obstacles are removed.

The first of these is our not understanding the scope and dignity of Decorative design. With all our talk about it, the very meaning of the words "Decorative art" remains confused and undecided. I want, if possible, to settle this question for you to-night, and to show you that the principles on which you must work are likely to be false, in proportion as they are narrow; true, only as they are founded on a perception of the connection of all branches of art with each other.

Observe, then, first—the only essential distinction between Decorative and other art is the being fitted for

a fixed place ; and in that place, related, either in subordination or in command, to the effect of other pieces of
art. And all the greatest art which the world has produced is thus fitted for a place, and subordinated to a
purpose. There is no existing highest-order art but is
decorative. The best sculpture yet produced has been
the decoration of a temple front—the best painting, the
decoration of a room. Raphael's best doing is merely
the wall-colouring of a suite of apartments in the Vatican,
and his cartoons were made for tapestries. Correggio's
best doing is the decoration of two small church cupolas
at Parma ; Michael Angelo's, of a ceiling in the Pope's
private chapel ; Tintoret's, of a ceiling and side wall
belonging to a charitable society at Venice ; while Titian
and Veronese threw out their noblest thoughts, not even
on the inside, but on the outside of the common brick
and plaster walls of Venice.

Get rid, then, at once of any idea of Decorative art
being a degraded or a separate kind of art. Its nature
or essence is simply its being fitted for a definite place ;
and, in that place, forming part of a great and harmonious whole, in companionship with other art ; and so
far from this being a degradation to it—so far from
Decorative art being inferior to other art because it is
fixed to a spot—on the whole it may be considered as
rather a piece of degradation that it should be portable.
Portable art—independent of all place—is for the most
part ignoble art. Your little Dutch landscape, which
you put over your sideboard to-day, and between the
windows to-morrow, is a far more contemptible piece of
work than the extents of field and forest with which
Benozzo has made green and beautiful the once melancholy arcade of the Campo Santo at Pisa ; and the wild
boar of silver which you use for a seal, or lock into a
velvet case, is little likely to be so noble a beast as the
bronze boar who foams forth the fountain from under his
tusks in the market-place of Florence. It is, indeed,
possible that the portable picture or image may be first-
rate of its kind, but it is not first-rate because it is

portable; nor are Titian's frescoes less than first-rate because they are fixed; nay, very frequently the highest compliment you can pay to a cabinet picture is to say— " It is as grand as a fresco."

Keeping, then, this fact fixed in our minds,—that all art *may* be decorative, and that the greatest art yet produced has been decorative,—we may proceed to distinguish the orders and dignities of Decorative art, thus :—

I. The first order of it is that which is meant for places where it cannot be disturbed or injured, and where it can be perfectly seen; and then the main parts of it should be, and have always been made, by the great masters, as perfect, and as full of nature as possible.

You will every day hear it absurdly said that room decoration should be by flat patterns—by dead colours —by conventional monotonies, and I know not what. Now, just be assured of this—nobody ever yet used conventional art to decorate with, when he could do anything better, and knew that what he did would be safe. Nay, a great painter will always give you the natural art, safe or not. Correggio gets a commission to paint a room on the ground floor of a palace at Parma : Any of our people—bred on our fine modern principles—would have covered it with a diaper, or with stripes or flourishes, or mosaic patterns. Not so Correggio :—he paints a thick trellis of vine-leaves, with oval openings, and lovely children leaping through them into the room ; and lovely children, depend upon it, are rather more desirable decorations than diaper, if you can do them—but they are not quite so easily done. In like manner Tintoret has to paint the whole end of the Council Hall at Venice. An orthodox decorator would have set himself to make the wall look like a wall— Tintoret thinks it would be rather better, if he can manage it, to make it look a little like Paradise ;— stretches his canvas right over the wall, and his clouds right over his canvas ; brings the light through his clouds—all blue and clear—zodiac beyond zodiac ; rolls away the vaporous flood from under the feet of saints, leaving them at last in infinitudes of light—unorthodox in the last degree, but, on the whole, pleasant.

And so in all other cases whatever, the greatest decorative art is wholly unconventional—downright, pure, good painting and sculpture, but always fitted for its place ; and subordinated to the purpose it has to serve in that place.

II. But if art is to be placed where it is liable to injury —to wear and tear ; or to alteration of its form ; as, for instance, on domestic utensils, and armour, and weapons, and dress ; in which either the ornament will be worn out by the usage of the thing, or will be cast into altered shape by the play of its folds ; then it is wrong to put beautiful and perfect art to such uses, and you want forms of inferior art, such as will be by their simplicity less liable to injury ; or, by reason of their complexity and continuousness, may show to advantage, however distorted by the folds they are cast into.

And thus arise the various forms of inferior decorative art, respecting which the general law is, that the lower the place and office of the thing, the less of natural or perfect form you should have in it ; a zigzag or a chequer is thus a better, because a more consistent ornament for a cup or platter than a landscape or portrait is : hence the general definition of the true forms of conventional ornament is, that they consist in the bestowal of as much beauty on the object as shall be consistent with its Material, its Place, and its Office.

Let us consider these three modes of consistency a little.

(A.) Conventionalism by cause of inefficiency of material.

If, for instance, we are required to represent a human figure with stone only, we cannot represent its colour ; we reduce its colour to whiteness. That is not elevating the human body, but degrading it ; only it would be a much greater degradation to give its colour falsely. Diminish beauty as much as you will, but do not misrepresent it. So again, when we are sculpturing a face,

we can't carve its eyelashes. The face is none the better
for wanting its eyelashes—it is injured by the want ; but
would be much more injured by a clumsy representation
of them.

Neither can we carve the hair. We must be content
with the conventionalism of vile solid knots and lumps
of marble, instead of the golden cloud that encompasses
the fair human face with its waving mystery. The lumps
of marble are not an elevated representation of hair—
they are a degraded one ; yet better than any attempt to
imitate hair with the incapable material.

In all cases in which such imitation is attempted,
instant degradation to a still lower level is the result.
For the effort to imitate shows that the workman has
only a base and poor conception of the beauty of the
reality—else he would know his task to be hopeless, and
give it up at once ; so that all endeavours to avoid conventionalism, when the material demands it, result from
insensibility to truth, and are among the worst forms of
vulgarity. Hence, in the greatest Greek statues, the
hair is very slightly indicated—not because the sculptor
disdained hair, but because he knew what it was too
well to touch it insolently. I do not doubt but that the
Greek painters drew hair exactly as Titian does. Modern
attempts to produce finished pictures on glass result from
the same base vulgarism. No man who knows what
painting means, can endure a painted glass window
which emulates painter's work. But he rejoices in a
glowing mosaic of broken colour : for that is what the
glass has the special gift and right of producing.[1]

(B.) Conventionalism by cause of inferiority of place.

When work is to be seen at a great distance, or in
dark places, or in some other imperfect way, it constantly
becomes necessary to treat it coarsely or severely, in
order to make it effective. The statues on cathedral
fronts, in good times of design, are variously treated
according to their distances : no fine execution is put

[1] See Appendix II., Sir Joshua Reynolds' disappointment.

into the features of the Madonna who rules the group of figures above the south transept of Rouen at 150 feet above the ground : but in base modern work, as Milan Cathedral, the sculpture is finished without any reference to distance ; and the merit of every statue is supposed to consist in the visitor's being obliged to ascend three hundred steps before he can see it.

(c.) Conventionalism by cause of inferiority of office.

When one piece of ornament is to be subordinated to another (as the moulding is to the sculpture it encloses, or the fringe of a drapery to the statue it veils), this inferior ornament needs to be degraded in order to mark its lower office ; and this is best done by refusing, more or less, the introduction of natural form. The less of nature it contains, the more degraded is the ornament, and the fitter for a humble place ; but, however far a great workman may go in refusing the higher organisms of nature, he always takes care to retain the magnificence of natural lines ; that is to say, of the infinite curves, such as I have analyzed in the fourth volume of "Modern Painters." His copyists, fancying that they can follow him without nature, miss precisely the essence of all the work ; so that even the simplest piece of Greek con· ventional ornament loses the whole of its value in any modern imitation of it, the finer curves being always missed. Perhaps one of the dullest and least justifiable mistakes which have yet been made about my writing, is the supposition that I have attacked or despised Greek work. I have attacked Palladian work, and modern imitation of Greek work. Of Greek work itself I have never spoken but with a reverence quite infinite : I name Phidias always in exactly the same tone with which I speak of Michael Angelo, Titian, and Dante. My first statement of this faith, now thirteen years ago, was surely clear enough. "We shall see by this light three colossal images standing up side by side, looming in their great rest of spirituality above the whole world horizon. Phidias, Michael Angelo, and Dante,—from these we may go down step by step among the mighty men of every age, securely and certainly observant of diminished lustre in every appearance of restlessness and effort, until the last trace of inspiration vanishes in the tottering affectation or tortured insanities of modern times." (Modern Painters, vol. ii., p. 221.) This was surely plain speaking enough, and from that day to this my effort has been not less continually to make the heart of Greek work known than the heart of Gothic : namely, the nobleness of conception of form derived from perpetual study of the figure ; and my complaint of the modern architect has been not that he followed the Greeks, but that he denied the first laws of life in theirs as in all other art.

The fact is, that all good subordinate forms of ornamentation ever yet existent in the world have been invented, and others as beautiful *can* only be invented, by men primarily exercised in drawing or carving the human figure. I will not repeat here what I have already twice insisted upon, to the students of London and of Manchester, respecting the degradation of temper and intellect which follows the pursuit of art without reference to natural form, as among the Asiatics : here, I will only trespass on your patience so far as to mark the inseparable connection between figure-drawing and good ornamental work, in the great European schools, and all that are connected with them.

Tell me, then, first of all, what ornamental work is usually put before our students as the type of decorative perfection ? Raphael's arabesques ; are they not ? Well, Raphael knew a little about the figure, I suppose, before he drew them. I do not say that I like those arabesques ; but there are certain qualities in them which are inimitable by modern designers ; and those qualities are just the fruit of the master's figure study. What is given the student as next to Raphael's work ? Cinquecento ornament generally. Well, cinquecento generally, with its birds, and cherubs, and wreathed foliage, and clustered fruit, was the amusement of men who habitually and easily carved the figure, or painted it. All the truly fine specimens of it have figures or animals as main parts of the design.

"Nay, but," some anciently or mediævally minded person will exclaim, "we don't want to study cinque-cento. We want severer, purer conventionalism." What will you have? Egyptian ornament? Why, the whole mass of it is made up of multitudinous human figures in every kind of action—and magnificent action; their kings drawing their bows in their chariots, their sheaves of arrows rattling at their shoulders; the slain falling under them as before a pestilence; their captives driven before them in astonied troops; and do you expect to imitate Egyptian ornament without knowing how to draw the figure? Nay, but you will take Christian ornament—purest mediæval Christian—thirteenth century! Yes: and do you suppose you will find the Christian less human? The least natural and most purely conventional ornament of the Gothic schools is that of their painted glass; and do you suppose painted glass, in the fine times, was ever wrought without figures? We have got into the way, among our other modern wretchednesses, of trying to make windows of leaf diapers, and of strips of twisted red and yellow bands, looking like the patterns of currant jelly on the top of Christmas cakes; but every casement of old glass contained a saint's history. The windows of Bourges, Chartres, or Rouen have ten, fifteen, or twenty medallions in each, and each medallion contains two figures at least, often six or seven, representing every event of interest in the history of the saint whose life is in question. Nay, but, you say, those figures are rude and quaint, and ought not to be imitated. Why, so is the leafage rude and quaint, yet you imitate that. The coloured border pattern of geranium or ivy leaf is not one whit better drawn, or more like geraniums and ivy, than the figures are like figures; but you call the geranium leaf idealized—why don't you call the figures so? The fact is, neither are idealized, but both are conventionalized on the same principles, and in the same way; and if you want to learn how to treat the leafage, the only way is to learn first how to treat the figure. And you may soon test your powers in this respect. Those old workmen were not afraid of the most familiar subjects. The windows of Chartres were presented by the trades of the town, and at the bottom of each window is a representation of the proceedings of the tradesmen at the business which enabled them to pay for the window. There are smiths at the forge, curriers at their hides, tanners looking into their pits, mercers selling goods over the counter—all made into beautiful medallions. Therefore, whenever you want to know whether you have got any real power of composition or adaptation in ornament, don't be content with sticking leaves together by the ends,—anybody can do that ; but try to conventionalize a butcher's or a green-grocer's, with Saturday night customers buying cabbage and beef. That will tell you if you can design or not.

I can fancy your losing patience with me altogether just now. "We asked this fellow down to tell our workmen how to make shawls, and he is only trying to teach them how to caricature." But have a little patience with me, and examine, after I have done, a little for yourselves into the history of ornamental art, and you will discover why I do this. You will discover, I repeat, that all great ornamental art whatever is founded on the effort of the workman to draw the figure, and, in the best school, to draw all that he saw about him in living nature. The best art of pottery is acknowledged to be that of Greece, and all the power of design exhibited in it, down to the merest zigzag, arises primarily from the workman having been forced to outline nymphs and knights ; from those helmed and draped figures he holds his power. Of Egyptian ornament I have just spoken. You have everything given there that the workman saw ; people of his nation employed in hunting, fighting, fishing, visiting, making love, building, cooking—everything they did is drawn, magnificently or familiarly, as was needed. In Byzantine ornament, saints, or animals which are types of various spiritual power, are the main subjects ; and from the church down to the piece of enamelled metal, figure, —figure,—figure, always principal. In Norman and

Gothic work you have, with all their quiet saints, also other much disquieted persons, hunting, feasting, fighting, and so on ; or whole hordes of animals racing after each other. In the Bayeux tapestry, Queen Matilda gave, as well as she could,—in many respects graphically enough, —the whole history of the conquest of England. Thence, as you increase in power of art, you have more and more finished figures, up to the solemn sculptures of Wells Cathedral, or the cherubic enrichments of the Venetian Madonna dei Miracoli. Therefore, I tell you fearlessly, for I know it is true, you must raise your workman up to life, or you will never get from him one line of well-imagined conventionalism. We have at present no good ornamental design. We can't have it yet, and we must be patient if we want to have it. Do not hope to feel the effect of your schools at once, but raise the men as high as you can, and then let them stoop as low as you need ; no great man ever minds stooping. Encourage the students, in sketching accurately and continually from nature anything that comes in their way—still life, flowers, animals ; but, above all, figures ; and so far as you allow of any difference between an artist's training and theirs, let it be, not in what they draw, but in the degree of conventionalism you require in the sketch. For my own part, I should always endeavour to give thorough artistical training first ; but I am not certain (the experiment being yet untried) what results may be obtained by a truly intelligent practice of conventional drawing, such as that of the Egyptians, Greeks, or thirteenth century French, which consists in the utmost possible rendering of natural form by the fewest possible lines. The animal and bird drawing of the Egyptians is, in their fine age, quite magnificent under its conditions ; magnificent in two ways—first, in keenest perception of the main forms and facts in the creature ; and, secondly, in the grandeur of line by which their forms are abstracted and insisted on, making every asp, ibis, and vulture a sublime spectre of asp or ibis or vulture power. The way for students to get some of this gift again (*some* only, for I believe the fulness of the gift itself to be connected with vital superstition, and with resulting intensity of reverence ; people were likely to know something about hawks and ibises, when to kill one was to be irrevocably judged to death) is never to pass a day without drawing some animal from the life, allowing themselves the fewest possible lines and colours to do it with, but resolving that whatever is characteristic of the animal shall in some way or other be shown.[1] I repeat, it cannot yet be judged what results might be obtained by a nobly practised conventionalism of this kind ; but, however that may be, the first fact,—the necessity of animal and figure drawing, is absolutely certain, and no person who shrinks from it will ever become a great designer.   One great good arises even from the first step in figure drawing, that it gets the student quit at once of the notion of formal symmetry. If you learn only to draw a leaf well, you are taught in some of our schools to turn it the other way, opposite to itself ; and the two leaves set opposite ways are called a " design : " and thus it is supposed possible to produce ornamentation, though you have no more brains than a looking-glass or a kaleidoscope has.   But if once you learn to draw the human figure, you will find that knocking two men's heads together does not necessarily constitute a good design ; nay, that it makes a very bad design, or no design at all ; and you will see at once that to arrange a group of two or more figures, you must, though perhaps it may be desirable to balance, or oppose them, at the same time vary their attitudes, and make one, not the reverse of the other, but the companion of the other.

I had a somewhat amusing discussion on this subject with a friend, only the other day ; and one of his retorts upon me was so neatly put, and expresses so completely all that can either be said or shown on the opposite side, that it is well worth while giving it you exactly in the form it was sent to me.   My friend had been maintaining that the essence of ornament consisted in three things :

[1] Plate 75 in Vol. V. of Wilkinson's " Ancient Egypt " will give the student an idea of how to set to work.

—contrast, series, and symmetry. I replied (by letter)

that " none of them, nor all of them
together, would produce ornament.
Here "—(making a ragged blot with
the back of my pen
on the paper)—"you
have contrast ; but it
isn't ornament : here,
—1, 2, 3, 4, 5, 6,"—(writing the
numerals)—"you have series ; but
it isn't ornament : and here,"—(sketching this figure at
the side)—" you have symmetry ; but it isn't ornament."

My friend replied :—" Your materials were not ornament, because you did not apply them. I send them to
you back, made up into a choice sporting neckerchief :—

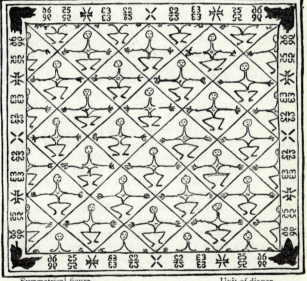

Symmetrical figure	.	.	.	.	.	Unit of diaper.
Contrast	.	.	.	.	.	Corner ornaments.
Series	.	.	.	.	.	Border ornaments.

Each figure is converted into a harmony by being revolved on its two axes, the whole opposed in contrasting series."

My answer was—or rather was to the effect (for I must expand it a little, here)—that his words, "because you did not apply them," contained the gist of the whole matter ;—that the application of them, or of any other things, was precisely the essence of design ;—the non-application, or wrong application, the negation of design : that his use of the poor materials was in this case admirable ; and that, if he could explain to me, in clear words, the principles on which he had so used them, he would be doing a very great service to all students of art.

"Tell me, therefore" (I asked), "these main points :

"1. How did you determine the number of figures you would put into the neckerchief ? Had there been more, it would have been mean and ineffective,—a pepper-and-salt sprinkling of figures. Had there been fewer, it would have been monstrous. How did you fix the number ?

"2. How did you determine the breadth of the border, and relative size of the numerals ?

"3. Why are there two lines outside of the border, and one only inside ? Why are there no more lines ? Why not three and two, or three and five ? Why lines at all to separate the barbarous figures ; and why, if lines at all, not double or treble instead of single ?

"4. Why did you put the double blots at the corners ? Why not at the angles of the chequers,—or in the middle of the border ?

"It is precisely your knowing why *not* to do these things, and why to do just what you have done, which constituted your power of design ; and like all the people I have ever known who had that power, you are entirely unconscious of the essential laws by which you work, and confuse other people by telling them that the design depends on symmetry and series, when, in fact, it depends entirely on your own sense and judgment."

This was the substance of my last answer—to which (as I knew beforehand would be the case) I got no reply ; but it still remains to be observed that with all the skill and taste (especially involving the architect's great trust, harmony of proportion), which my friend could bring to bear on the materials given him, the result is still only—a sporting neckerchief—that is to say, the materials addressed, first, to recklessness, in the shape of a mere blot ; then to computativeness, in a series of figures ; and then to absurdity and ignorance, in the shape of an ill-drawn caricature—such materials, however treated, can only work up into what will please reckless, computative, and vulgar persons,—that is to say, into a sporting neckerchief. The difference between this piece of ornamentation and Correggio's painting at Parma lies simply and wholly in the additions (somewhat large ones), of truth and of tenderness : in the drawing being lovely as well as symmetrical—and representative of realities as well as agreeably disposed. And truth, tenderness, and inventive application or disposition are indeed the roots of ornament—not contrast, nor symmetry.

It ought yet farther to be observed, that *the nobler the materials, the less their symmetry is endurable.* In the present case, the sense of fitness and order, produced by the repetition of the figures, neutralizes, in some degree, their reckless vulgarity ; and is wholly, therefore, beneficent to them. But draw the figures better, and their repetition will become painful. You may harmlessly balance a mere geometrical form, and oppose one quatrefoil or cusp by another exactly like it. But put two Apollo Belvideres back to back, and you will not think the symmetry improves them. *Whenever the materials of ornament are noble, they must be various ;* and repetition of parts is either the sign of utterly bad, hopeless, and base work ; or of the intended degradation of the parts in which such repetition is allowed, in order to foil others more noble.

Such, then, are a few of the great principles, by the

enforcement of which you may hope to promote the success of the modern student of design ; but remember, none of these principles will be useful at all, unless you understand them to be, in one profound and stern sense, useless.[1]

That is to say, unless you feel that neither you nor I nor any one, can, in the great ultimate sense, teach anybody how to make a good design.

If designing *could* be taught, all the world would learn ; as all the world reads—or calculates. But designing is not to be spelled, nor summed. My men continually come to me, in my drawing class in London, thinking I am to teach them what is instantly to enable them to gain their bread. " Please, sir, show us how to design." " Make designers of us." And you, I doubt not, partly expect me to tell you to-night how to make designers of your Bradford youths. Alas ! I could as soon tell you how to make or manufacture an ear of wheat, as to make a good artist of any kind. I can analyze the wheat very learnedly for you—tell you there is starch in it, and carbon, and silex. I can give you starch, and charcoal, and flint ; but you are as far from your ear of wheat as you were before. All that can possibly be done for any one who wants ears of wheat is to show them where to find grains of wheat, and how to sow them, and then, with patience, in Heaven's time, the ears will come—or will perhaps come—ground and weather permitting. So in this matter of making artists—first you must find your artist in the grain ; then you must plant him ; fence and weed the field about him ; and with patience, ground and weather permitting, you may get an artist out of him—not otherwise. And what I have to speak to you about, to-night, is mainly the ground and the weather, it being the first and quite most material question in this matter, whether the ground and weather of Bradford, or the ground and weather of England in general,—suit wheat.

[1] I shall endeavour for the future to put my self-contradictions in short sentences and direct terms, in order to save sagacious persons the trouble of looking for them.

And observe in the outset, it is not so much what the present circumstances of England are, as what we wish to make them, that we have to consider. If you will tell me what you ultimately intend Bradford to be, perhaps I can tell you what Bradford can ultimately produce. But you must have your minds clearly made up, and be distinct in telling me what you do want. At present I don't know what you are aiming at, and possibly on consideration you may feel some doubt whether you know yourselves. As matters stand, all over England, as soon as one mill is at work, occupying two hundred hands, we try, by means of it, to set another mill at work, occupying four hundred. That is all simple and comprehensive enough—but what is it to come to? How many mills do we want? or do we indeed want to end of mills? Let us entirely understand each other on this point before we go any farther. Last week, I drove from Rochdale to Bolton Abbey ; quietly, in order to see the country, and certainly it was well worth while. I never went over a more interesting twenty miles than those between Rochdale and Burnley. Naturally, the valley has been one of the most beautiful in the Lancashire hills ; one of the far away solitudes, full of old shepherd ways of life. At this time there are not,—I speak deliberately, and I believe quite literally,—there are not, I think, more than a thousand yards of road to be traversed anywhere, without passing a furnace or mill.

Now, is that the kind of thing you want to come to everywhere? Because, if it be, and you tell me so distinctly, I think I can make several suggestions to-night, and could make more if you give me time, which would materially advance your object. The extent of our operations at present is more or less limited by the extent of coal and ironstone, but we have not yet learned to make proper use of our clay. Over the greater part of England, south of the manufacturing districts, there are magnificent beds of various kinds of useful clay ; and I believe that it would not be difficult to point out

modes of employing it which might enable us to turn
nearly the whole of the south of England into a brickfield, as we have already turned nearly the whole of the
north into a coal-pit. I say "nearly" the whole, because, as you are doubtless aware, there are considerable
districts in the south composed of chalk renowned up to
the present time for their downs and mutton. But, I
think, by examining carefully into the conceivable uses
of chalk, we might discover a quite feasible probability
of turning all the chalk districts into a limekiln, as we
turn the clay districts into a brickfield. There would
then remain nothing but the mountain districts to be
dealt with; but, as we have not yet ascertained all the
uses of clay and chalk, still less have we ascertained
those of stone; and I think, by draining the useless
inlets of the Cumberland, Welsh, and Scotch lakes, and
turning them, with their rivers, into navigable reservoirs
and canals, there would be no difficulty in working the
whole of our mountain districts as a gigantic quarry of
slate and granite, from which all the rest of the world
might be supplied with roofing and building stone.

Is this, then, what you want? You are going straight
at it at present; and I have only to ask under what
limitations I am to conceive or describe your final
success? Or shall there be no limitations? There are
none to your powers; every day puts new machinery at
your disposal, and increases, with your capital, the vast-
ness of your undertakings. The changes in the state of
this country are now so rapid, that it would be wholly
absurd to endeavour to lay down laws of art education
for it under its present aspect and circumstances; and
therefore I must necessarily ask, how much of it do you
seriously intend within the next fifty years to be coal-pit,
brickfield, or quarry? For the sake of distinctness of
conclusion, I will suppose your success absolute: that
from shore to shore the whole of the island is to be set
as thick with chimneys as the masts stand in the docks
of Liverpool: and there shall be no meadows in it; no
trees; no gardens; only a little corn grown upon the

housetops, reaped and threshed by steam : that you do not leave even room for roads, but travel either over the roofs of your mills, on viaducts; or under their floors, in tunnels : that, the smoke having rendered the light of the sun unserviceable, you work always by the light of your own gas : that no acre of English ground shall be without its shaft and its engine; and therefore, no spot of English ground left, on which it shall be possible to stand, without a definite and calculable chance of being blown off it, at any moment, into small pieces.

Under these circumstances, (if this is to be the future of England,) no designing or any other development of beautiful art will be possible. Do not vex your minds, nor waste your money with any thought or effort in the matter. Beautiful art can only be produced by people who have beautiful things about them, and leisure to look at them ; and unless you provide some elements of beauty for your workmen to be surrounded by, you will find that no elements of beauty can be invented by them.

I was struck forcibly by the bearing of this great fact upon our modern efforts at ornamentation in an afternoon walk, last week, in the suburbs of one of our large manufacturing towns. I was thinking of the difference in the effect upon the designer's mind, between the scene which I then came upon, and the scene which would have presented itself to the eyes of any designer of the middle ages, when he left his workshop. Just outside the town I came upon an old English cottage, or mansion, I hardly know which to call it, set close under the hill, and beside the river, perhaps built somewhere in the Charles's times, with mullioned windows and a low arched porch ; round which, in the little triangular garden, one can imagine the family as they used to sit in old summer times, the ripple of the river heard faintly through the sweetbriar hedge, and the sheep on the far-off wolds shining in the evening sunlight. There, un-inhabited for many and many a year, it had been left in unregarded havoc of ruin; the garden-gate still swung

*F 219

loose to its latch; the garden, blighted utterly into a field of ashes, not even a weed taking root there; the roof torn into shapeless rents; the shutters hanging about the windows in rags of rotten wood; before its gate, the stream which had gladdened it now soaking slowly by, black as ebony, and thick with curdling scum; the bank above it trodden into unctuous, sooty slime: far in front of it, between it and the old hills, the fur-naces of the city foaming forth perpetual plague of sulphurous darkness; the volumes of their storm clouds coiling low over a waste of grassless fields, fenced from each other, not by hedges, but by slabs of square stone, like gravestones, riveted together with iron.

That was your scene for the designer's contemplation in his afternoon walk at Rochdale. Now fancy what was the scene which presented itself, in his afternoon walk, to a designer of the Gothic school of Pisa—Nino Pisano, or any of his men.

On each side of a bright river he saw rise a line of brighter palaces, arched and pillared, and inlaid with deep red porphyry, and with serpentine; along the quays before their gates were riding troops of knights, noble in face and form, dazzling in crest and shield; horse and man one labyrinth of quaint colour and gleaming light— the purple, and silver, and scarlet fringes flowing over the strong limbs and clashing mail, like sea-waves over rocks at sunset. Opening on each side from the river were gardens, courts, and cloisters; long successions of white pillars among wreaths of vine; leaping of fountains through buds of pomegranate and orange: and still along the garden-paths, and under and through the crimson of the pomegranate shadows, moving slowly, groups of the fairest women that Italy ever saw—fairest, because purest and thoughtfullest; trained in all high knowledge, as in all courteous art—in dance, in song, in sweet wit, in lofty learning, in loftier courage, in loftiest love—able alike to cheer, to enchant, or save, the souls of men. Above all this scenery of perfect human life, rose dome and bell-tower, burning with white

alabaster and gold : beyond dome and bell-tower the
slopes of mighty hills, hoary with olive ; far in the north,
above a purple sea of peaks of solemn Apennine, the
clear, sharp-cloven Carrara mountains sent up their steadfast flames of marble summit into amber sky ; the great
sea itself, scorching with expanse of light, stretching
from their feet to the Gorgonian isles ; and over all
these, ever present, near or far—seen through the leaves
of vine, or imaged with all its march of clouds in the
Arno's stream, or set with its depth of blue close against
the golden hair and burning cheek of lady and knight,—
that untroubled and sacred sky, which was to all men, in
those days of innocent faith, indeed the unquestioned
abode of spirits, as the earth was of men ; and which
opened straight through its gates of cloud and veils of
dew into the awfulness of the eternal world ;—a heaven
in which every cloud that passed was literally the chariot
of an angel, and every ray of its Evening and Morning
streamed from the throne of God.

What think you of that for a school of design ?

I do not bring this contrast before you as a ground of
hopelessness in our task ; neither do I look for any
possible renovation of the Republic of Pisa, at Bradford,
in the nineteenth century ; but I put it before you in
order that you may be aware precisely of the kind of
difficulty you have to meet, and may then consider with
yourselves how far you can meet it. To men surrounded
by the depressing and monotonous circumstances of
English manufacturing life, depend upon it, design is
simply impossible. This is the most distinct of all the
experiences I have had in dealing with the modern workman. He is intelligent and ingenious in the highest
degree—subtle in touch and keen in sight : but he is,
generally speaking, wholly destitute of designing power.
And if you want to give him the power, you must give
him the materials, and put him in the circumstances for
it. Design is not the offspring of idle fancy : it is the
studied result of accumulative observation and delightful
habit. Without observation and experience, no design—

without peace and pleasurableness in occupation, no design—and all the lecturings, and teachings, and prizes, and principles of art, in the world, are of no use, so long as you don't surround your men with happy influences and beautiful things. It is impossible for them to have right ideas about colour, unless they see the lovely colours of nature unspoiled; impossible for them to supply beautiful incident and action in their ornament, unless they see beautiful incident and action in the world about them. Inform their minds, refine their habits, and you form and refine their designs; but keep them illiterate, uncomfortable, and in the midst of un-beautiful things, and whatever they do will still be spurious, vulgar, and valueless.

I repeat, that I do not ask you nor wish you to build a new Pisa for them. We don't want either the life or the decorations of the thirteenth century back again; and the circumstances with which you must surround your workmen are those simply of happy modern English life, because the designs you have now to ask for from your workmen are such as will make modern English life beautiful. All that gorgeousness of the middle ages, beautiful as it sounds in description, noble as in many respects it was in reality, had, nevertheless, for foundation and for end, nothing but the pride of life—the pride of the so-called superior classes; a pride which supported itself by violence and robbery, and led in the end to the destruction both of the arts themselves and the States in which they flourished.

The great lesson of history is, that all the fine arts hitherto—having been supported by the selfish power of the noblesse, and never having extended their range to the comfort or the relief of the mass of the people—the arts, I say, thus practised, and thus matured, have only accelerated the ruin of the States they adorned; and at the moment when, in any kingdom, you point to the triumphs of its greatest artists, you point also to the determined hour of the kingdom's decline. The names of great painters are like passing bells: in the name of

Velasquez, you hear sounded the fall of Spain; in the name of Titian, that of Venice; in the name of Leonardo, that of Milan; in the name of Raphael, that of Rome. And there is profound justice in this; for in proportion to the nobleness of the power is the guilt of its use for purposes vain or vile; and hitherto the greater the art, the more surely has it been used, and used solely, for the decoration of pride,[1] or the provoking of sensuality. Another course lies open to us. We may abandon the hope—or if you like the words better—we may disdain the temptation, of the pomp and grace of Italy in her youth. For us there can be no more the throne of marble—for us no more the vault of gold—but for us there is the loftier and lovelier privilege of bringing the power and charm of art within the reach of the humble and the poor; and as the magnificence of past ages failed by its narrowness and its pride, ours may prevail and continue, by its universality and its lowliness.

And thus, between the picture of too laborious England, which we imagined as future, and the picture of too luxurious Italy, which we remember in the past, there may exist—there will exist, if we do our duty—an intermediate condition, neither oppressed by labour nor wasted in vanity—the condition of a peaceful and thoughtful temperance in aims, and acts, and arts.

We are about to enter upon a period of our world's history in which domestic life, aided by the arts of peace, will slowly, but at last entirely, supersede public life and the arts of war. For our own England, she will not, I believe, be blasted throughout with furnaces; nor will she be encumbered with palaces. I trust she will keep her green fields, her cottages, and her homes of middle life; but these ought to be, and I trust will be, enriched with a useful, truthful, substantial form of art. We want now no more feasts of the gods, nor martyrdoms of saints; we have no need of sensuality, no place for superstition, or for

---

[1] Whether religious or profane pride,—chapel—or banqueting room,—is no matter.

costly insolence. Let us have learned and faithful historical painting—touching and thoughtful representations
of human nature, in dramatic painting; poetical and
familiar renderings of natural objects and of landscape ;
and rational, deeply-felt realizations of the events which
are the subjects of our religious faith. And let these
things we want, as far as possible, be scattered abroad
and made accessible to all men.

So also, in manufacture : we require work substantial
rather than rich in make ; and refined, rather than
splendid in design. Your stuffs need not be such as
would catch the eye of a duchess ; but they should be such
as may at once serve the need, and refine the taste, of a
cottager. The prevailing error in English dress, especially
among the lower orders, is a tendency to flimsiness
and gaudiness, arising mainly from the awkward imitation
of their superiors.[1] It should be one of the first objects
of all manufacturers to produce stuffs not only beautiful
and quaint in design, but also adapted for every-day
service, and decorous in humble and secluded life.
And you must remember always that your business,
as manufacturers, is to form the market, as much as
to supply it. If, in shortsighted and reckless eagerness
for wealth, you catch at every humour of the populace

---

[1] If their superiors would give them simplicity and economy to
imitate, it would, in the issue, be well for themselves, as well as for
those whom they guide. The typhoid fever of passion for dress,
and all other display, which has struck the upper classes of Europe
at this time, is one of the most dangerous political elements we
have to deal with. Its wickedness I have shown elsewhere (Polit.
Economy of Art, p. 31, *et seq.*) ; but its wickedness is, in the
minds of most persons, a matter of no importance. I wish I had
time also to show them its danger. I cannot enter here into
political investigation ; but this is a certain fact, that the wasteful
and vain expenses at present indulged in by the upper classes are
hastening the advance of republicanism more than any other element
of modern change. No agitators, no clubs, no epidemical errors,
ever were, or will be, fatal to social order in any nation. Nothing
but the guilt of the upper classes, wanton, accumulated, reckless,
and merciless, ever overthrows them. Of such guilt they have now
much to answer for—let them look to it in time.

as it shapes itself into momentary demand—if, in jealous rivalry with neighbouring States, or with other producers, you try to attract attention by singularities, novelties, and gaudinesses—to make every design an advertisement, and pilfer every idea of a successful neighbour's, that you may insidiously imitate it, or pompously eclipse— no good design will ever be possible to you, or perceived by you. You may, by accident, snatch the market; or, by energy, command it; you may obtain the confidence of the public, and cause the ruin of opponent houses; or you may, with equal justice of fortune, be ruined by them. But whatever happens to you, this, at least, is certain, that the whole of your life will have been spent in corrupting public taste and encouraging public extravagance. Every preference you have won by gaudiness must have been based on the purchaser's vanity; every demand you have created by novelty has fostered in the consumer a habit of discontent; and when you retire into inactive life, you may, as a subject of consolation for your declining years, reflect that precisely according to the extent of your past operations, your life has been successful in retarding the arts, tarnishing the virtues, and confusing the manners of your country.

But, on the other hand, if you resolve from the first that, so far as you can ascertain or discern what is best, you will produce what is best, on an intelligent consideration of the probable tendencies and possible tastes of the people whom you supply, you may literally become more influential for all kinds of good than many lecturers on art, or many treatise-writers on morality. Considering the materials dealt with, and the crude state of art knowledge at the time, I do not know that any more wide or effective influence in public taste was ever exercised than that of the Staffordshire manufacture of pottery under William Wedgwood; and it only rests with the manufacturer in every other business to determine whether he will, in like manner, make his wares educational instruments, or mere drugs of the market. You all should be, in a certain sense, authors: you must, indeed, first catch the public eye, as an author must the public ear; but once gain your audience, or observance, and as it is in the writer's power thenceforward to publish what will educate as it amuses—so it is in yours to publish what will educate as it adorns. Nor is this surely a subject of poor ambition. I hear it said continually that men are too ambitious: alas! to me, it seems they are never enough ambitious. How many are content to be merely the thriving merchants of a state, when they might be its guides, counsellors, and rulers—wielding powers of subtle but gigantic beneficence, in restraining its follies while they supplied its wants. Let such duty, such ambition, be once accepted in their fulness, and the best glory of European art and of European manufacture may yet be to come. The paintings of Raphael and of Buonaroti gave force to the falsehoods of superstition, and majesty to the imaginations of sin; but the arts of England may have, for their task, to inform the soul with truth, and touch the heart with compassion. The steel of Toledo and the silk of Genoa did but give strength to oppression and lustre to pride: let it be for the furnace and for the loom of England, as they have already richly earned, still more abundantly to bestow, comfort on the indigent, civilization on the rude, and to dispense, through the peaceful homes of nations, the grace and the preciousness of simple adornment, and useful possession.

LECTURE IV

INFLUENCE OF IMAGINATION IN ARCHITECTURE

AN ADDRESS

Delivered to the Members of the Architectural Association, in Lyon's Inn Hall, 1857.

IF we were to be asked abruptly, and required to answer briefly, what qualities chiefly distinguish great artists from feeble artists, we should answer, I suppose, first, their sensibility and tenderness; secondly, their imagination; and thirdly, their industry. Some of us might, perhaps, doubt the justice of attaching so much importance to this last character, because we have all known clever men who were indolent, and dull men who were industrious. But though you may have known clever men who were indolent, you never knew a *great* man who was so; and, during such investigation as I have been able to give to the lives of the artists whose works are in all points noblest, no fact ever looms so large upon me—no law remains so steadfast in the universality of its application, as the fact and law that they are all great workers: nothing concerning them is matter of more astonishment than the quantity they have accomplished in the given length of their life; and when I hear a young man spoken of, as giving promise of high genius, the first question I ask about him is always—

Does he work?

But though this quality of industry is essential to an artist, it does not in anywise make an artist; many people are busy, whose doings are little worth. Neither does sensibility make an artist; since, as I hope, many can feel both strongly and nobly, who yet care nothing about art. But the gifts which distinctively mark the artist—*without* which he must be feeble in life, forgotten

161

in death—*with* which he may become one of the shakers of the earth, and one of the signal lights in heaven—are those of sympathy and imagination. I will not occupy your time, nor incur the risk of your dissent, by endeavouring to give any close definition of this last word. We all have a general and sufficient idea of imagination, and of its work with our hands and in our hearts : we understand it, I suppose, as the imaging or picturing of new things in our thoughts; and we always show an involuntary respect for this power, wherever we can recognize it, acknowledging it to be a greater power than manipulation, or calculation, or observation, or any other human faculty. If we see an old woman spinning at the fireside, and distributing her thread dexterously from the distaff, we respect her for her manipulation— if we ask her how much she expects to make in a year, and she answers quickly, we respect her for her calculation —if she is watching at the same time that none of her grandchildren fall into the fire, we respect her for her observation—yet for all this she may still be a commonplace old woman enough. But if she is all the time telling her grandchildren a fairy tale out of her head, we praise her for her imagination, and say, she must be a rather remarkable old woman.

Precisely in like manner, if an architect does his working-drawing well, we praise him for his manipulation—if he keeps closely within his contract, we praise him for his honest arithmetic—if he looks well to the laying of his beams, so that nobody shall drop through the floor, we praise him for his observation. But he must, somehow, tell us a fairy tale out of his head beside all this, else we cannot praise him for his imagination, nor speak of him as we did of the old woman, as being in any wise out of the common way, a rather remarkable architect. It seemed to me, therefore, as if it might interest you to-night, if we were to consider together what fairy tales are, in and by architecture, to be told— what there is for you to do in this severe art of yours " out of your heads," as well as by your hands.

Perhaps the first idea which a young architect is apt to be allured by, as a head-problem in these experimental days, is its being incumbent upon him to invent a " new style " worthy of modern civilization in general, and of England in particular; a style worthy of our engines and telegraphs; as expansive as steam, and as sparkling as electricity.

But, if there are any of my hearers who have been impressed with this sense of inventive duty, may I ask them, first, whether their plan is that every inventive architect among us shall invent a new style for himself, and have a county set aside for his conceptions, or a province for his practice? Or, must every architect invent a little piece of the new style, and all put it together at last like a dissected map? And if so, when the new style is invented, what is to be done next? I will grant you this Eldorado of imagination—but can you have more than one Columbus? Or, if you sail in company, and divide the prize of your discovery and the honour thereof, who is to come after you clustered Columbuses? to what fortunate islands of style are your architectural descendants to sail, avaricious of new lands. When our desired style is invented, will not the best we can all do be simply—to build in it?—and cannot you now do that in styles that are known? Observe, I grant, for the sake of your argument, what perhaps many of you know that I would not grant otherwise—that a new style *can* be invented. I grant you not only this, but that it shall be wholly different from any that was ever practised before. We will suppose that capitals are to be at the bottom of pillars instead of the top; and that buttresses shall be on the tops of pinnacles instead of at the bottom; that you roof your apertures with stones which shall neither be arched nor horizontal; and that you compose your decoration of lines which shall neither be crooked nor straight. The furnace and the forge shall be at your service: you shall draw out your plates of glass and beat out your bars of iron till you have encompassed us all,—if your style is of the practical kind,—with endless perspective of black skeleton and blinding square,—or if your style is to be of the ideal kind,—you shall wreath your streets with ductile leafage, and roof them with variegated crystal—you shall put, if you will, all London under one blazing dome of many colours that shall light the clouds round it with its flashing, as far as to the sea. And still, I ask you, What after this ? Do you suppose those imaginations of yours will ever lie down there asleep beneath the shade of your iron leafage, or within the coloured light of your enchanted dome ? Not so. Those souls, and fancies, and ambitions of yours, are wholly infinite ; and, whatever may be done by others, you will still want to do something for yourselves ; if you cannot rest content with Palladio, neither will you with Paxton : all the metal and glass that ever were melted have not so much weight in them as will clog the wings of one human spirit's aspiration.

If you will think over this quietly by yourselves, and can get the noise out of your ears of the perpetual, empty, idle, incomparably idiotic talk about the necessity of some novelty in architecture, you will soon see that the very essence of a Style, properly so called, is that it should be practised *for ages*, and applied to all purposes ; and that so long as any given style is in practice, all that is left for individual imagination to accomplish must be within the scope of that style, not in the invention of a new one. If there are any here, therefore, who hope to obtain celebrity by the invention of some strange way of building which must convince all Europe into its adoption, to them, for the moment, I must not be understood to address myself, but only to those who would be content with that degree of celebrity which an artist may enjoy who works in the manner of his fore-fathers ;—which the builder of Salisbury Cathedral might enjoy in England, though he did not invent Gothic ; and which Titian might enjoy at Venice, though he did not invent oil painting. Addressing myself then to those humbler, but wiser, or rather, only wise students who are content to avail themselves of some system of building already understood, let us consider together what room for the exercise of the imagination may be left to us under such conditions. And, first, I suppose it will be said, or thought, that the architect's principal field for exercise of his invention must be in the disposition of lines, mouldings, and masses, in agreeable proportions. Indeed, if you adopt some styles of architecture, you cannot exercise invention in any other way. And I admit that it requires genius and special gift to do this rightly. Not by rule, nor by study, can the gift of graceful proportionate design be obtained; only by the intuition of genius can so much as a single tier of façade be beautifully arranged; and the man has just cause for pride, as far as our gifts can ever be a cause for pride, who finds himself able, in a design of his own, to rival even the simplest arrangement of parts in one by Sanmicheli, Inigo Jones, or Christopher Wren.

Invention, then, and genius being granted, as necessary to accomplish this, let me ask you, What, after all, with this special gift and genius, you *have* accomplished, when you have arranged the lines of a building beautifully?

In the first place you will not, I think, tell me that the beauty there attained is of a touching or pathetic kind. A well-disposed group of notes in music will make you sometimes weep and sometimes laugh. You can express the depth of all affections by those dispositions of sound; you can give courage to the soldier, language to the lover, consolation to the mourner, more joy to the joyful, more humility to the devout. Can you do as much by your group of lines? Do you suppose the front of Whitehall, a singularly beautiful one, ever inspires the two Horse Guards, during the hour they sit opposite to it, with military ardour? Do you think that the lovers in our London walk down to the front of Whitehall for consolation when mistresses are

unkind ; or that any person wavering in duty, or feeble
in faith, was ever confirmed in purpose or in creed by
the pathetic appeal of those harmonious architraves?
You will not say so. Then, if they cannot touch, or
inspire, or comfort any one, can your architectural proportions amuse any one? Christmas is just over ; you
have doubtless been at many merry parties during the
period. Can you remember any in which architectural
proportions contributed to the entertainment of the
evening? Proportions of notes in music were, I am
sure, essential to your amusement ; the setting of flowers
in hair, and of ribands on dresses, were also subjects of
frequent admiration with you, not inessential to your
happiness. Among the juvenile members of your
society the proportion of currants in cake, and of sugar
in comfits, became subjects of acute interest ; and, when
such proportions were harmonious, motives also of
gratitude to cook and to confectioner. But, did you
ever see either young or old amused by the architrave
of the door? Or otherwise interested in the proportions
of the room than as they admitted more or fewer
friendly faces? Nay, if all the amusement that there is
in the best proportioned architecture of London could
be concentrated into one evening, and you were to issue
tickets for nothing to this great proportional entertainment ;—how do you think it would stand between you
and the Drury pantomime?

You are, then, remember, granted to be people of
genius—great and admirable ; and you devote your lives
to your art, but you admit that you cannot comfort
anybody, you cannot encourage anybody, you cannot
improve anybody, and you cannot amuse anybody. I
proceed then farther to ask, Can you inform anybody?
Many sciences cannot be considered as highly touching
or emotional; nay, perhaps not specially amusing ;
scientific men may sometimes, in these respects, stand
on the same ground with you. As far as we can judge
by the results of the late war, science helps our soldiers
about as much as the front of Whitehall ; and at the

Christmas parties, the children wanted no geologists to tell them about the behaviour of bears and dragons in Queen Elizabeth's time. Still, your man of science teaches you something ; he may be dull at a party, or helpless in a battle, he is not always that ; but he can give you, at all events, knowledge of noble facts, and open to you the secrets of the earth and air. Will your architectural proportions do as much ? Your genius is granted, and your life is given, and what do you teach us ?—Nothing, I believe, from one end of that life to the other, but that two and two make four, and that one is to two as three is to six.

You cannot, then, it is admitted, comfort any one, serve or amuse any one, nor teach any one. Finally, I ask, Can you be of *Use* to any one ? " Yes," you reply ; " certainly we are of some use—we architects—in a climate like this, where it always rains." You are of use, certainly ; but, pardon me, only as builders—not as proportionalists. We are not talking of building as a protection, but only of that special work which your genius is to do ; not of building substantial and comfortable houses like Mr. Cubitt, but of putting beautiful façades on them like Inigo Jones. And, again, I ask— Are you of use to any one ? Will your proportions of façade heal the sick, or clothe the naked ? Supposing you devoted your lives to be merchants, you might reflect at the close of them, how many, fainting for want, you had brought corn to sustain ; how many, infected with disease, you had brought balms to heal ; how widely, among multitudes of far-away nations, you had scattered the first seeds of national power, and guided the first rays of sacred light. Had you been, in fine, *anything* else in the world *but* architectural designers, you might have been of some use or good to people. Content to be petty tradesmen, you would have saved the time of mankind ;—rough-handed daily labourers, you would have added to their stock of food or of clothing. But, being men of genius, and devoting your lives to the exquisite exposition of this genius, on what achievements

do you think the memories of your old age are to fasten ?
Whose gratitude will surround you with its glow, or
on what accomplished good, of that greatest kind for
which men show *no* gratitude, will your life rest the con-
tentment of its close ? Truly, I fear that the ghosts
of proportionate lines will be thin phantoms at your
bedsides—very speechless to you ; and that on all the
emanations of your high genius you will look back
with less delight than you might have done on a cup of
cold water given to him who was thirsty, or to a single
moment when you had "prevented with your bread him
that fled."

Do not answer, nor think to answer, that with your
great works and great payments of workmen in them,
you would do this ; I know you would, and will, as
Builders ; but, I repeat, it is not your *building* that I am
talking about, but your *brains ;* it is your invention and
imagination of whose profit I am speaking. The good
done through the building, observe, is done by your
employers, not by you—you share in the benefit of it.
The good that *you* personally must do is by your
designing ; and I compare you with musicians who do
good by their pathetic composing, not as they do good
by employing fiddlers in the orchestra ; for it is the
public who in reality do that, not the musicians. So
clearly keeping to this one question, what good we
architects are to do by our genius ; and having found that
on our proportionate system we can do no good to
others, will you tell me, lastly, what good we can do to
ourselves ?

Observe, nearly every other liberal art or profession
has some intense pleasure connected with it, irrespective
of any good to others. As lawyers, or physicians, or
clergymen, you would have the pleasure of investigation,
and of historical reading, as part of your work : as men
of science you would be rejoicing in curiosity perpetually
gratified respecting the laws and facts of nature : as
artists you would have delight in watching the external
forms of nature : as day labourers or petty tradesmen,

supposing you to undertake such work with as much intellect as you are going to devote to your designing, you would find continued subjects of interest in the manufacture or the agriculture which you helped to improve ; or in the problems of commerce which bore on your business. But your architectural designing leads you into no pleasant journeys,—into no seeing of lovely things,—no discerning of just laws,—no warmths of compassion, no humilities of veneration, no progressive state of sight or soul. Our conclusion is—must be— that you will not amuse, nor inform, nor help anybody ; you will not amuse, nor better, nor inform yourselves ; you will sink into a state in which you can neither show, nor feel, nor see, anything, but that one is to two as three is to six. And in that state what should we call ourselves ? Men ? I think not. The right name for us would be—numerators and denominators. Vulgar Fractions.

Shall we, then, abandon this theory of the soul of architecture being in proportional lines, and look whether we can find anything better to exert our fancies upon ?

May we not, to begin with, accept this great principle —that, as our bodies, to be in health, must be *generally* exercised, so our minds, to be in health, must be *generally* cultivated ? You would not call a man healthy who had strong arms but was paralytic in his feet ; nor one who could walk well, but had no use of his hands ; nor one who could see well, if he could not hear. You would not voluntarily reduce your bodies to any such partially developed state. Much more, then, you would not, if you could help it, reduce your minds to it. Now, your minds are endowed with a vast number of gifts of totally different uses—limbs of mind as it were, which, if you don't exercise, you cripple. One is curiosity ; that is a gift, a capacity of pleasure in knowing ; which if you destroy, you make yourselves cold and dull. Another is sympathy ; the power of sharing in the feelings of living creatures, which if you destroy, you make yourselves hard and cruel. Another of your limbs of mind is admiration; the power of enjoying beauty or ingenuity, which if you destroy, you make yourselves base and irreverent. Another is wit; or the power of playing with the lights on the many sides of truth; which if you destroy, you make yourselves gloomy, and less useful and cheering to others than you might be. So that in choosing your way of work it should be your aim, as far as possible, to bring out all these faculties, as far as they exist in you; not one merely, nor another, but all of them. And the way to bring them out, is simply to concern yourselves attentively with the subjects of each faculty. To cultivate sympathy you must be among living creatures, and thinking about them; and to cultivate admiration, you must be among beautiful things and looking at them.

All this sounds much like truism, at least I hope it does, for then you will surely not refuse to act upon it; and to consider farther, how, as architects, you are to keep yourselves in contemplation of living creatures and lovely things.

You all probably know the beautiful photographs which have been published within the last year or two of the porches of the Cathedral of Amiens. I hold one of these up to you, (merely that you may know what I am talking about, as of course you cannot see the detail at this distance, but you will recognise the subject.) Have you ever considered how much sympathy, and how much humour, are developed in filling this single doorway[1] with these sculptures of the history of St. Honoré (and, by the way, considering how often we English are now driving up and down the Rue St. Honoré, we may as well know as much of the saint as the old architect cared to tell us). You know, in all legends of saints who ever were bishops, the first thing you are told of them is that they didn't want to be bishops. So here is St. Honoré, who doesn't want to be

---

[1] The tympanum of the south transept door; it is to be found generally among all collections of architectural photographs.

a bishop, sitting sulkily in the corner; he hugs his book with both hands, and won't get up to take his crosier; and here are all the city aldermen of Amiens come to *poke* him up; and all the monks in the town in a great puzzle what they shall do for a bishop if St. Honoré won't be; and here's one of the monks in the opposite corner who is quite cool about it, and thinks they'll get on well enough without St. Honoré,—you see that in his face perfectly. At last St. Honoré consents to be bishop, and here he sits in a throne, and has his book now grandly on a desk instead of his knees, and he directs one of his village curates how to find relics in a wood; here is the wood, and here is the village curate, and here are the tombs, with the bones of St. Victorien and Gentien in them.

After this, St. Honoré performs grand mass, and the miracle occurs of the appearance of a hand blessing the wafer, which occurrence afterwards was painted for the arms of the abbey. Then St. Honoré dies; and here is his tomb with his statue on the top; and miracles are being performed at it—a deaf man having his ear touched, and a blind man groping his way up to the tomb with his dog. Then here is a great procession in honour of the relics of St. Honoré; and under his coffin are some cripples being healed; and the coffin itself is put above the bar which separates the cross from the lower subjects, because the tradition is that the figure on the crucifix of the Church of St. Firmin bowed its head in token of acceptance, as the relics of St. Honoré passed beneath.

Now just consider the amount of sympathy with human nature, and observance of it, shown in this one bas-relief; the sympathy with disputing monks, with puzzled aldermen, with melancholy recluse, with triumphant pre-late, with palsy-stricken poverty, with ecclesiastical magni-ficence, or miracle-working faith. Consider how much intellect was needed in the architect, and how much observance of nature, before he could give the expres-sion to these various figures—cast these multitudinous draperies—design these rich and quaint fragments of tombs and altars—weave with perfect animation the entangled branches of the forest.

But you will answer me, all this is not architecture at all—it is sculpture. Will you then tell me precisely where the separation exists between one and the other? We will begin at the very beginning. I will show you a piece of what you will certainly admit to be a piece of pure architecture;[1] it is drawn on the back of another photograph, another of these marvellous tympana from Notre Dame, which you call, I suppose, impure. Well, look on this picture, and on this. Don't laugh; you must not laugh, that's very improper of you, this is classical architecture. I have taken it out of the essay on that subject in the " Encyclopædia Britannica."

Yet I suppose none of you would think yourselves particularly ingenious architects if you had designed nothing more than this; nay, I will even let you improve it into any grand proportion you choose, and add to it as many windows as you choose; the only thing I insist upon in our specimen of pure architecture is, that there shall be no mouldings nor ornaments upon it. And I suspect you don't quite like your architecture so "pure" as this. We want a few mouldings, you will say—just a few. Those who want mouldings, hold up their hands. We are unanimous, I think. Will you, then, design the profiles of these mouldings yourselves, or will you copy them? If you wish to copy them, and to copy them always, of course I leave you at once to your authorities, and your imaginations to their repose. But if you wish to design them yourselves, how do you do it? You draw the profile according to your taste, and you order your mason to cut it. Now, will you tell me the logical difference between drawing the profile of a moulding and giving *that* to be cut, and drawing the folds of the drapery of a statue and giving *those* to be cut. The last is much more difficult to do than the first; but degrees of

---

[1] See Appendix III., " Classical Architecture."

difficulty constitute no specific difference, and you will not accept it, surely, as a definition of the difference between architecture and sculpture, that "architecture is doing anything that is easy, and sculpture anything that is difficult."

It is true, also, that the carved moulding represents nothing, and the carved drapery represents something; but you will not, I should think, accept, as an explanation of the difference between architecture and sculpture, this any more than the other, that "sculpture is art which has meaning, and architecture art which has none."

Where, then, is your difference? In this, perhaps, you will say; that whatever ornaments we can direct ourselves, and get accurately cut to order, we consider architectural. The ornaments that we are obliged to leave to the pleasure of the workman, or the superintendence of some other designer, we consider sculptural, especially if they are more or less extraneous and incrusted—not an essential part of the building.

Accepting this definition, I am compelled to reply, that it is in effect nothing more than an amplification of my first one—that whatever is easy you call architecture, whatever is difficult you call sculpture. For you cannot suppose the arrangement of the place in which the sculpture is to be put is so difficult or so great a part of the design as the sculpture itself. For instance : you all know the pulpit of Niccolo Pisano, in the baptistry at Pisa. It is composed of seven rich *relievi*, surrounded by panel mouldings, and sustained on marble shafts. Do you suppose Niccolo Pisano's reputation—such part of it at least as rests on this pulpit (and much does) —depends on the panel mouldings, or on the relievi? The panel mouldings are by his hand; he would have disdained to leave even them to a common workman; but do you think he found any difficulty in them, or thought there was any credit in them? Having once done the sculpture, those enclosing lines were mere child's play to him; the determination of the diameter of shafts and height of capitals was an affair of minutes his *work* was in carving the Crucifixion and the Baptism.

Or, again, do you recollect Orcagna's tabernacle in the church of San Michele, at Florence? That, also, consists of rich and multitudinous bas-reliefs, enclosed in panel mouldings, with shafts of mosaic, and foliated arches sustaining the canopy. Do you think Orcagna, any more than Pisano, if his spirit could rise in the midst of us at this moment, would tell us that he had trusted his fame to the foliation, or had put his soul's pride into the panelling? Not so; he would tell you that his spirit was in the stooping figures that stand round the couch of the dying Virgin.

Or, lastly, do you think the man who designed the procession on the portal of Amiens was the subordinate workman? that there was an architect over *him*, restraining him within certain limits, and ordering of him his bishops at so much a mitre, and his cripples at so much a crutch? Not so. *Here*, on this sculptured shield, rests the Master's hand; *this* is the centre of the Master's thought: from this, and in subordination to this, waved the arch and sprang the pinnacle. Having done this, and being able to give human expression and action to the stone, all the rest—the rib, the niche, the foil, the shaft—were mere toys to his hand and accessories to his conception; and if once you also gain the gift of doing this, if once you can carve one fronton such as you have here, I tell you, you would be able—so far as it depended on your invention—to scatter cathedrals over England as fast as clouds rise from its streams after summer rain.

Nay, but perhaps you answer again, our sculptors at present do not design cathedrals, and could not. No, they could not; but that is merely because we have made architecture so dull that they cannot take any interest in it, and, therefore, do not care to add to their higher knowledge the poor and common knowledge of principles of building. You have thus separated building from sculpture, and you have taken away the power of both; for the sculptor loses nearly as much by never having room for the development of a continuous work, as you do from having reduced your work to a continuity of mechanism. You are essentially, and should always be, the same body of men, admitting only such difference in operation as there is between the work of a painter at different times, who sometimes labours on a small picture, and sometimes on the frescoes of a palace gallery.

This conclusion, then, we arrive at, *must* arrive at; the fact being irrevocably so :—that in order to give your imagination and the other powers of your souls full play, you must do as all the great architects of old time did— you must yourselves be your sculptors. Phidias, Michael Angelo, Orcagna, Pisano, Giotto,—which of these men, do you think, could not use his chisel? You say, "It is difficult; quite out of your way." I know it is; nothing that is great is easy; and nothing that is great, so long as you study building without sculpture, can be *in* your way. I want to put it in your way, and you to find your way to it. But, on the other hand, do not shrink from the task as if the refined art of perfect sculpture were always required from you. For, though architecture and sculpture are not separate arts, there is an architectural *manner* of sculpture; and it is, in the majority of its applications, a comparatively easy one. Our great mistake at present, in dealing with stone at all, is requiring to have all our work too refined; it is just the same mistake as if we were to require all our book illustrations to be as fine work as Raphael's. John Leech does not sketch so well as Leonardo da Vinci; but do you think that the public could easily spare him; or that he is wrong in bringing out his talent in the way in which it is most effective? Would you advise him, if he asked your advice, to give up his wood-blocks and take to canvas? I know you would not; neither would you tell him, I believe, on the other hand, that, because he could not draw as well as Leonardo, therefore he ought to draw nothing but straight lines with a ruler, and circles with compasses, and no figure-subjects at all. That would be some loss to you; would it not? You would all be vexed if next week's *Punch* had nothing in it but proportionate lines. And yet, do not you see that you are doing precisely the same thing with *your* powers of sculptural design that he would be doing with his powers of pictorial design, if he gave you nothing but such lines. You feel that you cannot carve like Phidias; therefore you will not carve at all, but only draw mouldings; and thus all that intermediate power which is of especial value in modern days,—that popular power of expression which is within the attainment of thousands, and would address itself to tens of thousands,—is utterly lost to us in stone, though in ink and paper it has become one of the most important engines, and one of the most desired luxuries, of modern civilization.

Here, then, is one part of the subject to which I would especially invite your attention, namely, the distinctive character which may be wisely permitted to belong to architectural sculpture, as distinguished from perfect sculpture on one side, and from mere geometrical decoration on the other.

And first, observe what an indulgence we have in the distance at which most work is to be seen. Supposing we were able to carve eyes and lips with the most exquisite precision, it would all be of no use as soon as the work was put far above the eye; but, on the other hand, as beauties disappear by being far withdrawn, so will faults; and the mystery and confusion which are the natural consequence of distance, while they would often render your best skill but vain, will as often render your worst errors of little consequence; nay, more than this, often a deep cut, or a rude angle, will produce in certain positions an effect of expression both startling and true, which you never hoped for. Not that mere distance will give animation to the work, if it has none in itself; but if it has life at all, the distance will make that life more perceptible and powerful by softening the defects of execution. So that you are placed, as workmen, in this position of singular advantage, that you may give your fancies free play, and strike hard for the expression that you want, knowing that, if you miss it, no one will detect you; if you at all touch it, nature herself will help you, and with every changing shadow and basking sunbeam bring forth new phases of your fancy.

But it is not merely this privilege of being imperfect which belongs to architectural sculpture. It has a true privilege of imagination, far excelling all that can be granted to the more finished work, which, for the sake of distinction, I will call,—and I don't think we can have a much better term—"furniture sculpture;" sculpture, that is, which can be moved from place to place to furnish rooms.

For observe, to that sculpture the spectator is usually brought in a tranquil or prosaic state of mind; he sees it associated rather with what is sumptuous than sublime, and under circumstances which address themselves more to his comfort than his curiosity. The statue which is to be pathetic, seen between the flashes of footmen's livery round the dining-table, must have strong elements of pathos in itself; and the statue which is to be awful, in the midst of the gossip of the drawing-room, must have the elements of awe wholly in itself. But the spectator is brought to *your* work already in an excited and imaginative mood. He has been impressed by the cathedral wall as it loomed over the low streets, before he looks up to the carving of its porch—and his love of mystery has been touched by the silence and the shadows of the cloister, before he can set himself to decipher the bosses on its vaulting. So that when once he begins to observe your doings, he will ask nothing better from you, nothing kinder from you, than that you would meet this imaginative temper of his half way;—that you would farther touch the sense of terror, or satisfy the expectation of things strange, which have been prompted by the mystery or the majesty of the surrounding scene. And thus, your leaving forms more or less undefined, or carrying out your fancies, however extravagant, in grotesqueness of shadow or shape, will be for the most part in accordance with the temper of the observer; and he is likely, therefore, much more willingly to use his fancy to help your meanings, than his judgment to detect your faults.

Again. Remember that when the imagination and feelings are strongly excited, they will not only bear with strange things, but they will *look* into *minute* things with a delight quite unknown in hours of tranquillity. You surely must remember moments of your lives in which, under some strong excitement of feeling, all the details of visible objects presented themselves with a strange intensity and insistance, whether you would or no ; urging themselves upon the mind, and thrust upon the eye, with a force of fascination which you could not refuse. Now, to a certain extent, the senses get into this state when-ever the imagination is strongly excited. Things trivial at other times assume a dignity or significance which we cannot explain ; but which is only the more attractive because inexplicable : and the powers of attention, quickened by the feverish excitement, fasten and feed upon the minutest circumstances of detail, and remotest traces of intention. So that what would at other times be felt as more or less mean or extraneous in a work of sculpture, and which would assuredly be offensive to the perfect taste in its moments of languor, or of critical judgment, will be grateful, and even sublime, when it meets this frightened inquisitiveness, this fascinated watchfulness, of the roused imagination. And this is all for your advantage ; for, in the beginnings of your sculpture, you will assuredly find it easier to imitate minute circumstances of costume or character, than to perfect the anatomy of simple forms or the flow of noble masses ; and it will be encouraging to remember that the grace you cannot perfect, and the simplicity you cannot achieve, would be in great part vain, even if you could achieve them, in their appeal to the hasty curiosity of passionate fancy ; but that the sympathy which would be refused to your science will be granted to your innocence ; and that the mind of the general observer, though wholly unaffected by correctness of anatomy or propriety of gesture, will follow you with fond and pleased concurrence, as you carve the knots of the hair, and the patterns of the vesture.

Farther yet.   We are to remember that not only do the associated features of the larger architecture tend to excite the strength of fancy, but the architectural laws to which you are obliged to submit your decoration stimulate its *ingenuity*.   Every crocket which you are to crest with sculpture,—every foliation which you have to fill, presents itself to the spectator's fancy, not only as a pretty thing, but as a *problematic* thing.   It contained, he perceives immediately, not only a beauty which you wished to display, but a necessity which you were forced to meet; and the problem, how to occupy such and such a space with organic form in any probable way, or how to turn such a boss or ridge into a conceivable image of life, becomes at once, to him as to you, a matter of amusement as much as of admiration.   The ordinary conditions of perfection in form, gesture, or feature, are willingly dispensed with, when the ugly dwarf and ungainly goblin have only to gather themselves into angles, or crouch to carry corbels; and the want of skill which, in other kinds of work, would have been required for the finishing of the parts, will at once be forgiven here, if you have only disposed ingeniously what you have executed roughly, and atoned for the rudeness of your hands by the quickness of your wits.

Hitherto, however, we have been considering only the circumstances in architecture favourable to the development of the *powers* of imagination.   A yet more important point for us seems, to me, the place which it gives to all the *objects* of imagination.

For, I suppose, you will not wish me to spend any time in proving, that imagination must be vigorous in proportion to the quantity of material which it has to handle; and that, just as we increase the range of what we see, we increase the richness of what we can imagine. Granting this, consider what a field is opened to your fancy merely in the subject matter which architecture admits. Nearly every other art is severely limited in its subjects— the landscape painter, for instance, gets little help from the aspects of beautiful humanity ; the historical painter, less, perhaps, than he ought, from the accidents of wild nature ; and the pure sculptor, still less, from the minor details of common life. But is there anything within range of sight, or conception, which may not be of use to *you*, or in which your interest may not be excited with advantage to your art ? From visions of angels, down to the least important gesture of a child at play, whatever may be conceived of Divine, or beheld of Human, may be dared or adopted by you ; throughout the kingdom of animal life, no creature is so vast, or so minute, that you cannot deal with it, or bring it into service ; the lion and the crocodile will couch about your shafts ; the moth and the bee will sun themselves upon your flowers ; for you, the fawn will leap ; for you, the snail be slow ; for you, the dove smooth her bosom ; and the hawk spread her wings toward the south. All the wide world of vegeta-tion blooms and bends for you ; the leaves tremble that you may bid them be still under the marble snow ; the thorn and the thistle, which the earth casts forth as evil, are to you the kindliest servants ; no dying petal, nor drooping tendril, is so feeble as to have no help for you ; no robed pride of blossom so kingly, but it will lay aside its purple to receive at your hands the pale immortality. Is there anything in common life too mean,—in common things too trivial,—to be ennobled by your touch ? As there is nothing in life, so there is nothing in lifelessness which has not its lesson for you, or its gift ; and when you are tired of watching the strength of the plume, and the tenderness of the leaf, you may walk down to your rough river-shore, or into the thickest markets of your thoroughfares ; and there is not a piece of torn cable that will not twine into a perfect moulding ; there is not a fragment of cast-away matting, or shattered basket-work, that will not work into a chequer or a capital. Yes : and if you gather up the very sand, and break the stone on which you tread, among its fragments of all but invisible shells you will find forms that will take their place, and that proudly, among the starred traceries of your vaulting; and you, who can crown the mountain with its fortress, and the city with its towers, are thus able also to give beauty to ashes, and worthiness to dust.

Now, in that your art presents all this material to you, you have already much to rejoice in. But you have more to rejoice in, because all this is submitted to you, not to be dissected or analyzed, but to be sympathized with, and to bring out, therefore, what may be accurately called the moral part of imagination. We saw that, if we kept ourselves among lines only, we should have cause to envy the naturalist, because he was conversant with facts; but you will have little to envy now, if you make yourselves conversant with the feelings that arise out of his facts. For instance, the naturalist, coming upon a block of marble, has to begin considering immediately how far its purple is owing to iron, or its whiteness to magnesia; he breaks his piece of marble, and at the close of his day, has nothing but a little sand in his crucible, and some data added to the theory of the elements. But *you* approach your marble to sympathize with it, and rejoice over its beauty. You cut it a little indeed; but only to bring out its veins more perfectly: and at the end of your day's work you leave your marble shaft with joy and complacency in its perfectness, as marble. When you have to watch an animal instead of a stone, you differ from the naturalist in the same way. He may, perhaps, if he be an amiable naturalist, take delight in having living creatures round him;—still, the major part of his work is, or has been, in counting feathers, separating fibres, and analyzing structures. But *your* work is always with the living creature; the thing you have to get at in him is his life, and ways of going about things. It does not matter to you how many cells there are in his bones, or how many filaments in his feathers; what you want is his moral character and way of behaving himself; it is just that which your imagination, if healthy, will first seize—just that which your chisel, if vigorous, will first cut. You must get the storm spirit into your eagles, and the lordliness into your lions, and the tripping fear into your fawns ; and in order to do this, you must be in continual sympathy with every fawn of them ; and be hand-in-glove with all the lions, and hand-in-claw with all the hawks. And don't fancy that you will lower your-selves by sympathy with the lower creatures ; you cannot sympathize rightly with the higher, unless you do with those : but you have to sympathize with the higher, too— with queens, and kings, and martyrs, and angels. Yes, and above all, and more than all, with simple humanity in all its needs and ways, for there is not one hurried face that passes you in the street that will not be impressive, if you can only fathom it. All history is open to you, all high thoughts and dreams that the past fortunes of men can suggest ; all fairy land is open to you—no vision that ever haunted forest, or gleamed over hill-side, but calls you to understand how it came into men's hearts, and may still touch them ; and all Paradise is open to you— yes, and the work of Paradise ; for in bringing all this, in perpetual and attractive truth, before the eyes of your fellow-men, you have to join in the employment of the angels, as well as to imagine their companies.

And observe, in this last respect, what a peculiar importance, and responsibility, are attached to your work, when you consider its permanence, and the multitudes to whom it is addressed. We frequently are led, by wise people, to consider what responsibility may some-times attach to words, which yet, the chance is, will be heard by few, and forgotten as soon as heard. But none of *your* words will be heard by few, and none will be forgotten, for five or six hundred years, if you build well. You will talk to all who pass by ; and all those little sympathies, those freaks of fancy, those jests in stone, those workings-out of problems in caprice, will occupy mind after mind of utterly countless multitudes, long after you are gone. You have not, like authors, to plead for a hearing, or to fear oblivion. Do but build large enough, and carve boldly enough, and all the world will hear you ; they cannot choose but look.

I do not mean to awe you by this thought; I do not mean that because you will have so many witnesses and watchers, you are never to jest, or do anything gaily or lightly; on the contrary, I have pleaded, from the beginning, for this art of yours, especially because it has room for the whole of your character—if jest is in you, let the jest be jested; if mathematical ingenuity is yours, let your problem be put, and your solution worked out, as quaintly as you choose; above all, see that your work is easily and happily done, else it will never make anybody else happy: but while you thus give the rein to all your impulses, see that those impulses be headed and centred by one noble impulse; and let that be Love—triple love—for the art which you practise, the creation in which you move, and the creatures to whom you minister.

I. I say, first, Love for the art which you practise. Be assured that if ever any other motive becomes a leading one in your mind, as the principal one for exertion, except your love of art, that moment it is all over with your art. I do not say you are not to desire money, nor to desire fame, nor to desire position; you cannot but desire all three; nay, you may—if you are willing that I should use the word Love in a desecrated sense—love all three; that is, passionately covet them, yet you must not covet or love them in the first place. Men of strong passions and imaginations must always care a great deal for anything they care for at all; but the whole question is one of first or second. Does your art lead you, or your gain lead you? You may like making money exceedingly; but if it come to a fair question, whether you are to make five hundred pounds less by this business, or to spoil your building, and you choose to spoil your building, there's an end of you. So you may be as thirsty for fame as a cricket is for cream; but, if it come to a fair question, whether you are to please the mob, or do the thing as you know it ought to be done; and you can't do both, and choose to please the mob,—it's all over with you;—there's no hope for you; nothing that you can do will ever be worth a man's glance as he passes by. The test is absolute, inevitable—Is your art first with you? Then you are artists; you may be, after you have made your money, misers and usurers; you may be, after you have got your fame, jealous, and proud, and wretched, and base :—but yet, *as long as you won't spoil your work*, you are artists. On the other hand—Is your money first with you, and your fame first with you? Then, you may be very charitable with your money, and very magnificent with your money, and very graceful in the way you wear your reputation, and very courteous to those beneath you, and very acceptable to those above you; but you are *not artists*. You are mechanics, and drudges.

II. You must love the creation you work in the midst of. For, wholly in proportion to the intensity of feeling which you bring to the subject you have chosen, will be the depth and justice of our perception of its character. And this depth of feeling is not to be gained on the instant, when you want to bring it to bear on this or that. It is the result of the general habit of striving to feel rightly; and, among thousands of various means of doing this, perhaps the one I ought specially to name to you, is the keeping yourselves clear of petty and mean cares. Whatever you do, don't be anxious, nor fill your heads with little chagrins and little desires. I have just said, that you may be great artists, and yet be miserly and jealous, and troubled about many things. So you may be; but I said also that the miserliness or trouble must not be in your hearts all day. It is possible that you may get a habit of saving money; or it is possible, at a time of great trial, you may yield to the temptation of speaking unjustly of a rival,—and you will shorten your powers and dim your sight even by this ;— but the thing that you have to dread far more than any such unconscious habit, or any such momentary fall—is the *constancy of small emotions ;*—the anxiety whether Mr. So-and-so will like your work ; whether such and such a workman will do all that you want of him, and

so on;—not wrong feelings or anxieties in themselves,
but impertinent, and wholly incompatible with the full
exercise of your imagination.

Keep yourselves, therefore, quiet, peaceful, with your
eyes open. It doesn't matter at all what Mr. So-and-so
thinks of your work; but it matters a great deal what
that bird is doing up there in its nest, or how that
vagabond child at the street corner is managing his
game of knuckle-down. And remember, you cannot
turn aside from your own interests, to the birds and the
children's interests, unless you have long before got into
the habit of loving and watching birds and children; so
that it all comes at last to the forgetting yourselves, and
the living out of yourselves, in the calm of the great
world, or if you will, in its agitation; but always in
a calm of your own bringing. Do not think it wasted
time to submit yourselves to any influence which may
bring upon you any noble feeling. Rise early, always
watch the sunrise, and the way the clouds break from
the dawn; you will cast your statue-draperies in quite
another than your common way, when the remembrance
of that cloud motion is with you, and of the scarlet
vesture of the morning. Live always in the spring-time
in the country; you do not know what leaf-form means,
unless you have seen the buds burst, and the young
leaves breathing low in the sunshine, and wondering at
the first shower of rain. But above all, accustom yourselves to look for, and to love, all nobleness of gesture
and feature in the human form; and remember that the
highest nobleness is usually among the aged, the poor,
and the infirm: you will find, in the end, that it is not
the strong arm of the soldier, nor the laugh of the young
beauty, that are the best studies for you. Look at them,
and look at them reverently; but be assured that endur-
ance is nobler than strength, and patience than beauty;
and that it is not in the high church pews, where the
gay dresses are, but in the church free seats, where the
widows' weeds are, that you may see the faces that will
fit best between the angels' wings, in the church porch.

III. And therefore, lastly, and chiefly, you must love
the creatures to whom you minister, your fellow-men ;
for, if you do not love them, not only will you be little
interested in the passing events of life, but in all your
gazing at humanity, you will be apt to be struck only by
outside form, and not by expression.   It is only kindness
and tenderness which will ever enable you to see what
beauty there is in the dark eyes that are sunk with
weeping, and in the paleness of those fixed faces which
the earth's adversity has compassed about, till they shine
in their patience like dying watchfires through twilight.
But it is not this only which makes it needful for you, if
you would be great, to be also kind ; there is a most
important and all-essential reason in the very nature of
your own art.   So soon as you desire to build largely,
and with addition of noble sculpture, you will find that
your work must be associative.   You cannot carve a
whole cathedral yourself—you can carve but few and
simple parts of it.   Either your own work must be
disgraced in the mass of the collateral inferiority, or you
must raise your fellow-designers to correspondence of
power.   If you have genius, you will yourselves take the
lead in the building you design ; you will carve its porch
and direct its disposition.   But for all subsequent advancement of its detail, you must trust to the agency and the
invention of others ; and it rests with you either to re-
press what faculties your workmen have, into cunning
subordination to your own ; or to rejoice in discovering
even the powers that may rival you, and leading forth
mind after mind into fellowship with your fancy, and
association with your fame.

I need not tell you that if you do the first—if you
endeavour to depress or disguise the talents of your
subordinates—you are lost ; for nothing could imply
more darkly and decisively than this, that your art and
your work were not beloved by you ; that it was your own
prosperity that you were seeking, and your own skill only
that you cared to contemplate.   I do not say that you
must not be jealous at all ; it is rarely in human nature to

be wholly without jealousy ; and you may be forgiven for going some day sadly home, when you find some youth, unpractised and unapproved, giving the life-stroke to his work which you, after years of training, perhaps, cannot reach ; but your jealousy must not conquer—your love of your building must conquer, helped by your kindness of heart. See—I set no high or difficult standard before you. I do not say that you are to surrender your pre-eminence in *mere* unselfish generosity. But I do say that you must surrender your pre-eminence in your love of your building helped by your kindness ; and that whomsoever you find better able to do what will adorn it than you,—that person you are to give place to : and to console your-selves for the humiliation, first, by your joy in seeing the edifice grow more beautiful under his chisel, and secondly, by your sense of having done kindly and justly. But if you are morally strong enough to make the kindness and justice the first motive, it will be better ;—best of all—if you do not consider it as kindness at all, but bare and stern justice ; for, truly, such help as we can give each other in this world is a *debt* to each other ; and the man who perceives a superiority or capacity in a subordinate, and neither confesses, nor assists it, is not merely the withholder of kindness, but the committer of injury. But be the motive what you will, only see that you do the thing ; and take the joy of the consciousness that, as your art embraces a wider field than all others—and addresses a vaster multitude than all others—and is surer of audience than all others—so it is profounder and holier in Fellowship than all others. The artist, when his pupil is perfect, must see him leave his side that he may declare his distinct, perhaps opponent, skill. Man of science wrestles with man of science for priority of discovery, and pursues in pangs of jealous haste his solitary inquiry. You alone are called by kindness,—by necessity,—by equity, to fraternity of toil ; and thus, in those misty and massive piles which rise above the domestic roofs of our ancient cities, there was—there may be again—a meaning more profound and true than any that fancy so commonly has attached to them.   Men say their pinnacles point to heaven.   Why, so does every tree that buds, and every bird that rises as it sings.   Men say their aisles are good for worship.   Why, so is every mountain glen, and rough sea-shore.   But this they have, of distinct and indisputable glory,—that their mighty walls were never raised, and never shall be, but by men who love and aid each other in their weakness ;—that all their interlacing strength of vaulted stone has its foundation upon the stronger arches of manly fellowship, and all their changing grace of depressed or lifted pinnacle owes its cadence and completeness to sweeter symmetries of human soul.

LECTURE V

A LECTURE

Delivered at Tunbridge Wells, February, 1858

WHEN first I heard that you wished me to address you this evening, it was a matter of some doubt with me whether I could find any subject that would possess any sufficient interest for you to justify my bringing you out of your comfortable houses on a winter's night. When I venture to speak about my own special business of art, it is almost always before students of art, among whom I may sometimes permit myself to be dull, if I can feel that I am useful: but a mere talk about art, especially without examples to refer to (and I have been unable to prepare any careful illustrations for this lecture), is seldom of much interest to a general audience. As I was considering what you might best bear with me in speaking about, there came naturally into my mind a subject connected with the origin and present prosperity of the town you live in ; and, it seemed to me, in the out-branchings of it, capable of a very general interest. When, long ago (I am afraid to think how long), Tunbridge Wells was my Switzerland, and I used to be brought down here in the summer, a sufficiently active child, rejoicing in the hope of clambering sandstone cliffs of stupendous height above the common, there used sometimes, as, I suppose, there are in the lives of all children at the Wells, to be dark days in my life—days of condemnation to the pantiles and band—under which calamities my only consolation used to be in watching, at every turn in my walk, the welling forth of the spring over the orange rim of its marble basin. The memory of the clear water, sparkling over its saffron stain came

189

back to me as the strongest image connected with the place; and it struck me that you might not be unwilling, to-night, to think a little over the full significance of that saffron stain, and of the power, in other ways and other functions, of the steely element to which so many here owe returning strength and life;—chief as it has been always, and is yet more and more markedly so day by day, among the precious gifts of the earth.

The subject is, of course, too wide to be more than suggestively treated; and even my suggestions must be few, and drawn chiefly from my own fields of work; nevertheless, I think I shall have time to indicate some courses of thought which you may afterwards follow out for yourselves if they interest you; and so I will not shrink from the full scope of the subject which I have announced to you—the functions of Iron, in Nature, Art, and Policy.

Without more preface, I will take up the first head.

I. IRON IN NATURE.—You all probably know that the ochreous stain, which, perhaps, is often thought to spoil the basin of your spring, is iron in a state of rust: and when you see rusty iron in other places you generally think, not only that it spoils the places it stains, but that it is spoiled itself—that rusty iron is spoiled iron.

For most of our uses it generally is so; and because we cannot use a rusty knife or razor so well as a polished one, we suppose it to be a great defect in iron that it is subject to rust. But not at all. On the contrary, the most perfect and useful state of it is that ochreous stain; and therefore it is endowed with so ready a disposition to get itself into that state. It is not a fault in the iron, but a virtue, to be so fond of getting rusted, for in that condition it fulfils its most important functions in the universe, and most kindly duties to mankind. Nay, in a certain sense, and almost a literal one, we may say that iron rusted is Living; but when pure or polished, Dead. You all probably know that in the mixed air we breathe, the part of it essentially needful to us is called oxygen; and that this substance is to all animals, in the most accurate sense of the word, "breath of life." The nervous power of life is a different thing; but the supporting element of the breath, without which the blood, and therefore the life, cannot be nourished, is this oxygen. Now it is this very same air which the iron breathes when it gets rusty. It takes the oxygen from the atmosphere as eagerly as we do, though it uses it differently. The iron keeps all that it gets; we, and other animals, part with it again; but the metal absolutely keeps what it has once received of this aërial gift; and the ochreous dust which we so much despise is, in fact, just so much nobler than pure iron, in so far as it is *iron and the air*. Nobler, and more useful —for, indeed, as I shall be able to show you presently—the main service of this metal, and of all other metals, to us, is not in making knives, and scissors, and pokers, and pans, but in making the ground we feed from, and nearly all the substances first needful to our existence. For these are all nothing but metals and oxygen—metals with breath put into them. Sand, lime, clay, and the rest of the earths—potash and soda, and the rest of the alkalies—are all of them metals which have undergone this, so to speak, vital change, and have been rendered fit for the service of man by permanent unity with the purest air which he himself breathes. There is only one metal which does not rust readily; and that, in its influence on Man hitherto, has caused Death rather than Life; it will not be put to its right use till it is made a pavement of, and so trodden under foot.

Is there not something striking in this fact, considered largely as one of the types, or lessons, furnished by the inanimate creation? Here you have your hard, bright, cold, lifeless metal—good enough for swords and scissors —but not for food. You think, perhaps, that your iron is wonderfully useful in a pure form, but how would you like the world, if all your meadows, instead of grass, grew nothing but iron wire—if all your arable ground, instead of being made of sand and clay, were suddenly turned into flat surfaces of steel—if the whole earth, instead of its green and glowing sphere, rich with forest and flower, showed nothing but the image of the vast furnace of a ghastly engine—a globe of black, lifeless, excoriated metal? It would be that,—probably it was once that; but assuredly it would be, were it not that all the substance of which it is made sucks and breathes the brilliancy of the atmosphere; and, as it breathes, softening from its merciless hardness, it falls into fruitful and beneficent dust; gathering itself again into the earths from which we feed, and the stones with which we build; —into the rocks that frame the mountains, and the sands that bind the sea.

Hence, it is impossible for you to take up the most insignificant pebble at your feet, without being able to read, if you like, this curious lesson in it. You look upon it at first as if it were earth only. Nay, it answers, "I am not earth—I am earth and air in one; part of that blue heaven which you love, and long for, is already in me; it is all my life—without it I should be nothing, and able for nothing; I could not minister to you, nor nourish you—I should be a cruel and helpless thing; but, because there is, according to my need and place in creation, a kind of soul in me, I have become capable of good, and helpful in the circles of vitality."

Thus far the same interest attaches to all the earths, and all the metals of which they are made; but a deeper interest, and larger beneficence belong to that ochreous earth of iron which stains the marble of your springs. It stains much besides that marble. It stains the great earth wheresoever you can see it, far and wide—it is the colouring substance appointed to colour the globe for the sight, as well as subdue it to the service of man. You have just seen your hills covered with snow, and, perhaps, have enjoyed, at first, the contrast of their fair white with the dark blocks of pine woods; but have you ever considered how you would like them always white—not pure white, but dirty white—the white of thaw, with all the chill of snow in it, but none of its brightness? That is what the colour of the earth would be without its iron; that would be its colour, not here or there only, but in all places,

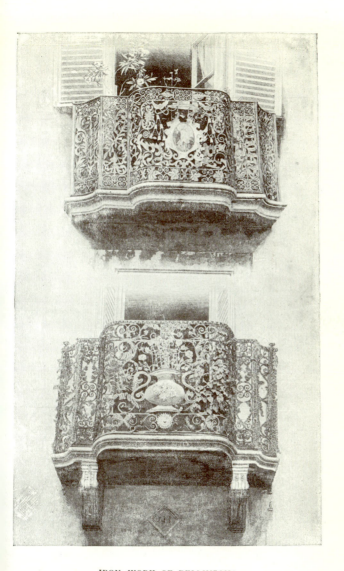

IRON WORK OF BELLINZONA

and at all times. Follow out that idea till you get it in some detail. Think first of your pretty gravel walks in your gardens, yellow and fine, like plots of sunshine between the flower-beds ; fancy them all suddenly turned to the colour of ashes. That is what they would be without iron ochre. Think of your winding walks over the common, as warm to the eye as they are dry to the foot, and imagine them all laid down suddenly with gray cinders. Then pass beyond the common into the country, and pause at the first ploughed field that you see sweeping up the hill sides in the sun, with its deep brown furrows, and wealth of ridges all a-glow, heaved aside by the ploughshare, like deep folds of a mantle of russet velvet—fancy it all changed suddenly into grisly furrows in a field of mud. That is what it would be without iron. Pass on, in fancy, over hill and dale, till you reach the bending line of the sea shore ; go down upon its breezy beach—watch the white foam flashing among the amber of it, and all the blue sea embayed in belts of gold : then fancy those circlets of far sweeping shore suddenly put into mounds of mourning—all those golden sands turned into gray slime ; the fairies no more able to call to each other, "Come unto these yellow sands ;" but, "Come unto these drab sands." That is what they would be, without iron.

Iron is in some sort, therefore, the sunshine and light of landscape, so far as that light depends on the ground ; but it is a source of another kind of sunshine, quite as important to us in the way we live at present—sunshine, not of landscape, but of dwelling-place.

In these days of swift locomotion I may doubtless assume that most of my audience have been somewhere out of England—have been in Scotland, or France, or Switzerland. Whatever may have been their impression, on returning to their own country, of its superiority or inferiority in other respects, they cannot but have felt one thing about it—the comfortable look of its towns and villages. Foreign towns are often very picturesque, very beautiful, but they never have quite that look of warm self-sufficiency and wholesome quiet with which our villages nestle themselves down among the green fields. If you will take the trouble to examine into the sources of this impression, you will find that by far the greater part of that warm and satisfactory appearance depends upon the rich scarlet colour of the bricks and tiles. It does not belong to the neat building—very neat building has an uncomfortable rather than a comfortable look—but it depends on the *warm* building; our villages are dressed in red tiles as our old women are in red cloaks; and it does not matter how worn the cloaks, or how bent and bowed the roof may be, so long as there are no holes in either one or the other, and the sobered but unextinguishable colour still glows in the shadow of the hood, and burns among the green mosses of the gable. And what do you suppose dyes your tiles of cottage roof? You don't paint them. It is nature who puts all that lovely vermilion into the clay for you; and all that lovely vermilion is this oxide of iron. Think, therefore, what your streets of towns would become—ugly enough, indeed, already, some of them, but still comfortable-looking—if instead of that warm brick red, the houses became all pepper-and-salt colour. Fancy your country villages changing from that homely scarlet of theirs which, in its sweet suggestion of laborious peace, is as honourable as the soldiers' scarlet of laborious battle—suppose all those cottage roofs, I say, turned at once into the colour of unbaked clay, the colour of street gutters in rainy weather. That's what they would be, without iron.

There is, however, yet another effect of colour in our English country towns which, perhaps, you may not all yourselves have noticed, but for which you must take the word of a sketcher. They are not so often merely warm scarlet as they are warm purple;—a more beautiful colour still: and they owe this colour to a mingling with the vermilion of the deep grayish or purple hue of our fine Welsh slates on the more respectable roofs, made more blue still by the colour of intervening atmosphere. If

you examine one of these Welsh slates freshly broken, you
will find its purple colour clear and vivid ; and although
never strikingly so after it has been long exposed to
weather, it always retains enough of the tint to give rich
harmonies of distant purple in opposition to the green of
our woods and fields. Whatever brightness or power
there is in the hue is entirely owing to the oxide of iron.
Without it the slates would either be pale stone colour,
or cold gray, or black.

Thus far we have only been considering the use and
pleasantness of iron in the common earth of clay. But
there are three kinds of earth which in mixed mass and
prevalent quantity, form the world. Those are, in
common language, the earths of clay, of lime, and of flint.
Many other elements are mingled with these in sparing
quantities ; but the great frame and substance of the
earth is made of these three, so that wherever you stand
on solid ground, in any country of the globe, the thing
that is mainly under your feet will be either clay, limestone, or some condition of the earth of flint, mingled
with both.

These being what we have usually to deal with, Nature
seems to have set herself to make these three substances
as interesting to us, and as beautiful for us, as she can.
The clay, being a soft and changeable substance, she
doesn't take much pains about, as we have seen, till it is
baked ; she brings the colour into it only when it receives
a permanent form. But the limestone and flint she
paints, in her own way, in their native state : and her
object in painting them seems to be much the same as
in her painting of flowers ; to draw us, careless and idle
human creatures, to watch her a little, and see what she
is about—that being on the whole good for us,—her
children. For Nature is always carrying on very strange
work with this limestone and flint of hers : laying down
beds of them at the bottom of the sea ; building islands
out of the sea ; filling chinks and veins in mountains with
curious treasures ; petrifying mosses, and trees, and shells ;
in fact, carrying on all sorts of business, subterranean

or submarine, which it would be highly desirable for us, who profit and live by it, to notice as it goes on. And apparently to lead us to do this, she makes picture-books for us of limestone and flint ; and tempts us, like foolish children as we are, to read her books by the pretty colours in them.   The pretty colours in her lime-stone-books form those variegated marbles which all mankind have taken delight to polish and build with from the beginning of time ; and the pretty colours in her flint-books form those agates, jaspers, cornelians, blood-stones, onyxes, cairngorms, chrysoprases, which men have in like manner taken delight to cut, and polish, and make ornaments of, from the beginning of time ; and yet, so much of babies are they, and so fond of looking at the pictures instead of reading the book, that I question whether, after six thousand years of cutting and polishing, there are above two or three people out of any given hundred, who know, or care to know, how a bit of agate or a bit of marble was made, or painted.

How it was made, may not be always very easy to say ; but with what it was painted there is no manner of question.   All those beautiful violet veinings and variega-tions of the marbles of Sicily and Spain, the glowing orange and amber colours of those of Siena, the deep russet of the Rosso antico, and the blood-colour of all the precious jaspers that enrich the temples of Italy ; and, finally, all the lovely transitions of tint in the pebbles of Scotland and the Rhine, which form, though not the most precious, by far the most interesting portion of our modern jewellers' work ;—all these are painted by nature with this one material only, variously proportioned and applied—the oxide of iron that stains your Tunbridge springs.

But this is not all, nor the best part of the work of iron.   Its service in producing these beautiful stones is only rendered to rich people, who can afford to quarry and polish them.   But Nature paints for all the world, poor and rich together ; and while, therefore, she thus adorns the innermost rocks of her hills, to tempt your investigation, or indulge your luxury,—she paints, far more carefully, the outsides of the hills, which are for the eyes of the shepherd and the ploughman. I spoke just now of the effect in the roofs of our villages of their purple slates ; but if the slates are beautiful even in their flat and formal rows on house-roofs, much more are they beautiful on the rugged crests and flanks of their native mountains. Have you ever considered, in speaking as we do so often of distant blue hills, what it is that makes them blue? To a certain extent it is distance ; but distance alone will not do it. Many hills look white, however distant. That lovely dark purple colour of our Welsh and Highland hills is owing, not to their distance merely, but to their rocks. Some of their rocks are, indeed, too dark to be beautiful, being black or ashy gray ; owing to imperfect and porous structure. But when you see this dark colour dashed with russet and blue, and coming out in masses among the green ferns, so purple that you can hardly tell at first whether it is rock or heather, then you must thank your old Tunbridge friend, the oxide of iron.

But this is not all. It is necessary for the beauty of hill scenery that Nature should colour not only her soft rocks, but her hard ones ; and she colours them with the same thing, only more beautifully. Perhaps you have wondered at my use of the word "purple," so often of stones ; but the Greeks, and still more the Romans, who had profound respect for purple, used it of stone long ago. You have all heard of "porphyry" as among the most precious of the harder massive stones. The colour which gave it that noble name, as well as that which gives the flush to all the rosy granite of Egypt—yes, and to the rosiest summits of the Alps themselves—is still owing to the same substance—your humble oxide of iron.

And last of all :

A nobler colour than all these—the noblest colour ever seen on this earth—one which belongs to a strength greater than that of the Egyptian granite, and to a beauty greater than that of the sunset or the rose—is still mysteriously connected with the presence of this dark iron. I believe it is not ascertained on what the crimson of blood actually depends; but the colour is connected, of course, with its vitality, and that vitality with the existence of iron as one of its substantial elements.

Is it not strange to find this stern and strong metal mingled so delicately in our human life, that we cannot even blush without its help? Think of it, my fair and gentle hearers; how terrible the alternative—sometimes you have actually no choice but to be brazen-faced, or iron-faced!

In this slight review of some of the functions of the metal, you observe that I confine myself strictly to its operations as a colouring element. I should only confuse your conception of the facts, if I endeavoured to describe its uses as a substantial element, either in strengthening rocks, or influencing vegetation by the decomposition of rocks. I have not, therefore, even glanced at any of the more serious uses of the metal in the economy of nature. But what I wish you to carry clearly away with you is the remembrance that in all these uses the metal would be nothing without the air. The pure metal has no power, and never occurs in nature at all except in meteoric stones, whose fall no one can account for, and which are useless after they have fallen: in the necessary work of the world, the iron is invariably joined with the oxygen, and would be capable of no service or beauty whatever without it.

II. IRON IN ART.—Passing, then, from the offices of the metal in the operations of nature to its uses in the hands of man, you must remember, in the outset, that the type which has been thus given you, by the lifeless metal, of the action of body and soul together, has noble antitype in the operation of all human power. All art worthy the name is the energy—neither of the human body alone, nor of the human soul alone, but of both united, one guiding the other: good craftsmanship and work of the fingers, joined with good emotion and work of the heart.

There is no good art, nor possible judgment of art, when these two are not united; yet we are constantly trying to separate them. Our amateurs cannot be persuaded but that they may produce some kind of art by their fancy or sensibility, without going through the necessary manual toil. That is entirely hopeless. Without a certain number, and that a very great number, of steady acts of hand—a practice as careful and constant as would be necessary to learn any other manual business —no drawing is possible. On the other side, the workman, and those who employ him, are continually trying to produce art by trick or habit of fingers, without using their fancy or sensibility. That also is hopeless. Without mingling of heart-passion with hand-power, no art is possible.[1] The highest art unites both in their intensest degrees: the action of the hand at its finest, with that of the heart at its fullest.

Hence it follows that the utmost power of art can only be given in a material capable of receiving and retaining the influence of the subtlest touch of the human hand. That hand is the most perfect agent of material power existing in the universe; and its full subtlety can only be shown when the material it works on, or with, is entirely yielding. The chords of a perfect instrument will receive it, but not of an imperfect one; the softly bending point of the hair pencil, and soft melting of colour, will receive it, but not even the chalk or pen point, still less the steel point, chisel, or marble. The hand of a sculptor may, indeed, be as subtle as that of a painter, but all its subtlety is not bestowable nor expressible: the touch of Titian, Correggio, or Turner[2] is a far more marvellous piece of nervous action than can be shown in anything but colour, or in the very highest conditions of executive expression in music. In proportion as the

[1] No fine art, that is. See the previous definition of fine art at p. 118.

[2] See Appendix IV. "Subtlety of Hand."

material worked upon is less delicate, the execution necessarily becomes lower, and the art with it. This is one main principle of all work. Another is, that whatever the material you choose to work with, your art is base if it does not bring out the distinctive qualities of that material.

The reason of this second law is, that if you don't want the qualities of the substance you use, you ought to use some other substance : it can be only affectation, and desire to display your skill that lead you to employ a refractory substance, and therefore your art will all be base. Glass, for instance, is eminently, in its nature, transparent. If you don't want transparency, let the glass alone. Do not try to make a window look like an opaque picture, but take an opaque ground to begin with. Again, marble is eminently a solid and massive substance. Unless you want mass and solidity, don't work in marble. If you wish for lightness, take wood ; if for freedom, take stucco ; if for ductility, take glass. Don't try to carve feathers, or trees, or nets, or foam, out of marble. Carve white limbs and broad breasts only out of that.

So again, iron is eminently a ductile and tenacious substance—tenacious above all things, ductile more than most. When you want tenacity, therefore, and involved form, take iron. It is eminently made for that. It is the material given to the sculptor as the companion of marble, with a message, as plain as it can well be spoken, from the lips of the earth-mother, "Here's for you to cut, and here's for you to hammer. Shape this, and twist that. What is solid and simple, carve out ; what is thin and entangled, beat out. I give you all kinds of forms to be delighted in ;—fluttering leaves as well as fair bodies ; twisted branches as well as open brows. The leaf and the branch you may beat and drag into their imagery : the body and brow you shall reverently touch into their imagery. And if you choose rightly and work rightly, what you do shall be safe afterwards. Your slender leaves shall not break off in my tenacious iron, though they may be rusted a little with an iron autumn. Your broad surfaces shall not be unsmoothed in my pure crystalline marble—no decay shall touch them. But if you carve in the marble what will break with a touch, or mould in the metal what a stain of rust or verdigris will spoil, it is your fault—not mine."

These are the main principles in this matter; which, like nearly all other right principles in art, we moderns delight in contradicting as directly and specially as may be. We continually look for, and praise, in our exhibitions, the sculpture of veils, and lace, and thin leaves, and all kinds of impossible things pushed as far as possible in the fragile stone, for the sake of showing the sculptor's dexterity.[1] On the other hand, we *cast* our iron into bars—brittle, though an inch thick—sharpen them at the ends, and consider fences, and other work, made of such materials, decorative! I do not believe it would be easy to calculate the amount of mischief done to our taste in England by that fence iron-work of ours alone. If it were asked of us, by a single characteristic, to distinguish the dwellings of a country into two broad sections; and to set, on one side, the places where people were, for the most part, simple, happy, benevolent, and honest; and, on the other side, the places where at least a great number of the people were sophisticated, unkind, uncomfortable, and unprincipled, there is, I think, one feature that you could fix upon as a positive test: the uncomfortable and unprincipled parts of a country would be the parts where people lived among

[1] I do not mean to attach any degree of blame to the effort to represent leafage in marble for certain expressive purposes. The later works of Mr. Munro have depended for some of their most tender thoughts on a delicate and skilful use of such accessories. And in general, leaf sculpture is good and admirable, if it renders, as in Gothic work, the grace and lightness of the leaf by the arrangement of light and shadow—supporting the masses well by strength of stone below; but all carving is base which proposes to itself *slightness* as an aim, and tries to imitate the absolute thinness of thin or slight things, as much modern wood-carving does. I saw in Italy, a year or two ago, a marble sculpture of birds' nests.

iron railings, and the comfortable and principled parts where they had none. A broad generalization, you will say! Perhaps a little too broad; yet, in all sobriety, it will come truer than you think. Consider every other kind of fence or defence, and you will find some virtue in it; but in the iron railing none. There is, first, your castle rampart of stone—somewhat too grand to be considered here among our types of fencing; next, your garden or park wall of brick, which has indeed often an unkind look on the outside, but there is more modesty in it than unkindness. It generally means, not that the builder of it wants to shut you out from the view of his garden, but from the view of himself: it is a frank statement that as he needs a certain portion of time to himself, so he needs a certain portion of ground to himself, and must not be stared at when he digs there in his shirt-sleeves, or plays at leapfrog with his boys from school, or talks over old times with his wife, walking up and down in the evening sunshine. Besides, the brick wall has good practical service in it, and shelters you from the east wind, and ripens your peaches and nectarines, and glows in autumn like a sunny bank. And, moreover, your brick wall, if you build it properly, so that it shall stand long enough, is a beautiful thing when it is old, and has assumed its grave purple red, touched with mossy green.

Next to your lordly wall, in dignity of enclosure, comes your close-set wooden paling, which is more objectionable, because it commonly means enclosure on a larger scale than people want. Still it is significative of pleasant parks, and well-kept field walks, and herds of deer, and other such aristocratic pastoralisms, which have here and there their proper place in a country, and may be passed without any discredit.

Next to your paling, comes your low stone dyke, your mountain fence, indicative at a glance either of wild hill country, or of beds of stone beneath the soil; the hedge of the mountains—delightful in all its associations, and yet more in the varied and craggy forms of the loose stones it is built of: and next to the low stone wall, your lowland hedge, either in trim line of massive green, suggestive of the pleasances of old Elizabethan houses, and smooth alleys for aged feet, and quaint labyrinths for young ones, or else in fair entanglement of eglantine and virgin's bower, tossing its scented luxuriance along our country waysides : — how many such you have here among your pretty hills, fruitful with black clusters of the bramble for boys in autumn, and crimson hawthorn-berries for birds in winter. And then last, and most difficult to class among fences, comes your handrail, expressive of all sorts of things ; sometimes having a knowing and vicious look, which it learns at race-courses ; sometimes an innocent and tender look, which it learns at rustic bridges over cressy brooks ; and sometimes a prudent and protective look, which it learns on passes of the Alps, where it has posts of granite and bars of pine, and guards the brows of cliffs and the banks of torrents. So that in all these kinds of defence there is some good, pleasant, or noble meaning. But what meaning has the iron railing ? Either, observe, that you are living in the midst of such bad characters that you must keep them out by main force of bar, or that you are yourself of a character requiring to be kept inside in the same manner. Your iron railing always means thieves outside, or Bedlam inside ;—it *can* mean nothing else than that. If the people outside were good for anything, a hint in the way of fence would be enough for them ; but because they are violent and at enmity with you, you are forced to put the close bars and the spikes at the top. Last summer I was lodging for a little while in a cottage in the country, and in front of my low window there were, first, some beds of daisies, then a row of gooseberry and currant bushes, and then a low wall about three feet above the ground, covered with stone-cress. Outside, a corn-field, with its green ears glistening in the sun, and a field path through it, just past the garden gate. From my window I could see every peasant of the village who passed that way, with basket on arm for market, or spade on shoulder for field. When I was inclined for society, I could lean over my wall, and talk to anybody; when I was inclined for science, I could botanize all along the top of my wall—there were four species of stone-cress alone growing on it; and when I was inclined for exercise, I could jump over my wall, backwards and forwards. That's the sort of fence to have in a Christian country; not a thing which you can't walk inside of without making yourself look like a wild beast, nor look at out of your window in the morning without expecting to see somebody impaled upon it in the night.

And yet farther, observe that the iron railing is a useless fence—it can shelter nothing, and support nothing; you can't nail your peaches to it, nor protect your flowers with it, nor make anything whatever out of its costly tyranny; and besides being useless, it is an insolent fence;—it says plainly to everybody who passes—"You may be an honest person,—but, also, you may be a thief: honest or not, you shall not get in here, for I am a respectable person, and much above you; you shall only see what a grand place I have got to keep you out of—look here, and depart in humiliation."

This, however, being in the present state of civilization a frequent manner of discourse, and there being unfortunately many districts where the iron railing is unavoidable, it yet remains a question whether you need absolutely make it ugly, no less than significative of evil. You must have railings round your squares in London, and at the sides of your areas; but need you therefore have railings so ugly that the constant sight of them is enough to neutralise the effect of all the schools of art in the kingdom? You need not. Far from such necessity, it is even in your power to turn all your police force of iron bars actually into drawing masters, and natural historians. Not, of course, without some trouble and some expense; you can do nothing much worth doing, in this world, without trouble, you can get nothing much worth having, without expense. The main question is only—what is worth doing and having :—Consider, therefore, if this be not. Here is your iron railing, as yet, an uneducated monster ; a sombre seneschal, incapable of any words, except his perpetual " Keep out ! " and " Away with you ! " Would it not be worth some trouble and cost to turn this ungainly ruffian porter into a well-educated servant ; who, while he was severe as ever in forbidding entrance to evilly disposed people, should yet have a kind word for well-disposed people, and a pleasant look, and a little useful information at his command, in case he should be asked a question by the passers-by ?

We have not time to-night to look at many examples of ironwork ; and those I happen to have by me are not the best ; ironwork is not one of my special subjects of study ; so that I only have memoranda of bits that happened to come into picturesque subjects which I was drawing for other reasons. Besides, external iron-work is more difficult to find good than any other sort of ancient art ; for when it gets rusty and broken, people are sure, if they can afford it, to send it to the old iron shop, and get a fine new grating instead ; and in the great cities of Italy, the old iron is thus nearly all gone : the best bits I remember in the open air were at Brescia ;—fantastic sprays of laurel-like foliage rising over the garden gates ; and there are a few fine frag-ments at Verona, and some good trellis-work enclosing the Scala tombs ; but on the whole, the most interesting pieces, though by no means the purest in style, are to be found in out-of-the-way provincial towns, where people do not care, or are unable, to make polite alterations. The little town of Bellinzona, for instance, on the south of the Alps, and that of Sion on the north, have both of them complete schools of ironwork in their balconies and vineyard gates. That of Bellinzona is the best, though not very old—I suppose most of it of the seventeenth century ; still it is very quaint and beautiful.

Here, for example, (facing page 192), are two balconies, from two different houses; one has been a cardinal's, and the hat is the principal ornament of the balcony; its tassels being wrought with delightful delicacy and freedom; and catching the eye clearly even among the mass of rich wreathed leaves. These tassels and strings are precisely the kind of subject fit for ironwork—noble in ironwork, they would have been entirely ignoble in marble, on the grounds above stated. The real plant of oleander standing in the window enriches the whole group of lines very happily.

The other balcony, from a very ordinary-looking house in the same street, is much more interesting in its details. It is shown in the plate as it appeared last summer, with convolvulus twined about the bars, the arrow-shaped living leaves mingled among the leaves of iron; but you may see in the centre of these real leaves a cluster of lighter ones, which are those of the ironwork itself. This cluster is worth giving a little larger to show its treatment. Fig. 2 (in Appendix V.) is the front view of it: Fig. 4, its profile. It is composed of a large tulip in the centre; then two turkscap lilies; then two pinks, a little conventionalized; then two narcissi; then two nondescripts, or, at least, flowers I do not know; and then two dark buds, and a few leaves. I say, *dark* buds, for all these flowers have been coloured in their original state. The plan of the group is exceedingly simple: it is all enclosed in a pointed arch (Fig. 3, Appendix V,): the large mass of the tulip forming the apex; a six-foiled star on each side; then a jagged star; then a five-foiled star; then an unjagged star or rose; finally a small bud, so as to establish relation and cadence through the whole group. The profile is very free and fine, and the upper bar of the balcony exceedingly beautiful in effect; —none the less so on account of the marvellously simple means employed. A thin strip of iron is bent over a square rod; out of the edge of this strip are cut a series of triangular openings—widest at top, leaving projecting teeth of iron (Appendix, Fig. 5); then each of these projecting pieces gets a little sharp tap with the hammer in front, which breaks its edge inwards, tearing it a little open at the same time, and the thing is done.

The common forms of Swiss ironwork are less naturalistic than these Italian balconies, depending more on beautiful arrangements of various curve; nevertheless, there has been a rich naturalist school at Fribourg, where a few bell-handles are still left, consisting of rods branched into laurel and other leafage. At Geneva, modern improvements have left nothing; but at Annecy, a little good work remains; the balcony of its old hôtel de ville especially, with a trout of the lake—presumably the town arms—forming its central ornament.

I might expatiate all night—if you would sit and hear me—on the treatment of such required subject, or introduction of pleasant caprice by the old workmen; but we have no more time to spare, and I must quit this part of our subject—the rather as I could not explain to you the intrinsic merit of such ironwork without going fully into the theory of curvilinear design; only let me leave with you this one distinct assertion—that the quaint beauty and character of many natural objects, such as intricate branches, grass, foliage (especially thorny branches and prickly foliage), as well as that of many animals, plumed, spined, or bristled, is sculpturally expressible in iron only, and in iron would be majestic and impressive in the highest degree; and that every piece of metal work you use might be, rightly treated, not only a superb decoration, but a most valuable abstract of portions of natural forms, holding in dignity precisely the same relation to the painted representation of plants, that a statue does to the painted form of man. It is difficult to give you an idea of the grace and interest which the simplest objects possess when their forms are thus abstracted from among the surrounding of rich circumstance which in nature disturbs the feebleness of our attention. In Plate 2 (facing page 209), a few blades of common green grass, and a wild leaf or two—just as they were thrown by nature,—are thus abstracted from the associated redundance of the forms about them, and shown on a dark ground : every cluster of herbage would furnish fifty such groups, and every such group would work into iron (fitting it, of course, rightly to its service) with perfect ease, and endless grandeur of result.

III. IRON IN POLICY.—Having thus obtained some idea of the use of iron in art, as dependent on its ductility, I need not, certainly, say anything of its uses in manufacture and commerce; we all of us know enough,—perhaps a little too much—about *them.* So I pass lastly to consider its uses in policy; dependent chiefly upon its tenacity—that is to say, on its power of bearing a pull, and receiving an edge. These powers, which enable it to pierce, to bind, and to smite, render it fit for the three great instruments, by which its political action may be simply typified; namely, the Plough, the Fetter, and the Sword.

On our understanding the right use of these three instruments, depend, of course, all our power as a nation, and all our happiness as individuals.

1. THE PLOUGH.—I say, first, on our understanding the right use of the plough, with which, in justice to the fairest of our labourers, we must always associate that feminine plough—the needle. The first requirement for the happiness of a nation is that it should understand the function in this world of these two great instruments : a happy nation may be defined as one in which the husband's hand is on the plough, and the housewife's on the needle ; so in due time reaping its golden harvest, and shining in golden vesture : and an unhappy nation is one which, acknowledging no use of plough nor needle, will assuredly at last find its storehouse empty in the famine, and its breast naked to the cold.

Perhaps you think this is a mere truism, which I am wasting your time in repeating. I wish it were.

By far the greater part of the suffering and crime which exist at this moment in civilized Europe, arises simply from people not understanding this truism—not knowing that produce or wealth is eternally connected by the laws

GRASS OF THE FIELD

of heaven and earth with resolute labour; but hoping in some way to cheat or abrogate this everlasting law of life, and to feed where they have not furrowed, and be warm where they have not woven.

I repeat, nearly all our misery and crime result from this one misapprehension. The law of nature is, that a certain quantity of work is necessary to produce a certain quantity of good, of any kind whatever. If you want knowledge, you must toil for it: if food, you must toil for it; and if pleasure, you must toil for it. But men do not acknowledge this law, or strive to evade it, hoping to get their knowledge, and food, and pleasure for nothing; and in this effort they either fail of getting them, and remain ignorant and miserable, or they obtain them by making other men work for their benefit; and then they are tyrants and robbers. Yes, and worse than robbers. I am not one who in the least doubts or disputes the progress of this century in many things useful to mankind; but it seems to me a very dark sign respecting us that we look with so much indifference upon dishonesty and cruelty in the pursuit of wealth. In the dream of Nebuchadnezzar it was only the *feet* that were part of iron and part of clay; but many of us are now getting so cruel in our avarice, that it seems as if, in us, the *heart* were part of iron, part of clay.

From what I have heard of the inhabitants of this town, I do not doubt but that I may be permitted to do here what I have found it usually thought elsewhere highly improper and absurd to do, namely, trace a few Bible sentences to their practical result.

You cannot but have noticed how often in those parts of the Bible which are likely to be oftenest opened when people look for guidance, comfort, or help in the affairs of daily life, namely, the Psalms and Proverbs, mention is made of the guilt attaching to the *Oppression* of the poor. Observe; not the neglect of them, but the *Oppression* of them: the word is as frequent as it is strange. You can hardly open either of those books, but somewhere in their pages you will find a description

I 219

of the wicked man's attempts against the poor : such as
—" He doth ravish the poor when he getteth him into
his net."

" He sitteth in the lurking places of the villages ; his
eyes are privily set against the poor."

" In his pride he doth persecute the poor, and blesseth
the covetous, whom God abhorreth."

" His mouth is full of deceit and fraud ; in the secret
places doth he murder the innocent.   Have the workers
of iniquity no knowledge, who eat up my people as they
eat bread ?   They have drawn out the sword, and bent
the bow, to cast down the poor and needy."

" They are corrupt, and speak wickedly concerning
oppression."

" Pride compasseth them about as a chain, and violence
as a garment."

" Their poison is like the poison of a serpent.   Ye
weigh the violence of your hands in the earth."

Yes :   " Ye weigh the violence of your hands : "—weigh
these words as well.   The last things we ever usually
think of weighing are Bible words.   We like to dream
and dispute over them ; but to weigh them, and see
what their true contents are—anything but that.   Yet,
weigh these ; for I have purposely taken all these verses,
perhaps more striking to you read in this connection,
than separately in their places, out of the Psalms, because, for all people belonging to the Established Church
of this country these Psalms are appointed lessons,
portioned out to them by their clergy to be read once
through every month.   Presumably, therefore, whatever
portions of Scripture we may pass by or forget, these, at
all events, must be brought continually to our observance
as useful for direction of daily life.   Now, do we ever
ask ourselves what the real meaning of these passages
may be, and who these wicked people are, who are
" murdering the innocent ? "   You know it is rather
singular language this !—rather strong language, we
might, perhaps, call it—hearing it for the first time.
Murder ! and murder of innocent people !—nay, even a

sort of cannibalism. Eating people,—yes, and God's people, too—eating *My* people as if they were bread! swords drawn, bows bent, poison of serpents mixed! violence of hands weighed, measured, and trafficked with as so much coin! where is all this going on? Do you suppose it was only going on in the time of David, and that nobody but Jews ever murder the poor? If so, it would surely be wiser not to mutter and mumble for our daily lessons what does not concern us; but if there be any chance that it may concern us, and if this description, in the Psalms, of human guilt is at all generally applicable, as the descriptions in the Psalms of human sorrow are, may it not be advisable to know wherein this guilt is being committed round about us, or by ourselves? and when we take the words of the Bible into our mouths in a congregational way, to be sure whether we mean merely to chant a piece of melodious poetry relating to other people—(we know not exactly to whom) —or to assert our belief in facts bearing somewhat stringently on ourselves and our daily business. And if you make up your minds to do this no longer, and take pains to examine into the matter, you will find that these strange words, occurring as they do, not in a few places only, but almost in every alternate psalm and every alternate chapter of proverb, or prophecy, with tremendous reiteration, were not written for one nation or one time only; but for all nations and languages, for all places and all centuries; and it is as true of the wicked man now as ever it was of Nabal or Dives. that "his eyes are set against the poor."

Set *against* the poor, mind you. Not merely set *away* from the poor, so as to neglect or lose sight of them, but set against, so as to afflict and destroy them. This is the main point I want to fix your attention upon. You will often hear sermons about neglect or carelessness of the poor. But neglect and carelessness are not at all the points. The Bible hardly ever talks about neglect of the poor. It always talks of *oppression* of the poor—a very different matter. It does not merely speak of passing by on the other side, and binding up no wounds, but of drawing the sword and ourselves smiting the men down. It does not charge us with being idle in the pest-house, and giving no medicine, but with being busy in the pest-house, and giving much poison.

May we not advisedly look into this matter a little, even to-night, and ask first, Who are these poor?

No country is, or ever will be, without them : that is to say, without the class which cannot, on the average, do more by its labour than provide for its subsistence, and which has no accumulations of property laid by on any considerable scale. Now there are a certain number of this class whom we cannot oppress with much severity. An able-bodied and intelligent workman—sober, honest, and industrious, will almost always command a fair price for his work, and lay by enough in a few years to enable him to hold his own in the labour market. But all men are not able-bodied, nor intelligent, nor industrious ; and you cannot expect them to be. Nothing appears to me at once more ludicrous and more melancholy than the way the people of the present age usually talk about the morals of labourers. You hardly ever address a labouring man upon his prospects in life, without quietly assuming that he is to possess, at starting, as a small moral capital to begin with, the virtue of Socrates, the philosophy of Plato, and the heroism of Epaminondas. "Be assured, my good man,"—you say to him,—"that if you work steadily for ten hours a day all your life long, and if you drink nothing but water, or the very mildest beer, and live on very plain food, and never lose your temper, and go to church every Sunday, and always remain content in the position in which Providence has placed you, and never grumble, nor swear ; and always keep your clothes decent, and rise early, and use every opportunity of improving yourself, you will get on very well, and never come to the parish."

All this is exceedingly true ; but before giving the advice so confidently, it would be well if we sometimes tried it practically ourselves, and spent a year or so at some hard manual labour, not of an entertaining kind—ploughing or digging, for instance, with a very moderate allowance of beer; nothing but bread and cheese for dinner; no papers nor muffins in the morning; no sofas nor magazines at night; one small room for parlour and kitchen; and a large family of children always in the middle of the floor. If we think we could, under these circumstances, enact Socrates or Epaminondas entirely to our own satisfaction, we shall be somewhat justified in requiring the same behaviour from our poorer neighbours; but if not, we should surely consider a little whether among the various forms of the oppression of the poor, we may not rank as one of the first and likeliest—the oppression of expecting too much from them.

But let this pass; and let it be admitted that we never can be guilty of oppression towards the sober, industrious, intelligent, exemplary labourer. There will always be in the world some who are not altogether intelligent and exemplary; we shall, I believe, to the end of time find the majority somewhat unintelligent, a little inclined to be idle, and occasionally, on Saturday night, drunk; we must even be prepared to hear of reprobates who like skittles on Sunday morning better than prayers; and of unnatural parents who send their children out to beg instead of to go to school.

Now these are the kind of people whom you *can* oppress, and whom you do oppress, and that to purpose,—and with all the more cruelty and the greater sting, because it is just their own fault that puts them into your power. You know the words about wicked people are, " He doth ravish the poor when he getteth him *into his net*." This getting into the net is constantly the fault or folly of the sufferer—his own heedlessness or his own indolence; but after he is once in the net, the oppression of him, and making the most of his distress, are ours. The nets which we use against the poor are just those worldly embarrassments which either their ignorance or their improvidence are almost certain at some time or other to bring them into: then, just at the time when we ought to hasten to help them, and disentangle them, and teach them how to manage better in future, we rush forward to *pillage* them, and force all we can out of them in their adversity. For, to take one instance only, remember this is literally and simply what we do, whenever we buy, or try to buy, cheap goods—goods offered at a price which we know cannot be remunerative for the labour involved in them. Whenever we buy such goods, remember we are stealing somebody's labour. Don't let us mince the matter. I say, in plain Saxon, STEALING—taking from him the proper reward of his work, and putting it into our own pocket. You know well enough that the thing could not have been offered you at that price, unless distress of some kind had forced the producer to part with it. You take advantage of this distress, and you force as much out of him as you can under the circumstances. The old barons of the middle ages used, in general, the thumbscrew to extort property; we moderns use, in preference, hunger, or domestic afflic- tion: but the fact of extortion remains precisely the same. Whether we force the man's property from him by pinching his stomach, or pinching his fingers, makes some differ- ence anatomically;—morally, none whatsoever: we use a form of torture of some sort in order to make him give up his property; we use, indeed, the man's own anxieties, instead of the rack; and his immediate peril of starvation, instead of the pistol at the head; but otherwise we differ from Front de Bœuf, or Dick Turpin, merely in being less dexterous, more cowardly, and more cruel. More cruel, I say, because the fierce baron and the redoubted highwayman are reported to have robbed, at least by pre- ference, only the rich; *we* steal habitually from the poor. We buy our liveries, and gild our prayer-books, with pil- fered pence out of children's and sick men's wages, and thus ingeniously dispose a given quantity of Theft, so that it may produce the largest possible measure of delicately- distributed suffering.

But this is only one form of common oppression of the poor—only one way of taking our hands off the plough- handle, and binding another's upon it. This first way of

doing it is the economical way—the way preferred by
prudent and virtuous people. The bolder way is the ac-
quisitive way :—the way of speculation. You know we are
considering at present the various modes in which a nation
corrupts itself, by not acknowledging the eternal connection between its plough and its pleasure ;—by striving
to get pleasure, without working for it. Well, I say the
first and commonest way of doing so is to try to get the
product of other people's work, and enjoy it ourselves, by
cheapening their labour in times of distress ; then the
second way is that grand one of watching the chances of
the market ;—the way of speculation. Of course there
are some speculations that are fair and honest—speculations made with our own money, and which do not involve
in their success the loss, by others, of what we gain.
But generally modern speculation involves much risk to
others, with chance of profit only to ourselves : even
in its best conditions it is merely one of the forms of
gambling or treasure-hunting : it is either leaving the
steady plough and the steady pilgrimage of life, to look
for silver mines beside the way ; or else it is the full stop
beside the dice-tables in Vanity Fair—investing all the
thoughts and passions of the soul in the fall of the cards,
and choosing rather the wild accidents of idle fortune
than the calm and accumulative rewards of toil. And
this is destructive enough, at least to our peace and
virtue. But is usually destructive of far more than *our*
peace, or *our* virtue. Have you ever deliberately set
yourselves to imagine and measure the suffering, the
guilt, and the mortality caused necessarily by the failure
of any large-dealing merchant, or largely-branched bank ?
Take it at the lowest possible supposition—count, at the
fewest you choose, the families whose means of support
have been involved in the catastrophe. Then, on the
morning after the intelligence of ruin, let us go forth
amongst them in earnest thought ; let us use that imagination which we waste so often on fictitious sorrow, to
measure the stern facts of that multitudinous distress ;
strike open the private doors of their chambers, and enter

silently into the midst of the domestic misery; look upon
the old men, who had reserved for their failing strength
some remainder of rest in the evening-tide of life, cast
helplessly back into its trouble and tumult; look upon
the active strength of middle age suddenly blasted into
incapacity—its hopes crushed, and its hardly-earned
rewards snatched away in the same instant—at once the
heart withered, and the right arm snapped; look upon
the piteous children, delicately nurtured, whose soft eyes,
now large with wonder at their parents' grief, must soon
be set in the dimness of famine; and, far more than all
this, look forward to the length of sorrow beyond—to
the hardest labour of life, now to be undergone either in
all the severity of unexpected and inexperienced trial, or
else, more bitter still, to be begun again, and endured
for the second time, amidst the ruins of cherished hopes
and the feebleness of advancing years, embittered by
the continual sting and taunt of the inner feeling that
it has all been brought about, not by the fair course of
appointed circumstance, but by miserable chance and
wanton treachery; and, last of all, look beyond this—to
the shattered destinies of those who have faltered under
the trial, and sunk past recovery to despair.   And then
consider whether the hand which has poured this poison
into all the springs of life be one whit less guiltily red
with human blood than that which literally pours the
hemlock into the cup, or guides the dagger to the heart?
We read with horror of the crimes of a Borgia or a
Tophana; but there never lived Borgias such as live now
in the midst of us.   The cruel lady of Ferrara slew only
in the strength of passion—she slew only a few, those
who thwarted her purposes or who vexed her soul; she
slew sharply and suddenly, embittering the fate of her
victims with no foretastes of destruction, no prolongations
of pain; and, finally and chiefly, she slew, not without
remorse, nor without pity.   But *we*, in no storm of
passion—in no blindness of wrath,—we, in calm and
clear and untempted selfishness, pour our poison—not
for a few only, but for multitudes;—not for those who

have wronged us, or resisted,—but for those who have trusted us and aided ;—we, not with sudden gift of merciful and unconscious death, but with slow waste of hunger and weary rack of disappointment and despair ;— we, last and chiefly, do our murdering, not with any pauses of pity or scorching of conscience, but in facile and forgetful calm of mind—and so, forsooth, read day by day, complacently, as if they meant any one else than ourselves, the words that for ever describe the wicked : "The *poison of asps* is under their lips, and their *feet are swift to shed blood.*"

You may indeed, perhaps, think there is some excuse for many in this matter, just because the sin is so un-conscious ; that the guilt is not so great when it is unap-prehended, and that it is much more pardonable to slay heedlessly than purposefully. I believe no feeling can be more mistaken, and that in reality, and in the sight of heaven, the callous indifference which pursues its own interests at any cost of life, though it does not definitely adopt the purpose of sin, is a state of mind at once more heinous and more hopeless than the wildest aberrations of ungoverned passion. There may be, in the last case, some elements of good and of redemption still mingled in the character ; but, in the other, few or none. There may be hope for the man who has slain his enemy in anger ;—hope even for the man who has betrayed his friend in fear ; but what hope for him who trades in unregarded blood, and builds his fortune on unrepented treason ?

But, however this may be, and wherever you may think yourselves bound in justice to impute the greater sin, be assured that the question is one of responsibilities only, not of facts. The definite result of all our modern haste to be rich is assuredly, and constantly, the murder of a certain number of persons by our hands every year. I have not time to go into the details of another—on the whole, the broadest and terriblest way in which we cause the destruction of the poor—namely, the way of luxury and waste, destroying, in improvidence, what might have

been the support of thousands ;[1] but if you follow out the
subject for yourselves at home—and what I have endeavoured to lay before you to-night will only be useful
to you if you do—you will find that wherever and
whenever men are endeavouring to *make money hastily*,
and to avoid the labour which Providence has appointed
to be the only source of honourable profit ;—and also
wherever and whenever they permit themselves to *spend
it luxuriously*, without reflecting how far they are misguiding the labour of others ;—there and then, in either
case, they are literally and infallibly causing, for their own
benefit or their own pleasure, a certain annual number of
human deaths ; that, therefore, the choice given to every
man born into this world is, simply, whether he will be a
labourer, or an assassin ; and that whosoever has not his
hand on the Stilt of the plough, has it on the Hilt of the
dagger.

It would also be quite vain for me to endeavour to
follow out this evening the lines of thought which would
be suggested by the other two great political uses of iron
in the Fetter and the Sword : a few words only I must
permit myself respecting both.

2. THE FETTER.—As the plough is the typical instrument of industry, so the fetter is the typical instrument
of the restraint or subjection necessary in a nation—
either literally, for its evil-doers, or figuratively, in
accepted laws, for its wise and good men   You have to
choose between this figurative and literal use ; for depend
upon it, the more laws you accept, the fewer penalties

---

[1] The analysis of this error will be found completely carried out
in my lectures on the political economy of art.   And it is an error
worth analyzing ; for until it is finally trodden under foot, no
healthy political, economical, or moral action is *possible* in any state.
I do not say this impetuously or suddenly, for I have investigated
this subject as deeply, and as long, as my own special subject of
art ; and the principles of political economy which I have stated in
those lectures are as sure as the principles of Euc'id.   Foolish
readers doubted their certainty, because I told them I had "never
read any books on Political Economy."   Did they suppose I had
got **my** knowledge of art by reading books?

you will have to endure, and the fewer punishments to enforce. For wise laws and just restraints are to a noble nation not chains, but chain mail—strength and defence, though something also of an incumbrance. And this necessity of restraint, remember, is just as honourable to man as the necessity of labour. You hear every day greater numbers of foolish people speaking about liberty, as if it were such an honourable thing : so far from being that, it is, on the whole, and in the broadest sense, dishonourable, and an attribute of the lower creatures. No human being, however great, or powerful, was ever so free as a fish. There is always something that he must, or must not do ; while the fish may do whatever he likes. All the kingdoms of the world put together are not half so large as the sea, and all the railroads and wheels that ever were, or will be, invented are not so easy as fins. You will find, on fairly thinking of it, that it is his Restraint which is honourable to man, not his Liberty ; and, what is more, it is restraint which is honourable even in the lower animals. A butterfly is much more free than a bee ; but you honour the bee more, just because it is subject to certain laws which fit it for orderly function in bee society. And throughout the world, of the two abstract things, liberty and restraint, restraint is always the more honourable. It is true, indeed, that in these and all other matters you never can reason finally from the abstraction, for both liberty and restraint are good when they are nobly chosen, and both are bad when they are basely chosen ; but of the two, I repeat, it is restraint which characterizes the higher creature, and betters the lower creature : and, from the ministering of the archangel to the labour of the insect,—from the poising of the planets to the gravitation of a grain of dust,—the power and glory of all creatures, and all matter, consist in their obedience, not in their freedom. The Sun has no liberty—a dead leaf has much. The dust ot which you are formed has no liberty. Its liberty will come—with its corruption.

And, therefore, I say boldly, though it seems a strange

thing to say in England, that as the first power of a nation consists in knowing how to guide the Plough, its second power consists in knowing how to wear the Fetter :—

3. THE SWORD.—And its third power, which perfects it as a nation, consists in knowing how to wield the sword, so that the three talismans of national existence are expressed in these three short words—Labour, Law, and Courage.

This last virtue we at least possess ; and all that is to be alleged against us is that we do not honour it enough. I do not mean honour by acknowledgment of service, though sometimes we are slow in doing even that. But we do not honour it enough in consistent regard to the lives and souls of our soldiers. How wantonly we have wasted their lives you have seen lately in the reports of their mortality by disease, which a little care and science might have prevented ; but we regard their souls less than their lives, by keeping them in ignorance and idleness, and regarding them merely as instruments of battle. The argument brought forward for the maintenance of a standing army usually refers only to expediency in the case of unexpected war, whereas, one of the chief reasons for the maintenance of an army is the advantage of the military system as a method of education. The most fiery and headstrong, who are often also the most gifted and generous of your youths, have always a tendency both in the lower and upper classes to offer themselves for your soldiers : others, weak and unserviceable in a civil capacity, are tempted or entrapped into the army in a fortunate hour for them : out of this fiery or uncouth material, it is only soldier's discipline which can bring the full value and power. Even at present, by mere force of order and authority, the army is the salvation of myriads ; and men who, under other circumstances, would have sunk into lethargy or dissipation, are redeemed into noble life by a service which at once summons and directs their energies. How much more than this military education is capable of doing, you will find only when you make it education indeed. We have no excuse for leaving our private soldiers at their present level of ignorance and want of refinement, for we shall invariably find that, both among officers and men, the gentlest and best informed are the bravest; still less have we excuse for diminishing our army, either in the present state of political events, or, as I believe, in any other conjunction of them that for many a year will be possible in this world.

You may, perhaps, be surprised at my saying this; perhaps surprised at my implying that war itself can be right, or necessary, or noble at all. Nor do I speak of all war as necessary, nor of all war as noble. Both peace and war are noble or ignoble according to their kind and occasion. No man has a profounder sense of the horror and guilt of ignoble war than I have: I have personally seen its effects, upon nations, of unmitigated evil, on soul and body, with perhaps as much pity, and as much bitterness of indignation, as any of those whom you will hear continually declaiming in the cause of peace. But peace may be sought in two ways. One way is as Gideon s ght it, when he built his altar in Ophrah, naming it, "God send peace," yet sought this peace that he loved, as he was ordered to seek it, and the peace was sent, in God's way :—"the country was in quietness forty years in the days of Gideon." And the other way of seeking peace is as Menahem sought it, when he gave the King of Assyria a thousand talents of silver, that "his hand might be with him." That is, you may either win your peace, or buy it :—win it, by resistance to evil ;—buy it, by compromise with evil. You may buy your peace, with silenced consciences ;—you may buy it, with broken vows, — buy it, with lying words,—buy it, with base connivances,—buy it, with the blood of the slain, and the cry of the captive, and the silence of lost souls—over hemispheres of the earth, while you sit smiling at your serene hearths, lisping comfortable prayers evening and morning, and counting your pretty Protestant beads (which are flat, and of gold, instead of round, and of ebony, as the monks' ones were), and so mutter continually to yourselves, " Peace, peace," when there is No peace; but only captivity and death, for you, as well as for those you leave unsaved;—and yours darker than theirs.

I cannot utter to you what I would in this matter; we all see too dimly, as yet, what our great world-duties are, to allow any of us to try to outline their enlarging shadows. But think over what I *have* said, and as you return to your quiet homes to-night, reflect that their peace was not won for you by your own hands; but by theirs who long ago jeoparded their lives for you, their children; and remember that neither this inherited peace, nor any other, can be kept, but through the same jeopardy. No peace was ever won from Fate by subterfuge or agreement; no peace is ever in store for any of us, but that which we shall win by victory over shame or sin;—victory over the sin that oppresses, as well as over that which corrupts. For many a year to come, the sword of every righteous nation must be whetted to save or to subdue; nor will it be by patience of others' suffering, but by the offering of your own, that you will ever draw nearer to the time when the great change shall pass upon the iron of the earth;—when men shall beat their swords into ploughshares, and their spears into pruning-hooks; neither shall they learn war any more.

APPENDICES

TO THE TWO PATHS

APPENDIX I

RIGHT AND WRONG

READERS who are using my " Elements of Drawing " may be surprised by my saying here that Tintoret may lead them wrong ; while at page 196 of the " Elements," he is one of the six men named as being " always right."

I bring the apparent inconsistency forward at the beginning of this Appendix, because the illustration of it will be farther useful in showing the real nature of the self-contradiction which is often alleged against me by careless readers.

It is not only possible, but a frequent condition of human action, to *do* right and *be* right—yet so as to mislead other people if they rashly imitate the thing done. For there are many rights which are not absolutely, but relatively right— right only for *that* person to do under those circumstances,— not for *this* person to do under other circumstances.

Thus it stands between Titian and Tintoret. Titian is always absolutely Right. You may imitate him with entire security that you are doing the best thing that can possibly be done for the purpose in hand. Tintoret is always relatively Right—relatively to his own aims and peculiar powers. But you must quite understand Tintoret before you can be sure what his aim was, and why he was then right in doing what would not be right always. If, however, you take the pains thus to understand him, he becomes entirely instructive and exemplary, just as Titian is ; and therefore I have placed him among those who are " always right," and you can only study him rightly with that reverence for him.

Then the artists who are named as " admitting question or right and wrong," are those who from some mischance of circumstance or short-coming in their education, do not always do right, even with relation to their own aims and powers.

Take for example the quality of imperfection in drawing

form. There are many pictures of Tintoret in which the trees are drawn with a few curved flourishes of the brush instead of leaves. That is (absolutely) wrong. If you copied the tree as a model, you would be going very wrong indeed. But it is relatively, and for Tintoret's purposes, right. In the nature of the superficial work you will find there must have been a cause for it. Somebody perhaps wanted the picture in a hurry to fill a dark corner. Tintoret good-naturedly did all he could—painted the figures tolerably— had five minutes left only for the trees, when the servant came. "Let him wait another five minutes." And this is the best foliage we can do in the time. Entirely, admirably, unsurpassably right, under the conditions. Titian would not have worked under them, but Tintoret was kinder and humbler; yet he may lead you wrong if you don't understand him. Or, perhaps, another day, somebody came in while Tintoret was at work, who tormented Tintoret. An ignoble person! Titian would have been polite to him, and gone on steadily with his trees. Tintoret cannot stand the ignoble-ness; it is unendurably repulsive and discomfiting to him. "The Black P ague take him—and the trees, too! Shall such a fellow see me paint!" And the trees go all to pieces. This, in you, would be mere ill-breeding and ill temper. In Tintoret it was one of the necessary conditions of his intense sensibility; had he been capable, then, of keeping his temper, he could never have done his greatest works. Let the trees go to pieces by all means; it is quite right they should; he is always right.

But in a background of Gainsborough you would find the trees unjustifiably gone to pieces. The carelessness of form there is definitely purposed by him ;—adopted as an advisable thing ; and therefore it is both absolutely and relatively wrong :—it indicates his being imperfectly educated as a painter, and not having brought out all his powers. It may still happen that the man whose work is thus partially erroneous is greater far, than others who have fewer faults. Gainsborough's and Reynolds' wrongs are more charming than almost anybody else's right. Still, they occasionally *are* wrong—but the Venetians and Velasquez,[1] never

I ought, perhaps, to have added in that Manchester address (only one does not like to say things that shock people) some words of warning against painters likely to

---

[1] At least after his style was formed ; early pictures, like the Adoration of the Magi in our Gallery, are of little value.

mislead the student. For indeed, though here and there something may be gained by looking at inferior men, there is always more to be gained by looking at the best ; and there is not time, with all the looking of human life, to exhaust even one great painter's instruction. How then shall we dare to waste our sight and thoughts on inferior ones, even if we could do so, which we rarely can, without danger of being led astray? Nay, strictly speaking, what people call inferior painters are in general *no* painters. Artists are divided by an impassable gulf into the men who can paint, and who cannot. The men who can paint often fall short of what they should have done ;—are repressed, or defeated, or otherwise rendered inferior one to another : still there is an everlasting barrier between them and the men who cannot paint—who can only in various popular ways pretend to paint. And if once you know the difference, there is always some good to be got by looking at a real painter—seldom anything but mischief to be got out of a false one ; but do not suppose real painters are common. I do not speak of living men ; but among those who labour no more, in this England of ours, since it first had a school, we have had only five real painters ;—Reynolds, Gainsborough, Hogarth, Richard Wilson, and Turner.

The reader may, perhaps, think I have forgotten Wilkie. No. I once much overrated him as an expressional draughtsman, not having then studied the figure long enough to be able to detect superficial sentiment. But his colour I have never praised ; it is entirely false and valueless. And it would be unjust to English art if I did not here express my regret that the admiration of Constable, already harmful enough in England, is extending even into France. There was, perhaps, the making, in Constable, of a second or third-rate painter, if any careful discipline had developed in him the instincts which, though unparalleled for narrowness, were, as far as they went, true. But as it is, he is nothing more than an industrious and innocent amateur, blundering his way to a superficial expression of one or two popular aspects of common nature.

And my readers may depend upon it, that all blame which I express in this sweeping way is trustworthy. I have often had to repent of over-praise of inferior men ; and continually to repent of insufficient praise of great men ; but of broad condemnation, never. For I do not speak it but after the most searching examination of the matter, and under stern sense of need for it : so that whenever the reader is entirely shocked by what I say, he may be assured every word is true.[1] It is just because it so much offends him, that it was necessary : and knowing that it must offend him, I should not have ventured to say it, without certainty of its truth. I say "certainty," for it is just as possible to be certain whether the drawing of a tree or a stone is true or false, as whether the drawing of a triangle is ; and what I mean primarily by saying that a picture is in all respects worthless, is that it is in all respects False : which is not a matter of opinion at all, but a matter of ascertainable fact, such as I never assert till I *have* ascertained. And the thing so commonly said about my writings, that they are rather persuasive than just ; and that though my "language" may be good, I am an unsafe guide in art criticism, is, like many other popular estimates in such matters, not merely untrue, but precisely the reverse of the truth ; it is truth, like reflections in water, distorted much by the shaking receptive surface, and in every particular, upside down. For my "language," until within the last six or seven years, was loose, obscure, and more or less feeble ; and still, though I have tried hard to mend it, the best I can do is inferior to much contemporary work. No description that I have ever given of anything is worth four lines of Tennyson ; and in serious thought, my half-pages are generally only worth about as much as a single sentence either of his, or of Carlyle's. They are, I well trust, as true and necessary; but they are neither so concentrated nor so well put. But I am an entirely safe guide in art judgment : and that simply as the necessary result of my having given the labour of life to the determination of facts, rather than to the following of feelings or theories. Not, indeed, that my work is free from mistakes ; it admits many, and always must admit many, from its scattered range ; but, in the long run, it will be found to enter sternly and searchingly into the nature of what it deals with, and the kind of mistake it admits is never dangerous—consisting, usually, in pressing the truth too far. It is quite easy, for instance, to take an accidental irregularity in a piece of architecture, which less careful examination would never have detected at all, for an intentional irregularity ; quite

[1] He must, however, be careful to distinguish blame—however strongly expressed, of some special fault or error in a true painter,—from these general statements of inferiority or worthlessness. Thus he will find me continually laughing at Wilson's tree-painting ; not because Wilson could not paint, but because he had never looked at a tree.

possible to misinterpret an obscure passage in a picture, which a less earnest observer would never have tried to interpret. But mistakes of this kind—honest, enthusiastic mistakes—are never harmful; because they are always made in a true direction,—falls forward on the road, not into the ditch beside it; and they are sure to be corrected by the next comer. But the blunt and dead mistakes made by too many other writers on art—the mistakes of sheer inattention, and want of sympathy—are mortal. The entire purpose of a great thinker may be difficult to fathom, and we may be over and over again more or less mistaken in guessing at his meaning; but the real, profound, nay, quite bottomless, and unredeemable mistake, is the fool's thought —that he had *no* meaning.

I do not refer, in saying this, to any of my statements respecting subjects which it has been my main work to study: as far as I am aware, I have never yet misinterpreted any picture of Turner's, though often remaining blind to the half of what he had intended: neither have I as yet found anything to correct in my statements respecting Venetian architecture;[1] but in casual references to what has been quickly seen, it is impossible to guard wholly against error, without losing much valuable observation, true in ninety-nine cases out of a hundred, and harmless even when erroneous.

APPENDIX II

REYNOLDS' DISAPPOINTMENT

IT is very fortunate that in the fragment of Mason's MSS., published lately by Mr. Cotton in his " Sir Joshua Reynolds' Notes,"[2] record is preserved of Sir Joshua's feelings respecting the paintings in the window of New College, which might otherwise have been supposed to give his full sanction to this mode of painting on glass. Nothing can possibly be

[1] The subtle portions of the Byzantine Palaces, given in precise measurements in the second volume of the " Stones of Venice," were alleged by architects to be accidental irregularities. They will be found, by every one who will take the pains to examine them, most assuredly and indisputably intentional,—and not only so, but one of the principal subjects of the designer's care.

[2] Smith, Soho Square, 1859.

more curious, to my mind, than the great painter's expectations ; or his having at all entertained the idea that the qualities of colour which are peculiar to opaque bodies could be obtained in a transparent medium ; but so it is : and with the simplicity and humbleness of an entirely great man he hopes that Mr. Jervas on glass is to excel Sir Joshua on canvas. Happily, Mason tells us the result.

" With the copy Jervas made of this picture he was grievously disappointed. 'I had frequently,' he said to me, 'pleased myself by reflecting, after I had produced what I thought a brilliant effect of light and shadow on my canvas, how greatly that effect would be heightened by the transparency which the painting on glass would be sure to produce. It turned out quite the reverse.'"

APPENDIX III

CLASSICAL ARCHITECTURE

THIS passage in the lecture was illustrated by an enlargement of the woodcut, fig. 1 ; but I did not choose to disfigure the middle of this book with it. It is copied from the 49th

FIG. I.

plate of the third edition of the " Encyclopædia Britannica" (Edinburgh, 1797), and represents an English farmhouse arranged on classical principles. If the reader cares to consult the work itself, he will find in the same plate another composition of similar propriety, and dignified by the addition of a pediment, beneath the shadow of which " a private gentleman who has a small family may find conveniency."

APPENDIX IV

SUBTLETY OF HAND

I HAD intended in one or other of these lectures to have spoken at some length of the quality of refinement in Colour, but found the subject would lead me too far. A few words are, however, necessary in order to explain some expressions in the text.

"Refinement in colour" is indeed a tautological expression, for colour, in the true sense of the word, does not exist until it *is* refined. Dirt exists, — stains exist, — and pigments exist, easily enough in all places ; and are laid on easily enough by all hands ; but colour exists only where there is tenderness, and can be laid on only by a hand which has strong life in it. The law concerning colour is very strange, very noble, in some sense almost awful. In every given touch laid on canvas, if one grain of the colour is inoperative, and does not take its full part in producing the hue, the hue will be imperfect. The grain of colour which does not work is dead. It infects all about it with its death. It must be got quit of, or the touch is spoiled. We acknowledge this instinctively in our use of the phrases "dead colour," "killed colour," "foul colour." These words are, in some sort, literally true. If more colour is put on than is necessary, a heavy touch when a light one would have been enough, the quantity of colour that was not wanted, and is overlaid by the rest, is as dead, and it pollutes the rest. There will be no good in the touch.

The art of painting, properly so called, consists in laying on the least possible colour that will produce the required result, and this measurement, in all the ultimate, that is to say, the principal, operations of colouring, is so delicate that not one human hand in a million has the required lightness.

The final touch of any painter properly so named, of Correggio
—Titian—Turner—or Reynolds—would be always quite invisible to any one watching the progress of the work, the
films of hue being laid thinner than the depths of the grooves
in mother-of pearl. The work may be swift, apparently careless, nay, to the painter himself almost unconscious. Great
painters are so organized that they do their best work without effort ; but analyze the touches afterwards, and you will
find the structure and depth of the colour laid mathematically
demonstrable to be of literally infinite fineness, the last
touches passing away at their edges by untraceable gradation.
The very essence of a master's work may thus be removed
by a picture-cleaner in ten minutes.

Observe, however, this thinness exists only in portions of
the ultimate touches, for which the preparation may often
have been made with solid colours, commonly, and literally,
called "dead colouring," but even that is always subtle if a
master lays it—subtle at least in drawing, if simple in hue;
and farther, observe that the refinement of work consists not
in laying absolutely *little* colour, but in always laying precisely the right quantity. To lay on little needs indeed
the rare lightness of hand ; but to lay much,—yet not one
atom *too* much, and obtain subtlety, not by withholding
strength, but by precision of pause,—that is the master's
final sign-manual—power, knowledge, and tenderness all
united. A great deal of colour may often be wanted; perhaps quite a mass of it, such as shall project fiom the
canvas ; but the real painter lays this mass of its required
thickness and shape with as much precision as if it were a
bud of a flower which he had to touch into blossom : one of
Turner's loaded fragments of white cloud is modelled and
gradated in an instant, as if it alone were the subject of the
picture, when the same quantity of colour, under another
hand, would be a lifeless lump.

The following extract from a letter in the *Literary Gazette*
of 13th November, 1858, which I was obliged to write to
defend a questioned expression respecting Turner's subtlety
of hand from a charge of hyperbole, contains some interesting
and conclusive evidence on the point, though it refers to
pencil and chalk drawing only :—

"I must ask you to allow me yet leave to reply to the
objections you make to two statements in my catalogue, as
those objections would otherwise diminish its usefulness. I
have asserted that, in a given drawing (named as one of the
chief in the series), Turner's pencil did not move over the

thousandth of an inch without meaning; and you charge this expression with extravagant hyperbole. On the contrary, it is much within the truth, being merely a mathematically accurate description of fairly good execution in either drawing or engraving. It is only necessary to measure a piece of any ordinary good work to ascertain this. Take, for instance, Finden's engraving at the 180th page of Rogers' poems; in which the face of the figure, from the chin to the top of the brow, occupies just a quarter of an inch. and the space between the upper lip and chin as nearly as possible one-seventeenth of an inch. The whole mouth occupies one-third of this space, say one-fiftieth of an inch, and within that space both the lips and the much more difficult inner corner of the mouth are perfectly drawn and rounded, with quite successful and sufficiently subtle expression. Any artist will assure you that in order to draw a mouth as well as this, there must be more than twenty gradations of shade in the touches; that is to say, in this case, gradations changing, with meaning, within less than the thousandth of an inch.

" But this is mere child's play compared to the refinement of any first-rate mechanical work—much more of brush or pencil drawing by a master's hand. In order at once to furnish you with authoritative evidence on this point, I wrote to Mr. Kingsley, tutor of Sidney-Sussex College, a friend to whom I always have recourse when I want to be precisely right in any matter; for his great knowledge both of mathematics and of natural science is joined, not only with singular powers of delicate experimental manipulation, but with a keen sensitiveness to beauty in art. His answer, in its final statement respecting Turner's work, is amazing even to me, and will, I should think, be more so to your readers. Observe the successions of measured and tested refinement : here is No. 1 :—

" ' The finest mechanical work that I know, which is not optical, is that done by Nobert in the way of ruling lines. I have a series ruled by him on glass, giving actual scales from ·000024 and ·000016 of an inch, perfectly correct to these places of decimals, and he has executed others as fine as ·000012, though I do not know how far he could repeat these last with accuracy.'

" This is No. 1, of precision. Mr. Kingsley proceeds to No. 2 :—

" ' But this is rude work compared to the accuracy necessary for the construction of the object-glass of a microscope such as Rosse turns out.'

" I am sorry to omit the explanation which follows of the ten lenses composing such a glass, 'each of which must be exact in radius and in surface, and all have their axes coincident :' but it would not be intelligible without the figure by which it is illustrated ; so I pass to Mr. Kingsley's No. 3 :—

" ' I am tolerably familiar,' he proceeds, ' with the actual grinding and polishing of lenses and specula, and have produced by my own hand some by no means bad optical work, and I have copied no small amount of Turner's work, and *I still look with awe at the combined delicacy and precision of his hand;* IT BEATS OPTICAL WORK OUT OF SIGHT. In optical work, as in refined drawing, the hand goes beyond the eye, an i one has to depend upon the feel ; and when one has once learned what a delicate affair touch is, one gets a horror of all coarse work, and is ready to forgive any amount of feebleness, sooner than that boldness which is akin to impudence. In optics the distinction is easily seen when the work is put to trial ; but here too, as in drawing, it requires an educated eye to tell the difference when the work is only moderately bad ; but with "bold" work, nothing can be seen but distortion and fog ; and I heartily wish the same result would follow the same kind of handling in drawing ; but here, the boldness cheats the unlearned by looking like the precision of the true man. It is very strange how much better our ears are than our eyes in this country : if an ignorant man were to be "bold " with a violin, he would not get many admirers, though his boldness was far below that of ninety nine out of a hundred drawings one sees.'

" The words which I have put in italics in the above extract are those which were surprising to me. I knew that Turner's was as refined as any optical work, but had no idea of its going beyond it. Mr. Kingsley's word ' awe ' occurring just before, is, however, as I have often felt, precisely the right one. When once we begin at all to understand the handling of any truly great executor, such as that of any of the three great Venetians, of Correggio, or Turner, the awe of it is something greater than can be felt from the most stupendous natural scenery. For the creation of such a system as a high human intelligence, endowed with its ineffably perfect instruments of eye and hand, is a far more appalling manifestation of Infinite Power, than the making either of seas or mountains.

" After this testimony to the completion of Turner's work, I need not at length defend myself from the charge of hyper-

bole in the statement that, ' as far as I know, the galleries of
Europe may be challenged to produce one sketch [1] that shall
equal the chalk study No. 45, or the feeblest of the memoranda in the 71st and following frames ;' which memoranda,
however, it should have been observed, are stated at the
44th page to be in some respects ' the grandest work in grey
that he did in his life.' For I believe that, as manipulators,
none but the four men whom I have just named (the three
Venetians and Correggio) were equal to Turner ; and, as far
as I know, none of those four ever put their full strength into
sketches. But whether they did or not, my statement in
the catalogue is limited by my own knowledge : and, as far
as I can trust that knowledge, it is not an enthusiastic statement, but an entirely calm and considered one. It may be
a mistake, but it is not a hyperbole."

APPENDIX V

I CAN only give, to illustrate this balcony, fac-similes of
rough memoranda made on a single leaf of my note-book,
with a tired hand ; but it may be useful to young students to
see them, in order that they may know the difference between notes made to get at the gist and heart of a thing, and
notes made merely to look neat. Only it must be observed
that the best characters of free drawing are always lost even
in the most careful fac-simile ; and I should not show even
these slight notes in wood-cut imitation, unless the reader
had it in his power, by a glance at the 21st or 35th plates in
Modern Painters, (and yet better, by trying to copy a piece
of either of them,) to ascertain how far I can draw or not. I
refer to these plates, because, though I distinctly stated in
the preface that they, together with the 12th, 20th, 34th, and
37th, were executed on the steel by my own hand, (the use
of the dry point in the foregrounds of the 12th and 21st
plates being moreover wholly different from the common

---

[1] A sketch, observe,—not a finished drawing. Sketches are only
proper subjects of comparison with each other when they contain
about the same quantity of work : the test of their merit is the
quantity of truth told with a given number of touches. The assertion in the Catalogue which this letter was written to defend, was
made respecting the sketch of Rome, No. 101.

processes of etching,) I find it constantly assumed that they were engraved for me—as if direct lying in such matters were a thing of quite common usage.

Fig. 2 is the centre-piece of the balcony, but a leaf-spray

FIG. 2.

G. 3.

is omitted on the right-hand side, having been too much buried among the real leaves to be drawn.

Fig. 3 shows the intended general effect of its masses, the five-leaved and six-leaved flowers being clearly distinguishable at any distance.

Fig. 4 is its profile, rather carefully drawn at the top, to show the tulip and turkscap lily leaves. Underneath there is a plate of iron beaten into broad thin leaves, which gives the centre of the balcony a gradual sweep outwards, like the side of a ship of war. The central profile is of the greatest importance in iron-work, as the flow of it affects the curves of the whole design, not merely in surface, as in marble carving, but in their intersections, when the side is seen through the front. The lighter leaves, *b b*, are real bindweed.

Fig. 5 shows two of the teeth of the border, illustrating

Fig. 4.

their irregularity of form, which takes place quite to the
extent indicated.

Fig. 6 is the border at the side of the balcony, showing the most interesting circumstance in the treatment of the whole, namely, the enlargement and retraction of the teeth of the cornice, as it approaches the wall. This treatment

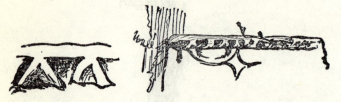

FIG. 5.   FIG. 6.

of the whole cornice as a kind of wreath round the balcony, having its leaves flung loose at the back, and set close at the front, as a girl would throw a wreath of leaves round her hair, is precisely the most finished indication of a good workman's mind to be found in the whole thing.

Fig. 7 shows the outline of the retracted leaves accurately.

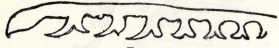

FIG. 7.

It was noted in the text that the whole of this ironwork had been coloured. The difficulty of colouring ironwork rightly, and the necessity of doing it in some way or other, have been the principal reasons for my never having entered heartily into this subject; for all the ironwork I have ever seen look beautiful was rusty, and rusty iron will not answer modern purposes. Nevertheless it may be painted; but it needs some one to do it who knows what painting means, and few of us do—certainly none, as yet, of our restorers of decoration or writers on colour.

It is a marvellous thing to me that book after book should appear on this last subject, without apparently the slightest consciousness on the part of the writers that the first necessity of beauty in colour is gradation, as the first necessity of beauty in line is curvature,—or that the second necessity in colour is mystery or subtlety, as the second necessity in line is softness. Colour ungradated is wholly valueless ; colour unmysterious is wholly barbarous. Unless it loses itself and melts away towards other colours, as a true line loses itself and melts away towards other lines, colour has no proper existence, in the noble sense of the word. What a cube, or tetrahedron, is to organic form, ungradated and unconfused colour is to organic colour ; and a person who attempts to arrange colour harmonies without gradation of tint is in precisely the same category, as an artist who should try to compose a beautiful picture out of an accumulation of cubes and parallelopipeds.

The value of hue in all illuminations on painted glass of fine periods depends primarily on the expedients used to make the colours palpitate and fluctuate ; *inequality* of brilliancy being the *condition* of brilliancy, just as inequality of accent is the condition of power and loveliness in sound. The skill with which the thirteenth century illuminators in books, and the Indians in shawls and carpets, use the minutest atoms of colour to gradate other colours, and confuse the eye, is the first secret in their gift of splendour : associated, however, with so many other artifices which are quite instinctive and unteachable, that it is of little use to dwell upon them. Delicacy of organization in the designer given, you will soon have all, and without it, nothing. However, not to close my book with desponding words, let me set down, as many of us like such things, five Laws to which there is no exception whatever, and which, if they can enable no one to produce good colour, are at least, as far as they reach, accurately condemnatory of bad colour.

1. ALL GOOD COLOUR IS GRADATED. A blush rose (or, better still, a blush itself,) is the type of rightness in arrangement of pure hue.

2. ALL HARMONIES OF COLOUR DEPEND FOR THEIR VITALITY ON THE ACTION AND HELPFUL OPERATION OF EVERY PARTICLE OF COLOUR THEY CONTAIN

3. THE FINAL PARTICLES OF COLOUR NECESSARY TO THE COMPLETENESS OF A COLOUR HARMONY ARE ALWAYS INFINITELY SMALL ; either laid by immeasurably subtle touches of the pencil, or produced by portions of the colouring substance, however distributed, which are so absolutely small as to become at the intended distance infinitely so to the eye.

4. NO COLOUR HARMONY IS OF HIGH ORDER UNLESS IT

INVOLVES INDESCRIBABLE TINTS. It is the best possible sign of a colour when nobody who sees it knows what to call it, or how to give an idea of it to any one else. Even among simple hues the most valuable are those which cannot be defined ; the most precious purples will look brown beside pure purple, and purple beside pure brown ; and the most precious greens will be called blue if seen beside pure green, and green if seen beside pure blue.

5. THE FINER THE EYE FOR COLOUR, THE LESS IT WILL REQUIRE TO GRATIFY IT INTENSELY. But that little must be supremely good and pure, as the finest notes of a great singer, which are so near to silence. And a great colouri t will make even the absence of colour lovely, as the fading of the perfect voice, makes silence sacred.

THE

KING OF THE GOLDEN RIVER

OR

THE BLACK BROTHERS

A LEGEND OF STIRIA

ILLUSTRATED BY RICHARD DOYLE

1851

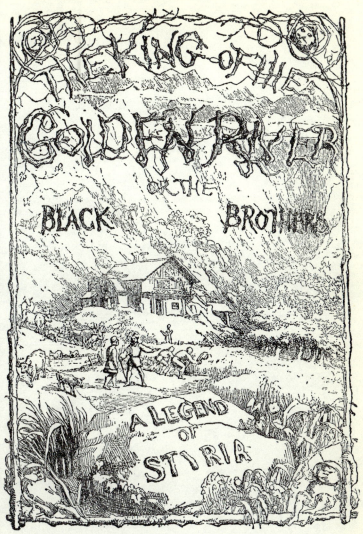

THE KING OF THE
GOLDEN RIVER

OR THE

BLACK BROTHERS

A LEGEND
OF
STIRIA

ADVERTISEMENT

TO FIRST EDITION

THE Publishers think it due to the Author of this Fairy Tale, to state the circumstances under which it appears.

THE KING OF THE GOLDEN RIVER was written in 1841, at the request of a very young lady, and solely for her amusement, without any idea of publication. It has since remained in the possession of a friend, to whose suggestion, and the passive assent of the Author, the Publishers are indebted for the opportunity of printing it.

The Illustrations, by Mr. Richard Doyle, will, it is hoped, be found to embody the Author's ideas with characteristic spirit.

CONTENTS

CHAPTER I

CHAPTER II

CHAPTER III

CHAPTER IV

CHAPTER V

LIST OF ILLUSTRATIONS

DESIGNED AND DRAWN ON WOOD BY
RICHARD DOYLE

NOTE.—The illustrations in this edition have been reproduced from the woodcuts in the original edition.

247

CHAPTER I

HOW THE AGRICULTURAL SYSTEM OF THE BLACK BROTHERS WAS INTERFERED WITH BY SOUTH WEST WIND, ESQUIRE

A secluded and mountainous part of Stiria, there was, in old time, a valley of the most surprising and luxuriant fertility. It was surrounded, on all sides, by steep and rocky mountains, rising into peaks, which were always covered with snow, and from which a number of torrents descended in constant cataracts. One of these fell westward, over the face of a crag so high, that, when the sun had set to everything else, and all below was darkness, his beams still shone full upon this waterfall, so that it looked like a shower of gold. It was, therefore,

called by the people of the neighbourhood, the Golden
River. It was strange that none of these streams fell
into the valley itself. They all descended on the other
side of the mountains, and wound away through broad
plains and by populous cities. But the clouds were
drawn so constantly to the snowy hills, and rested so
softly in the circular hollow, that in time of drought and
heat, when all the country round was burnt up, there
was still rain in the little valley; and its crops were so
heavy, and its hay so high, and its apples so red, and its
grapes so blue, and its wine so rich, and its honey so
sweet, that it was a marvel to every one who beheld it,
and was commonly called the Treasure Valley. The
whole of this little valley belonged to three brothers,
called Schwartz, Hans, and Gluck. Schwartz and Hans,
the two elder brothers, were very ugly men, with over-
hanging eyebrows and small dull eyes, which were always
half shut, so that you couldn't see into *them*, and always
fancied they saw very far into *you*. They lived by
farming the Treasure Valley, and very good farmers they
were. They killed everything that did not pay for its
eating. They shot the blackbirds, because they pecked
the fruit; and killed the hedgehogs, lest they should
suck the cows; they poisoned the crickets for eating the
crumbs in the kitchen, and smothered the cicadas, which
used to sing all summer in the lime trees. They worked
their servants without any wages, till they would not
work any more, and then quarrelled with them, and
turned them out of doors without paying them. It
would have been very odd, if with such a farm, and such
a system of farming, they hadn't got very rich; and very
rich they *did* get. They generally contrived to keep
their corn by them till it was very dear, and then sell it
for twice its value; they had heaps of gold lying about on
their floors, yet it was never known that they had given
so much as a penny or a crust in charity; they never
went to mass; grumbled perpetually at paying tithes;
and were, in a word, of so cruel and grinding a temper,
as to receive from all those with whom they had any

dealings, the nick-name of the " Black Brothers." The youngest brother, Gluck, was as completely opposed, in both appearance and character, to his seniors as could possibly be imagined or desired. He was not above twelve years old, fair, blue eyed, and kind in temper to every living thing. He did not, of course, agree particularly well with his brothers, or rather, they did not agree with *him*. He was usually appointed to the honourable office of turnspit, when there was anything to roast, which was not often ; for, to do the brothers justice, they were hardly less sparing upon themselves than upon other people. At other times he used to clean the shoes, floors, and sometimes the plates, occasionally getting what was left on them, by way of encouragement, and a wholesome quantity of dry blows, by way of education.

Things went on in this manner for a long time. At last came a very wet summer, and everything went wrong in the country round. The hay had hardly been got in, when the haystacks were floated bodily down to the sea by an inundation ; the vines were cut to pieces with the hail ; the corn was all killed by a black blight ; only in the Treasure Valley, as usual, all was safe. As it had rain when there was rain no where else, so it had sun when there was sun no where else. Every body came to buy corn at the fa m, and went away pouring maledictions on the Black Brothers. They asked what they liked, and got it, except from the poor people, who could only beg, and several of whom were starved at their very door, without the slightest regard or notice.

It was drawing towards winter, and very cold weather, when one day the two elder brothers had gone out, with their usual warning to little Gluck, who was left to mind the roast, that he was to let nobody in, and give nothing out. Gluck sat down quite close to the fire, for it was raining very hard, and the kitchen walls were by no means dry or comfortable looking. He turned and turned, and the roast got nice and brown. " What a pity," thought Gluck, " my brothers never ask any body to dinner. I'm sure, when they've got such a nice piece of mutton as this, and nobody else has got so much as a piece of dry bread, it would do their hearts good to have somebody to eat it with them."

Just as he spoke, there came a double knock at the house door, yet heavy and dull, as though the knocker had been tied up—more like a puff than a knock. "It must be the wind," said Gluck; "nobody else would venture to knock double knocks at our door." No it wasn't the wind : there it came again very hard, and what was particularly astounding, the knocker seemed to be in a hurry, and not to be in the least afraid of the consequences. Gluck went to the window, opened it, and put his head out to see who it was. It was the most extraordinary looking little gentleman he had ever seen in his life. He had a very long nose, slightly brass-coloured, and expanding towards its termination into a development not unlike the lower extremity of a key bugle. His cheeks were very round, and very red, and might have warranted a supposition that he had been blowing a refractory fire for the last eight-and-forty hours. His eyes twinkled merrily through long silky eyelashes, his mustaches curled twice round like a cork-screw on each side of his mouth, and his hair, of a curious mixed pepper and salt colour, descended far over his shoulders. He was about four feet six in height, and wore a conical pointed cap of nearly the same altitude, decorated with a black feather some three feet long. His doublet was prolonged behind into something resembling a violent exaggeration of what is now termed a "swallow tail," but was much obscured by the swelling folds of an enormous black, glossy looking cloak, which must have been very much too long in calm weather, as the wind, whistling round the old house, carried it clear out from the wearer's shoulders to about four times his own length.

Gluck was so perfectly paralyzed by the singular ap-pearance of his visitor, that he remained fixed without uttering a word, until the old gentleman, having per-formed another, and a more energetic concerto on the

knocker, turned round to look after his fly-away cloak.
In so doing he caught sight of Gluck's little yellow head
jammed in the window, with its mouth and eyes very
wide open indeed.

"Hollo!" said the little gentleman, "that's not the
way to answer the door: I'm wet, let me in."

To do the little gentleman justice, he *was* wet. His
feather hung down between his legs like a beaten puppy's
tail, dripping like an umbrella; and from the ends of his
mustaches the water was running into his waistcoat
pockets, and out again like a mill stream.

"I beg pardon, sir," said Gluck, "I'm very sorry, but
I really can't."

"Can't what?" said the old gentleman.

"I can't let you in, sir,—I can't indeed; my brothers
would beat me to death, sir, if I thought of such a thing.
What do you want, sir?"

"Want?" said the old gentleman petulantly. "I want
fire, and shelter; and there's your great fire there blazing,
crackling, and dancing on the walls, with nobody to
feel it. Let me in I say; I only want to warm
myself."

Gluck had had his head, by this time, so long out of
the window, that he began to feel it was really un-
pleasantly cold, and when he turned, and saw the beautiful
fire rustling and roaring, and throwing long bright tongues
up the chimney, as if it were licking its chops at the
savoury smell of the leg of mutton, his heart melted within
him that it should be burning away for nothing. "He
does look *very* wet," said little Gluck; "I'll just let him
in for a quarter of an hour." Round he went to the door,
and opened it; and as the little gentleman walked in,
there came a gust of wind through the house, that made
the old chimneys totter.

"That's a good boy," said the little gentleman.
"Never mind your brothers. I'll talk to them."

"Pray, sir, don't do any such thing;" said Gluck. "I
can't let you stay till they come; they'd be the death of
me."

"Dear me," said the old gentleman, "I'm very sorry to hear that. How long may I stay?"

"Only till the mutton's done, sir," replied Gluck, "and it's very brown."

Then the old gentleman walked into the kitchen, and sat himself down on the hob, with the top of his cap accommodated up the chimney, for it was a great deal too high for the roof.

"You'll soon dry there, sir," said Gluck, and sat down

again to turn the mutton. But the old gentleman did *not* dry there, but went on drip, drip, dripping among the cinders, and the fire fizzed, and sputtered, and began to look very black, and uncomfortable; never was such a cloak; every fold in it ran like a gutter.

"I beg pardon, sir," said Gluck at length, after watching the water spreading in long, quick-silver like streams over the floor for a quarter of an hour; "mayn't I take your cloak?"

"No, thank you," said the old gentleman.

"Your cap, sir?"

"I am all right, thank you," said the old gentleman rather gruffly.

"But,—sir,—I'm very sorry," said Gluck, hesitatingly; "but—really, sir,—you're—putting the fire out."

"It'll take longer to do the mutton then," replied his visitor drily.

Gluck was very much puzzled by the behaviour of his guest; it was such a strange mixture of coolness and humility. He turned away at the string meditatively for another five minutes.

"That mutton looks very nice," said the old gentleman at length. "Can't you give me a little bit?"

"Impossible, sir," said Gluck.

"I'm very hungry," continued the old gentleman. "I've had nothing to eat yesterday, nor to-day. They surely couldn't miss a bit from the knuckle!"

He spoke in so very melancholy a tone, that it quite melted Gluck's heart. "They promised me one slice to-day, sir," said he. "I can give you that, but not a bit more."

"That's a good boy," said the old gentleman again.

Then Gluck warmed a plate, and sharpened a knife. "I don't care if I do get beaten for it," thought he. Just as he had cut a large slice out of the mutton, there came a tremendous rap at the door. The old gentleman jumped off the hob, as if it had suddenly become inconveniently warm. Gluck fitted the slice into the mutton again, with desperate efforts at exactitude, and ran to open the door.

"What did you keep us waiting in the rain for?" said Schwartz, as he walked in, throwing his umbrella in Gluck's face. "Ay! what for, indeed, you little vagabond?" said Hans, administering an educational box on the ear, as he followed his brother into the kitchen.

"Bless my soul!" said Schwartz when he opened the door.

"Amen," said the little gentleman, who had taken his

cap off, and was standing in the middle of the kitchen, bowing with the utmost possible velocity.

"Who's that?" said Schwartz, catching up a rolling-pin, and turning to Gluck with a fierce frown.

"I don't know, indeed, brother," said Gluck in great terror.

"How did he get in?" roared Schwartz.

"My dear brother," said Gluck, deprecatingly, "he was so *very* wet!"

The rolling-pin was descending on Gluck's head; but, at the instant, the old gentleman interposed his conical cap, on which it crashed with a shock that shook the water out of it all over the room. What was very odd, the rolling-pin no sooner touched the cap, than it flew out of Schwartz's hand, spinning like a straw in a high wind, and fell into the corner at the further end of the room.

"Who are you, sir?" demanded Schwartz, turning upon him.

"What's your business?" snarled Hans.

"I'm a poor old man, sir," the little gentleman began

very modestly, "and I saw your fire through the window, and begged shelter for a quarter of an hour."

"Have the goodness to walk out again, then," said Schwartz. "We've quite enough water in our kitchen, without making it a drying house."

"It is a cold day to turn an old man out in, sir; look at my grey hairs." They hung down to his shoulders, as I told you before.

"Ay!" said Hans, "there are enough of them to keep you warm. Walk!"

"I'm very, very hungry, sir; couldn't you spare me a bit of bread before I go?"

"Bread, indeed!" said Schwartz; "do you suppose we've nothing to do with our bread, but to give it to such red-nosed fellows as you?"

"Why don't you sell your feather?" said Hans, sneeringly. "Out with you."

"A little bit," said the old gentleman.

"Be off!" said Schwartz.

"Pray, gentlemen."

"Off, and be hanged!" cried Hans, seizing him by the collar. But he had no sooner touched the old gentleman's collar, than away he went after the rolling-pin, spinning round and round, till he fell into the corner on the top of it. Then Schwartz was very angry, and ran at the old gentleman to turn him out; but he also had hardly touched him, when away he went after Hans and the rolling-pin, and hit his head against the wall as he tumbled into the corner. And so there they lay, all three.

Then the old gentleman spun himself round with velocity in the opposite direction; continued to spin until his long cloak was all wound neatly about him; clapped his cap on his head, very much on one side, (for it could not stand upright without going through the ceiling,) gave an additional twist to his cork-screw mustaches, and replied with perfect coolness: "Gentlemen, I wish you a very good morning. At twelve o'clock to-night, I'll call again; after such a refusal of hospitality as I have just experienced, you will not be surprised if that visit is the last I ever pay you."

"If ever I catch you here again," muttered Schwartz, coming half frightened, out of the corner—but, before he could finish his sentence, the old gentleman had shut the house door behind him with a great bang: and there drove past the window, at the same instant, a wreath of ragged cloud, that whirled and rolled away down the valley in all manner of shapes; turning over and over in the air; and melting away at last in a gush of rain.

"A very pretty business, indeed, Mr. Gluck!" said Schwartz. "Dish the mutton, sir. If ever I catch you at such a trick again—bless me, why the mutton's been cut!"

"You promised me one slice, brother, you know," said Gluck.

"Oh! and you were cutting it hot, I suppose, and going to catch all the gravy. It'll be long before I promise you such a thing again. Leave the room, sir; and have the kindness to wait in the coal-cellar till I call you."

Gluck left the room, melancholy enough. The brothers ate as much mutton as they could, locked the rest in the cupboard, and proceeded to get very drunk after dinner.

Such a night as it was! Howling wind, and rushing rain, without intermission. The brothers had just sense enough left to put up all the shutters, and double bar the door, before they went to bed. They usually slept in the same room. As the clock struck twelve, they were both awakened by a tremendous crash. Their door burst open with a violence that shook the house from top to bottom.

"What's that?" cried Schwartz, starting up in his bed.

"Only I," said the little gentleman.

The two brothers sat up on their bolster, and stared into the darkness. The room was full of water, and by a misty moon-beam, which found its way through a hole in the shutter, they could see in the midst of it, an enormous foam globe, spinning round, and bobbing up and down like a cork, on which, as on a most luxurious cushion, reclined the little old gentleman, cap and all. There was plenty of room for it now, for the roof was off.

"Sorry to incommode you," said their visitor, ironically. " I'm afraid your beds are dampish; perhaps you had better go to your brother's room: I've left the ceiling on, there."

They required no second admonition, but rushed into Gluck's room, wet through, and in an agony of terror.

"You'll find my card on the kitchen table," the old gentleman called after them. "Remember, the *last* visit."

"Pray Heaven it may!" said Schwartz, shuddering. And the foam globe disappeared.

Dawn came at last, and the two brothers looked out of Gluck's little window in the morning. The Treasure Valley was one mass of ruin, and desolation. The inundation had swept away trees, crops, and cattle, and left in their stead, a waste of red sand, and grey mud.

The two brothers crept shivering and horror-struck into the kitchen. The water had gutted the whole first floor; corn, money, almost every moveable thing had been swept away, and there was left only a small white card on the kitchen table. On it, in large, breezy, long-legged letters, were engraved the words:—

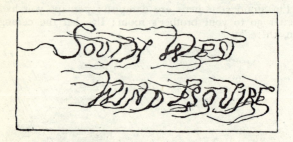

CHAPTER II

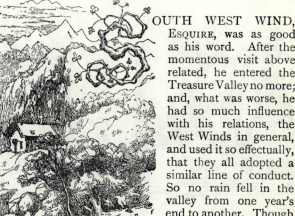

OUTH WEST WIND, ESQUIRE, was as good as his word. After the momentous visit above related, he entered the Treasure Valley no more; and, what was worse, he had so much influence with his relations, the West Winds in general, and used it so effectually, that they all adopted a similar line of conduct. So no rain fell in the valley from one year's end to another. Though everything remained green and flourishing in the plains below, the inheritance of the Three Brothers was a desert. What had once been the richest soil in the kingdom, became a shifting heap of red sand; and the brothers, unable longer to contend with the adverse skies, abandoned their valueless patrimony in despair, to seek some means of gaining a livelihood among the cities and people of the plains. All their money was gone, and they had nothing left but some curious old-fashioned pieces of gold plate, the last remnants of their ill-gotten wealth.

"Suppose we turn goldsmiths?" said Schwartz to Hans, as they entered the large city. "It is a good knave's trade; we can put a great deal of copper into the gold, without any one's finding it out."

The thought was agreed to be a very good one; they hired a furnace, and turned goldsmiths. But two slight circumstances affected their trade: the first, that people did not approve of the coppered gold; the second, that the two elder brothers, whenever they had sold anything, used to leave little Gluck to mind the furnace, and go

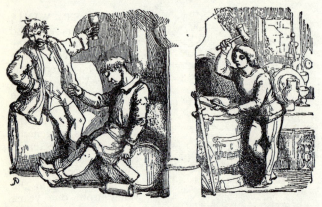

and drink out the money in the ale-house next door. So they melted all their gold, without making money enough to buy more, and were at last reduced to one large drinking-mug, which an uncle of his had given to little Gluck, and which he was very fond of, and would not have parted with for the world; though he never drank anything out of it but milk and water. The mug was a very odd mug to look at. The handle was formed of two wreaths of flowing golden hair, so finely spun that it looked more like silk than metal, and these wreaths descended into, and mixed with a beard and whiskers, of the same exquisite workmanship, which surrounded

and decorated a very fierce little face, of the reddest
gold imaginable, right in the front of the mug, with
a pair of eyes in it which seemed to command its whole
circumference. It was impossible to drink out of the
mug without being subjected to an intense gaze out
of the side of these eyes; and Schwartz positively
averred, that once, after emptying it, full of Rhenish
seventeen times, he had seen them wink! When it
came to the mug's turn to be made into spoons, it
half broke poor little Gluck's heart; but the brothers
only laughed at him, tossed the mug into the melting pot, and staggered out to the ale-house; leaving
him, as usual, to pour the gold into bars, when it was
all ready.

When they were gone, Gluck took a farewell look at
his old friend in the melting-pot. The flowing hair was
all gone; nothing remained but the red nose, and the
sparkling eyes, which looked more malicious than ever.
"And no wonder," thought Gluck, "after being treated
in that way." He sauntered
disconsolately to the window,
and sat himself down to catch
the fresh evening air, and
escape the hot breath of the
furnace. Now this window
commanded a direct view of
the range of mountains, which,
as I told you before, overhung
the Treasure Valley, and
more especially of the peak from
which fell the Golden River.
It was just at the close of the
day, and, when Gluck sat down
at the window, he saw the
rocks of the mountain tops, all crimson, and purple with
the sunset; and there were bright tongues of fiery
cloud burning and quivering about them; and the river,
brighter than all, fell, in a waving column of pure gold,
from precipice to precipice, with the double arch of

a broad purple rainbow stretched across it, flushing and
fading alternately in the wreaths of spray.

"Ah!" said Gluck aloud, after he had looked at it for
a little while, "if that river were really all gold, what
a nice thing it would be."

"No it wouldn't, Gluck," said a clear metallic voice,
close at his ear.

"Bless me, what's that?" exclaimed Gluck, jumping
up. There was nobody there. He looked round the
room, and under the table, and a great many times
behind him, but there was certainly nobody there, and
he sat down again at the window. This time he didn't
speak, but he couldn't help thinking again that it would
be very convenient if the river were really all gold.

"Not at all, my boy," said the same voice, louder
than before.

"Bless me!" said Gluck again, "what *is* that?" He
looked again into all the corners, and cupboards, and
then began turning round, and round, as fast as he
could, in the middle of the room, thinking there was
somebody behind him, when the same voice struck
again on his ear. It was singing now very merrily
"Lala-lira-la;" no words, only a soft running effervescent
melody, something like that of a kettle on the boil.
Gluck looked out of the window. No, it was certainly
in the house. Up stairs, and down stairs. No, it was
certainly in that very room, coming in quicker time, and
clearer notes, every moment. "Lala-lira-la." All at
once it struck Gluck, that it sounded louder near the
furnace. He ran to the opening, and looked in: yes,
he saw right, it seemed to be coming, not only out of
the furnace, but out of the pot. He uncovered it, and
ran back in a great fright, for the pot was certainly
singing! He stood in the farthest corner of the room,
with his hands up, and his mouth open, for a minute
or two, when the singing stopped, and the voice became
clear, and pronunciative.

"Hollo!" said the voice.

Gluck made no answer.

"Hollo! Gluck, my boy," said the pot again.

Gluck summoned all his energies, walked straight up to the crucible, drew it out of the furnace, and looked in. The gold was all melted, and its surface as smooth and polished as a river; but instead of reflecting little Gluck's head, as he looked in, he saw meeting his glance, from beneath the gold, the red nose, and sharp eyes of his old friend of the mug, a thousand times redder, and sharper than ever he had seen them in his life.

"Come Gluck, my boy," said the voice out of the pot again, " I'm all right; pour me out."

But Gluck was too much astonished to do anything of the kind.

"Pour me out, I say," said the voice rather gruffly.

Still Gluck couldn't move.

" *Will* you pour me out?" said the voice passionately, "I'm too hot."

By a violent effort, Gluck recovered the use of his limbs, took hold of the crucible, and sloped it, so as to pour out the gold. But instead of a liquid stream, there came out, first, a pair of pretty little yellow legs, then some coat tails, then a pair of arms stuck a kimbo, and, finally, the well known head of his friend the mug; all which articles, uniting as they rolled out, stood up energetically on the floor, in the shape of a little golden dwarf, about a foot and a half high.

"That's right!" said the dwarf, stretching out first his legs, and then his arms, and then shaking his head up and down, and as far round as it would go, for five minutes, without stopping; apparently with the view of ascertaining if he were quite correctly put together, while Gluck stood contemplating him in speechless amazement. He was dressed in a slashed doublet of spun gold, so fine in its texture, that the prismatic colours gleamed over it, as if on a surface of mother of pearl; and, over this brilliant doublet, his hair and beard fell full half way to the ground, in waving curls, so exquisitely delicate, that Gluck could hardly tell where they ended; they seemed to melt into air. The features of the face, however, were by no means finished with the same delicacy; they were rather coarse, slightly inclining to coppery in complexion, and indicative, in expression, of a very pertinacious and intractable disposition in their small proprietor. When the dwarf had finished

his self-examination, he turned his small sharp eyes full on Gluck, and stared at him deliberately for a minute or two. "No it wouldn't, Gluck, my boy," said the little man.

This was certainly rather an abrupt, and unconnected mode of commencing conversation. It might indeed be supposed to refer to the course of Gluck's thoughts, which had first produced the dwarf's observations out of the pot; but whatever it referred to, Gluck had no inclination to dispute the dictum.

"Wouldn't it, sir?" said Gluck, very mildly, and submissively indeed.

"No," said the dwarf, conclusively. "No it wouldn't." And with that, the dwarf pulled his cap hard over his brows, and took two turns, of three feet long, up and down the room, lifting his legs up very high, and setting them down very hard. This pause gave time for Gluck to collect his thoughts a little; and, seeing no great reason to view his diminutive visitor with dread, and feeling his curiosity overcome his amazement, he ventured on a question of peculiar delicacy.

"Pray, sir," said Gluck, rather hesitatingly, "were you my mug?"

On which the little man turned sharp round, walked straight up to Gluck, and drew himself up to his full height. "I," said the little man, "am the King of the Golden River." Whereupon he turned about again, and took two more turns, some six feet long, in order to allow time for the consternation which this announcement produced in his auditor to evaporate. After which, he again walked up to Gluck and stood still, as if expecting some comment on his communication.

Gluck determined to say something at all events. "I hope your majesty is very well," said Gluck.

"Listen!" said the little man, deigning no reply to this polite inquiry. "I am the King of what you mortals call the Golden River. The shape you saw me in, was owing to the malice of a stronger king, from whose enchantments you have this instant freed me. What I have seen of you, and your conduct to your wicked brothers, renders me willing to serve you; therefore attend to what I tell you. Whoever shall climb to the top of that mountain from which you see the Golden River issue, and shall cast into the stream at its source, three drops of holy water, for him, and for him only, the river shall turn to gold. But no one failing in his first, can succeed in a second attempt; and if any one shall cast unholy water into the river, it will overwhelm him, and he will become a black stone." So saying, the King of the Golden River turned away, and deliberately walked into the centre of the hottest flame of the furnace. His figure became red, white, transparent, dazzling—a blaze of intense light—rose, trembled, and disappeared. The King of the Golden River had evaporated.

"Oh!" cried poor Gluck, running to look up the chimney after him; "Oh, dear, dear, dear me! My mug! my mug! my mug!"

CHAPTER III

HOW MR. HANS SET OFF ON AN EXPEDITION TO THE
GOLDEN RIVER, AND HOW HE PROSPERED THEREIN

THE King of the Golden River had hardly made the extraordinary exit related in the last chapter, before Hans and Schwartz came roaring into the house, very savagely drunk. The discovery of the total loss of their last piece of plate had the effect of sobering them just enough to enable them to stand over Gluck, beating him very steadily for a quarter of an hour; at the expiration of which period they dropped into a couple of chairs, and requested to know what he had got to say for himself. Gluck told them his story, of which of course they did not believe a word. They beat him again, till their arms were tired, and staggered to bed. In the morning, however, the steadiness with which he adhered to his story obtained him some degree of credence; the immediate consequence of which was, that the two brothers, after wrangling a long time on the knotty question, which of them should try his fortune first, drew their swords, and began fighting. The noise of the fray alarmed the neighbours, who, finding they could not pacify the combatants, sent for the constable.

Hans, on hearing this, contrived to escape, and hid

himself; but Schwartz was taken before the magistrate, fined for breaking the peace, and, having drunk out his last

penny the evening before, was thrown into prison till he should pay.

When Hans heard this, he was much delighted, and determined to set out immediately for the Golden River.

How to get the holy water, was the question. He went to the priest, but the priest could not give any holy water to so abandoned a character. So Hans went to vespers in the evening for the first time in his life, and, under pretence of crossing himself, stole a cupful, and returned home in triumph.

Next morning he got up before the sun rose, put the holy water into a strong flask, and two bottles of wine and some meat in a basket, slung them over his back, took his alpine staff in his hand, and set off for the mountains.

On his way out of the town he had to pass the prison, and as he looked in at the windows, whom should he see but Schwartz himself peeping out of the bars, and looking very disconsolate.

"Good morning, brother," said Hans; "have you any message for the King of the Golden River?"

Schwartz gnashed his teeth with rage, and shook the bars with all his strength; but Hans only laughed at him, and, advising him to make himself comfortable till he came back again, shouldered his basket, shook the bottle of holy water in Schwartz's face till it frothed again, and marched off in the highest spirits in the world.

It was, indeed, a morning that might have made any one happy, even with no Golden River to seek for. Level lines of dewy mist lay stretched along the valley, out of which rose the massy mountains—their lower cliffs in pale grey shadow, hardly distinguishable from the floating vapour, but gradually ascending till they caught the sunlight, which ran in sharp touches of ruddy colour, along the angular crags, and pierced, in long level rays, through their fringes of spear-like pine. Far above, shot up red splintered masses of castellated rock, jagged and shivered into myriads of fantastic forms, with here and there a streak of sunlit snow, traced down their chasms like a line of forked lightning; and, far beyond, and far above all these, fainter than the morning cloud, but purer and changeless, slept, in the blue sky, the utmost peaks of the eternal snow.

The Golden River, which sprang from one of the lower and snowless elevations, was now nearly in shadow; all but the uppermost jets of spray, which rose like slow smoke above the undulating line of the cataract, and floated away in feeble wreaths upon the morning wind.

On this object, and on this alone, Hans' eyes and

thoughts were fixed ; forgetting the distance he had to traverse, he set off at an imprudent rate of walking, which greatly exhausted him before he had scaled the first range of the green and low hills.   He was, moreover, surprised, on surmounting them, to find that a large glacier, of whose existence, notwithstanding his previous knowledge of the mountains, he had been absolutely ignorant, lay between him and the source of the Golden River.   He entered on it with the boldness of a practised mountaineer ; yet he thought he had never traversed so strange, or so dangerous a glacier in his life.   The ice was excessively slippery, and out of all its chasms came wild sounds of gushing water ; not monotonous or low, but changeful and loud, rising occasionally into drifting passages of wild melody, then breaking off into short, melancholy tones, or sudden shrieks, resembling those of human voices in distress or pain.   The ice was broken into thousands of confused shapes, but none, Hans thought, like the ordinary forms of splintered ice.   There seemed a curious *expression* about all their outlines—a perpetual resemblance to living features, distorted and scornful.   Myriads of deceitful shadows, and lurid lights, played and floated about and through the pale blue pinnacles, dazzling and confusing the sight of the traveller ; while his ears grew dull and his head giddy with the constant gush and roar of the concealed waters. These painful circumstances increased upon him as he advanced ; the ice crashed and yawned into fresh chasms at his feet, tottering spires nodded around him, and fell thundering across his path ; and though he had repeatedly faced these dangers on the most terrific glaciers, and in the wildest weather, it was with a new and oppressive feeling of panic terror that he leaped the last chasm, and flung himself, exhausted and shuddering, on the firm turf of the mountain.

He had been compelled to abandon his basket of food, which became a perilous incumbrance on the glacier, and had now no means of refreshing himself but by breaking off and eating some of the pieces of ice.   This, however, relieved his thirst ; an hour's repose recruited his hardy frame, and, with the indomitable spirit of avarice, he resumed his laborious journey.

His way now lay straight up a ridge of bare red rocks, without a blade of grass to ease the foot, or a projecting angle to afford an inch of shade from the south sun. It was past noon, and the rays beat intensely upon the steep path, while the whole atmosphere was motionless, and penetrated with heat. Intense thirst was soon added to the bodily fatigue with which Hans was now afflicted; glance after glance he cast on the flask of water which hung at his belt. "Three drops are enough," at

last thought he; "I may, at least, cool my lips with it."

He opened the flask, and was raising it to his lips, when his eye fell on an object lying on the rock beside him; he thought it moved. It was a small dog, apparently in the last agony of death from thirst. Its tongue was out, its jaws dry, its limbs extended lifelessly, and a swarm of black ants were crawling about its lips and throat. Its eye moved to the bottle which Hans held in his hand. He raised it, drank, spurned the animal with his foot, and passed on. And he did not know how it was, but he thought that a strange shadow had suddenly come across the blue sky.

The path became steeper and more rugged every moment; and the high hill air, instead of refreshing him, seemed to throw his blood into a fever. The noise of the hill cataracts sounded like mockery in his ears : they were all distant, and his thirst increased every moment. Another hour passed, and he again looked down to the flask at his side ; it was half empty, but there was much more than three drops in it. He stopped to open it, and again, as he did so, something moved in the path above him. It was a fair child, stretched nearly lifeless on the rock, its breast heaving with thirst, its eyes closed, and its lips parched and burning. Hans eyed it deliberately, drank, and passed on. And a dark grey cloud came over the sun, and long, snake-like shadows crept up along the mountain sides. Hans struggled on. The sun was sinking, but its descent seemed to bring no coolness ; the leaden weight of the dead air pressed upon his brow and heart, but the goal was near. He saw the cataract of the Golden River springing from the hill-side, scarcely five hundred feet above him. He paused for a moment to breathe, and sprang on to complete his task.

At this instant a faint cry fell on his ear. He turned, and saw a grey haired old man extended on the rocks. His eyes were sunk, his features deadly pale, and gathered into an expression of despair. "Water !" he stretched his arms to Hans, and cried feebly, "Water ! I am dying."

"I have none," replied Hans ; "thou hast had thy share of life." He strode over the prostrate body, and darted on. And a flash of blue lightning rose out of the East, shaped like a sword ; it shook thrice over the whole heaven, and left it dark with one heavy, impenetrable shade. The sun was setting ; it plunged towards the horizon like a red-hot ball.

The roar of the Golden River rose on Hans' ear. He stood at the brink of the chasm through which it ran.

Its waves were filled with the red glory of the sunset: they shook their crests like tongues of fire, and flashes of bloody light gleamed along their foam. Their sound came mightier and mightier on his senses; his brain grew giddy with the prolonged thunder. Shuddering, he drew the flask from his girdle, and hurled it into the centre of the torrent. As he did so, an icy chill shot through his limbs; he staggered, shrieked, and fell. The waters closed over his cry. And the moaning of the river rose wildly into the night, as it gushed over

THE BLACK STONE.

CHAPTER IV

HOW MR. SCHWARTZ SET OFF ON AN EXPEDITION TO THE GOLDEN RIVER, AND HOW HE PROSPERED THEREIN

POOR little Gluck waited very anxiously alone in the house, for Hans' return. Finding he did not come back, he was terribly frightened, and went and told Schwartz in the prison, all that had happened. Then Schwartz was very much pleased, and said that Hans must certainly have been turned into a black stone, and he should have all the gold to himself. But Gluck was very sorry, and cried all night. When he got up in the morning, there was no bread in the house, nor any money; so Gluck went, and hired himself to another goldsmith, and he worked so hard, and so neatly, and so long every day, that he soon got money enough together, to pay his brother's fine, and he went, and gave it all to Schwartz, and Schwartz got out of prison. Then Schwartz was quite pleased, and said he should have some of the gold of the river. But Gluck only begged he would go and see what had become of Hans.

Now when Schwartz had heard that Hans had stolen the holy water, he thought to himself that such a proceeding might not be considered altogether correct by the King of the Golden River, and determined to manage

matters better.   So he took some more of Gluck's money, and went to a bad priest, who gave him some holy water very readily for it.
Then Schwartz was sure it was all quite right. So Schwartz got up early in the morning before the sun rose, and took some bread and wine, in a basket, and put his holy water in a flask, and set off for the mountains. Like his brother he was much surprised at the sight of the glacier, and had great difficulty in crossing it, even after leaving his basket behind him. The day was cloudless, but not bright: there was a heavy purple haze hanging over the sky, and the hills looked lowering and gloomy. And as Schwartz climbed the steep rock path, the thirst came upon him, as it had upon his brother, until he

lifted his flask to his lips to drink.   Then he saw the fair child lying near him on the rocks, and it cried to h:m, and moaned for water.
  "Water indeed," said Schwartz; "I haven't half enough for myself," and passed on.   And as he went he

thought the sunbeams grew more dim, and he saw a low bank of black cloud rising out of the West; and, when he had climbed for another hour, the thirst overcame him again, and he would have drunk. Then he saw the old man lying before him on the path, and heard him cry out for water. "Water, indeed," said Schwartz, "I haven't half enough for myself," and on he went.

Then again the light seemed to fade from before his eyes, and he looked up, and, behold, a mist, of the colour of blood, had come over the sun; and the bank of black cloud had risen very high, and its edges were tossing and tumbling like the waves of the angry sea. And they cast long shadows, which flickered over Schwartz's path.

Then Schwartz climbed for another hour, and again his thirst returned; and as he lifted his flask to his lips, he thought he saw his brother Hans lying exhausted on the path before him, and, as he gazed, the figure stretched its arms to him, and cried for water. "Ha, ha," laughed Schwartz, "are you there? remember the prison bars, my boy. Water, indeed! do you suppose I carried it all the way up here for *you*?" And he strode over the figure; yet, as he passed, he thought he saw a strange expression of mockery about its lips. And, when he had gone a few yards farther, he looked back; but the figure was not there.

And a sudden horror came over Schwartz, he knew not why; but the thirst for gold prevailed over his fear, and he rushed on. And the bank of black cloud rose to the zenith, and out of it came bursts of spiry lightning, and waves of darkness seemed to heave and float, between their flashes, over the whole heavens. And the sky where the sun was setting was all level, and like a lake of blood; and a strong wind came out of that sky, tearing its crimson clouds into fragments, and scattering them far into the darkness. And when Schwartz stood by the brink of the Golden River, its waves were black, like thunder clouds, but their foam was like fire; and the roar of the waters below, and the thunder above met, as he cast the flask into the stream. And, as he did so, the lightning glared in his eyes, and the earth gave way beneath him, and the waters closed over his cry. And the moaning of the river rose wildly into the night, as it gushed over the

TWO BLACK STONES.

CHAPTER V

WHEN Gluck found that Schwartz did not come back, he was very sorry, and did not know what to do. He had no money, and was obliged to go and hire himself again to the gold-smith, who worked him very hard, and gave him very little money. So, after a month, or two, Gluck grew tired, and made up his mind to go and try his fortune with the Golden River. "The little king looked very kind," thought he. " I don't think he will turn me into a black stone." So he went to the priest, and the priest gave him some holy water as soon as he asked for it. Then Gluck took some bread in his basket, and the bottle of water, and set off very early for the mountains.

If the glacier had occasioned a great deal of fatigue to his brothers, it was twenty times worse for him, who was neither so strong nor so practised on the mountains. He had several very bad falls, lost his basket, and bread, and was very much frightened at the strange noises under the ice. He lay a long time to rest on the grass, after he had got over, and began to climb the hill just in the hottest part of the day. When he had climbed for an hour, he got dreadfully thirsty, and was going to drink like his brothers, when he saw an old man coming down the path above him, looking very feeble, and leaning on a staff. " My son," said the old man, " I am faint with thirst, give me some of that water." Then Gluck looked at him, and when he saw that he was pale and weary, he gave him the water : " Only pray don't drink it all," said Gluck. But the old man drank a great deal, and gave him back the bottle two-thirds empty. Then he bade him good speed, and Gluck went on again merrily. And the path became easier to his feet, and two or three blades of grass appeared

upon it, and some grasshoppers began singing on the bank beside it ; and Gluck thought he had never heard such merry singing.

Then he went on for another hour, and the thirst increased on him so that he thought he should be forced to drink. But, as he raised the flask, he saw a little child lying panting by the road-side, and it cried out piteously for water. Then Gluck struggled with himself, and determined to bear the thirst a little longer ; and he put the bottle to the child's lips, and it drank it all but a few drops. Then it smiled on him, and got up, and ran down the hill ; and Gluck looked after it, till it became as small

*L 219

as a little star, and then turned, and began climbing again.

And then there were all kinds of sweet flowers growing on the rocks, bright green moss, with pale pink starry flowers, and soft belled gentians, more blue than the sky at its deepest, and pure white transparent lilies. And crimson and purple butterflies darted hither and thither, and the sky sent down such pure light, that Gluck had never felt so happy in his life.

Yet, when he had climbed for another hour, his thirst became intolerable again; and, when he looked at his bottle, he saw that there were only five or six drops left in it, and he could not venture to drink. And, as he was hanging the flask to his belt again, he saw a little dog lying on the rocks, gasping for breath—just as Hans had seen it on the day of his ascent. And Gluck stopped and looked at it, and then at the Golden River, not five hundred yards above him ; and he thought of the dwarf's words, "that no one could succeed, except in their first attempt" ; and he tried to pass the dog, but it whined piteously, and Gluck stopped again. " Poor beastie," said Gluck, "it'll be dead when I come down again, if I don't help it." Then he looked closer and closer at it, and its eye turned on him so mournfully, that he could not stand it. "Confound the King and his gold too," said Gluck ; and he opened the flask, and poured all the water into the dog's mouth.

The dog sprang up and stood on its hind legs. Its tail disappeared, its ears became long, longer, silky, golden ; its nose became very red, its eyes became very twinkling ; in three seconds the dog was gone, and before Gluck stood his old acquaintance, the King of the Golden River.

" Thank you," said the monarch, " but don't be frightened, it's all right" ; for Gluck showed manifest symptoms of consternation at this unlooked-for reply to his last observation. "Why didn't you come before," continued the dwarf, "instead of sending me those rascally brothers of yours, for me to have the trouble of turning into stones? Very hard stones they make too."

" Oh dear me ! " said Gluck, "have you really been so cruel ? "

" Cruel ! " said the dwarf, " they poured unholy water into my stream : do you suppose I'm going to allow that ? "

" Why," said Gluck, " I am sure, sir—your majesty, I mean—they got the water out of the church font."

" Very probably," replied the dwarf ; "but," and his countenance grew stern as he spoke, " the water which has been refused to the cry of the weary and dying, is unholy, though it had been blessed by every saint in

heaven ; and the water which is found in the vessel of
mercy is holy, though it had been defiled with corpses."

So saying, the dwarf stooped and plucked a lily that
grew at his feet.   On its white leaves there hung three
drops of clear dew.   And the dwarf shook them into
the flask which Gluck held in his hand.   "Cast these
into the river," he said, "and descend on the other
side of the mountains into the Treasure Valley.   And
so good speed."

As he spoke, the figure of the dwarf became indistinct.
The playing colours of his robe formed themselves into
a prismatic mist of dewy light : he stood for an instant
veiled with them as with the belt of a broad rainbow.
The colours grew faint, the mist rose into the air ; the
monarch had evaporated.

And Gluck climbed to the brink of the Golden River,
and its waves were as clear as crystal, and as brilliant
as the sun.   And, when he cast the three drops of dew
into the stream, there opened where they fell, a small
circular whirlpool, into which the waters descended with
a musical noise.   Gluck stood watching it for some
time, very much disappointed, because not only the
river was not turned into gold, but its waters seemed
much diminished in quantity.   Yet he obeyed his friend
the dwarf, and descended the other side of the mountains, towards the Treasure Valley ; and, as he went,
he thought he heard the noise of water working its way
under the ground.   And, when he came in sight of the
Treasure Valley, behold, a river, like the Golden River,
was springing from a new cleft of the rocks above it, and
was flowing in innumerable streams among the dry heaps
of red sand.   And as Gluck gazed, fresh grass sprang
beside the new streams, and creeping plants grew, and
climbed among the moistening soil.   Young flowers
opened suddenly along the river sides, as stars leap out
when twilight is deepening, and thickets of myrtle, and
tendrils of vine, cast lengthening shadows over the valley
as they grew.   And thus the Treasure Valley became a
garden again, and the inheritance, which had been lost

by cruelty, was regained by love.   And Gluck went, and
dwelt in the valley, and the poor were never driven
from his door; so that his barns became full of corn,
and his house of treasure.   And, for him, the river had,
according to the dwarf's promise, become a River of
Gold.   And, to this day, the inhabitants of the valley
point to the place, where the three drops of holy dew
were cast into the stream, and trace the course of the
Golden River under the ground, until it emerges in the
Treasure Valley.   And, at the top of the cataract of the
Golden River, are still to be seen two BLACK STONES
round which the waters howl mournfully every day at
sunset; and these stones are still called by the people of
the valley,

THE BLACK BROTHERS.

INDEX

TO THE TWO PATHS

BIOGRAPHY

ESSAYS AND CRITICISM

FICTION

4

HISTORY

LEGENDS AND SAGAS

POETRY AND DRAMA

6

REFERENCE

Reader's Guide to Everyman's Library. Compiled by *A. J. Hoppé*. This volume is a new compilation and gives in one alphabetical sequence the names of all the authors, titles and subjects in Everyman's Library.   (An Everyman Paperback, 1889).
Many volumes formerly included in Everyman's Library reference section are now included in Everyman's Reference Library and are bound in larger format.

RELIGION AND PHILOSOPHY

SCIENCE

TRAVEL AND TOPOGRAPHY